Yes! Youth-Led Changemaking

A Game-Changer In The Field Of Youth Development

This book contains the secret of turning young people into changemakers and has been recently tested with 16,000 young people from almost every walk of life.

By:

Ali Raza Khan & Thomas G. Jakel

YES! Youth-Led Changemaking
A Game-Changer in the Field of Youth Development
by Ali Raza Khan and Thomas Jakel

Published by YES Founders Foundation gUG (haftungsbeschränkt)
Eichborndamm 167 G55
13403 Berlin, Germany
www.yesfoundersfoundation.org

© 2017 Ali Raza Khan and Thomas Jakel

All rights reserved. This book or any portion thereof
may not be reproduced or used in any manner whatsoever
without the express written permission of the publisher
except for the use of brief quotations in a book review. For permissions contact:

book@youthledchangemaking.com

SEE MORE INFORMATION ABOUT THIS BOOK AND
DOWNLOAD ADDITIONAL RESOURCES AND WORKSHEETS:
www.youthledchangemaking.com

Read more about YES Network Pakistan and case studies here: www.yesnetworkpakistan.org
Read more about YES Founders Foundation here: www.yesfoundersfoundation.org

Ebook ISBN: 978-3-9819792-0-6
Paperback ISBN: 978-3-9819792-1-3
Hardcover ISBN: 978-3-9819792-2-0

YES! YOUTH-LED CHANGEMAKING

"The changemaking potential is latent in all young people. It is the paradigm of mistrust which veils it. When the paradigm of mistrust is shredded, the changemaking potential of young people surprises everyone."
—Ali Raza Khan

TESTIMONIALS

"Does Your Daughter Have Her Power? In today's world, where success comes from changemaking, not repetition, every teen needs to be a changemaker, actually to build a team and cause a change. Once a young person has this experience, they will have their power for life. Ali Raza Khan is an amazing world pioneer in moving society to this very different definition of success in growing up. He demonstrated how thousands of poor young people, of whom little was expected, could almost immediately, if challenged respectfully, create teams and substantial changes and profits. Does your daughter have this power? If you care for her or for your society, please read this book carefully."

Bill Drayton, CEO Ashoka: Innovators for the Public

"This is not only a splendid read about the author's 21-year journey of working with young people, but also a spectacular and insightful book about the power of youth-led changemaking. As the president of a public leadership program that has engaged over 800 next-generation youth leaders from 70 countries around the world, I have seen first-hand how employing unique youth-led changemaking models can transform outstanding young change agents into self-actualized, globally-minded public leaders and game changers. The book provides compelling evidence because it is based on facts and not assumptions. It is not only informative for stakeholders who wish to design, align, and deliver structures that can support youth, but most importantly, it is also an excellent tool for young people who wish to start a changemaking journey in their own communities and countries around the world. Outstanding and highly recommended!"

Diane de Mailly Nesle Sauvé,
President of the Jeanne Sauvé Foundation

"Ali Raza Khan's work over many years to empower young people to make a positive difference in their communities through YES has been an inspiration to me and many others in the youth civic engagement field globally. With YES, Ali has tapped into an enormous reservoir of young people's desperation to make a difference, rather than to exist in a state of despair. *YES! Youth-Led Changemaking* not only serves as a much-needed guidebook on effective programming, but it also describes Ali's personal journey over the past two decades. This is important, because we often fail to look behind the programs to understand the very personal values and decisions that have been the generators of successful programs. I also admire Ali for having figured out how to take YES to scale. There are many examples of excellent youth empowerment programs in countries around the world, but very few social entrepreneurs have figured out how to scale them up, which Ali has done. How many people can claim to have provided an opportunity to so many young people to change their lives and their communities? Ali deserves our congratulations and our support."

Susan Stroud, CEO, Innovations in Civic Participation (ICP)

"This is the journey of a visionary young man, Ali Raza Khan, whose first job as a government employee exposed him to a national resource and treasure: the youth of Pakistan. This generation, he observed, lacked faith and confidence in their abilities and were uncertain about their future. Using the foundation of his own upbringing and the inspiring example of his own mother, Khan established a non-profit called Youth Engagement Services (YES). This book describes the creative approach to youth empowerment, and its implementation of a mission to create the space in which the next generation of Pakistani citizens can actualize their true desire for a future with dignity and hope."

Dr. Amir Lakhani, Chairman, Sumar Lakhani Foundation, USA

"In a world that demands more and more positive changemakers, Ali and Thomas represent two young and energetic entrepreneurs who impacted the lives of countless young people. This book is testimony to a long and challenging journey to build YES and to let young people in Pakistan discover their true passion. Ultimately, I believe the world would be a better place if people were given the opportunity to discover their true compass. In that sense, traditional education fails all over the world, and often literally kills the creativity and innovation that children are naturally equipped with."

Christoph von Toggenburg, Head of Social Engagement,
World Economic Forum

"Since 2005, when Ali Khan was elected as an Ashoka Fellow, we have been celebrating and learning from his work. YES is not just an incredibly impactful organization, but it is also a harbinger of the global youth movement from powerlessness to changemaking. Through his work, Ali saw over two decades ago that young people everywhere have the power to transform themselves and their societies, even in parts of the world known more for their challenges than their opportunities. Since then, Ali's work has contributed to grow this power exponentially, aided by the historical shifts in technology, media, and the global economy. Now, it is absolutely vital to equip young people everywhere to channel the power to take charge of their future, and this is why YES is not just relevant to Pakistan today, but absolutely necessary to the world. Ali says, '*We must challenge every young person every day to become a changemaker.*' This is a core part of Ashoka's mission, and this book, *YES! Youth-Led Changemaking*, serves as an essential blueprint for all youth organizations seeking to change systems and mindsets, and for any social change leader who wants to catalyze the kind of transformation that Ali has. In my interactions with Ali, I have always been amazed by his

humility and his appetite for learning, and as I read this book and reflect on the totality of Ali's journey, I see this thread in every aspect of his life and work. We are grateful and honored to have him as part of our community."

Maria Clara Pinheiro, Director, Ashoka's Global Fellowship

"Mr. Khan has written a success story of a young man's belief in the potential of other young men. He initiated the idea to introduce 'youth-led changemaking projects', and ultimately, YES (Youth Engagement Services). The author has shed light on various aspects of youth, ranging from definition, dimensions, feelings, problems, and challenges, and has also covered all facets of youth-led changemaking. This book is a guideline for all those who want to be a changemaker and those who wish to take the responsibility of driving youth to create a difference. It will definitely be helpful in impacting the lives of both the youth and those who want to give youth a chance. As a teacher and a researcher, I strongly believe that encouragement and confidence in someone's capabilities can enhance the performance of that individual. I am a witness of many such transformations, but that's just a matter of accepting a challenge to change their mind-set. We are all living in a less trustful environment, which is not always about others, but ourselves, too. We need to rewrite the software of our beliefs. I agree with Ali when he says, 'It's time for us to be open and brave.' So, by selecting the choice of changemaking, we can create value, make progress, and break barriers. Well done, Ali Raza Khan. Many young souls are following you for good."

Prof. Dr. Azra Yasmin, Dean, Fatima Jinnah
Women University, Rawalpindi, Pakistan

"This book is a commendable effort of translating the outcome of the author's over twenty-year long journey of youth engagement. It is a creative blend of the knowledge, skill, and attitude of youth-led changemaking, as well as a practical manifestation of his strong belief system, conviction, and enthusiasm. Ali Raza has successfully proved the importance of youth engagement in social entrepreneurship as a single remedy for many social, economic, and moral ills. He has presented the "what, why, how, and by whom" of youth engagement remarkably well in this book. His youth-led changemaking model is surely evidence of seeing the youth as a solution rather than a problem. I am optimistic that this book can surely be a guiding document for many stakeholders, including policy makers, governmental and non-governmental agencies, university authorities, parents, and social activists to come forward and channel the unprecedented energies of youth."

Dr. Marium Din, Assistant Professor,
National University of Modern Languages, Islamabad

"It is really a praiseworthy initiative and a successful accomplishment. I also appreciate your capability in writing and compiling such a knowledgeable, well-informed, highly valuable, and supportive document. Really, you have completed a great task which will accord a positive result in the youth development curriculum and the model of Youth-Led Changemaking to countries and communities worldwide. My sincere salute to you, my friend."

Dulal Biswas, President, National Federation
of Youth Organizations in Bangladesh

"As someone who has met Ali Raza many times and examined his programs on youth entrepreneurs, I feel that I am in a good position to comment on this book. This manuscript covering Ali Raza's personal inspiring journey and details of his lifelong mission of youth empowerment is a much-needed and timely initiative. In Pakistan, where roughly half of the country's population falls within the youth bracket, it is important to benefit from this demographic dividend. Therefore, Raza's book can inspire many more young change agents from Pakistan."

Dr. Zahid Shahab Ahmed, Deakin University, Australia

"Ali's book is a much-needed road map which restores people's confidence in the latent and untapped talent, and the infinite potential of the youth of Pakistan. These young people include boys and girls who may not be educated, but are intelligent enough to create opportunities, not only for themselves, but also to address the social issues of the community. The book is a step-by-step guide to the road of success. It identifies the gaps in the social and educational system, and emphasizes the critical measures necessary to mobilize and harness youth talent and energy in a productive direction to abate destructive aggression and channel it into building peaceful and productive communities. It reminds the stakeholders to step up and take their roles and responsibilities seriously in creating bright future for these young people of Pakistan. Highly recommended!"

Kaukab Usman, Former National Deputy Manager, FIT, GIZ

"Reading this book is like witnessing Ali's journey of change, first-hand. The greatest achievement of this book, in my opinion, is that it has taken the amorphous concept of 'youth empowerment' and turned it into a tangible and achievable reality. Youth everywhere will find outlined in this book the steps that need to be taken for living a life that is not just productive, but also meaningful."

Rafia Rauf, Senior Grants Officer,
National Rural Support Program (NRSP)

"Around our planet, growing smaller and closer with each technological advancement, people seem to focus on the problems, especially the societal challenges, concerning marginalized people. Ali Raza Khan looks across the same landscape others deem to be bleak and sees possibilities. This visionary has spent his career demonstrating that the solution is all around us; the solution is our young people. Through the YES Network in Pakistan, Ali has demonstrated again and again that those with the fewest resources and the greatest need can also be the most remarkable source of viable solutions. These solutions, in the form of socially and environmentally conscious entrepreneurial endeavors, are transformative for individuals and communities! In their new book, *YES! Youth-Led Changemaking*, Ali Raza Khan and Thomas G. Jakel show anyone invested in youth how they, too, can empower youth to be positive changemakers wherever they may be!

This book will uplift, encourage, and energize you as you learn the easy process for transforming young people from passive recipients of programs designed to address societal problems into active and engaged community members who come to understand that they have the creative capabilities within themselves to make positive changes in their lives and communities!

I met the young ladies of the YES! Network of Pakistan at the SAGE (Students for the Global Entrepreneurship) Competition in Moscow, Russia in 2014. The Pakistani team was professional, intelligent, creative, determined, and caring. Outstanding representatives of their country and the YES! program. Our team of urban youth from Pittsburgh,

PA, in the United States, found them to be friendly, interesting, and inspirational. Through this experience, I reached out to Ali Raza Khan to learn more about his program and inquire if there was any way to facilitate a connection between his young people and ours. Over the years, I have learned more about Ali, his career trajectory, and his passion for positive and empowering change and youth engagement, and I was happy to find a kindred spirit.

Join us! It is my dream that the fruits of our collective labors, multiplied by all of the youth our work touches, will become the catalyst, and these young, empowered, positive changemakers from every walk of life will create a better future for our planet and all of its people, creatures, and places."

Maureen Anderson, M. Ed. Activities Manager
& SAGE Adviser, City Charter High School

"With over 60% of its population under 25, Pakistan's youth is its asset. Enough has been said about the role of youth in the country's growth and development; Ali and the YES Network's work in Pakistan has contributed practically to enable young people to strengthen their sense of agency, develop their skills, and motivate them to become change agents in their communities. The British Council is pleased to have collaborated with Ali Raza on the Changemaker Institute Project which helped develop youth-led social entrepreneurship in higher education institutions across Pakistan. This book is a testament to Ali's commitment and leadership to supporting young people in realizing their potential and contributing to their country."

Nishat Riaz
Director of Education, British Council

"What is the biggest challenge facing our youth today? Our limiting beliefs about who they are and what they can achieve. Ali Raza Khan's groundbreaking work with youth in Pakistan shows why many of our assumptions are wrong, and how *little* it takes to unleash the changemaking potential inherent in young people."

Charles Tsai
Sr. Manager, Social Innovation Partnerships Fossil Group

"Having known Ali for the past few years, I have seen firsthand his commitment to the youth of Pakistan. This book is a testament to his years of on-the-ground work with youth across Pakistan. He not only clearly lays out the shortfalls of Pakistani society, but also provides solutions. The book is a toolkit for every youth to become a changemaker. We need more Ali Raza Khans in Pakistan!"

Huma Haque, Former Associate Director,
South Asia Center, Atlantic Council

"I am a witness to Ali Raza Khan's pioneer work over the last several years in the field of youth-led changemaking in Pakistan. He has facilitated several thousand students of the Punjab Vocational Training Council to go from being victims to becoming changemakers in a short time. The Youth-Led Changemaking idea has the potential to overcome the unwanted poverty that young people impose upon themselves. This book provides compelling evidence and huge amount of insight into the ways that schools and parents can best support children in becoming changemakers. This book has all the new and invigorating ideas that we need to end negativity against young people. It is refreshingly rigorous."

Faisal Ijaz Khan
Chairman, Punjab Vocational Training Council

"Ali Raza Khan has always been an extremely motivated and talented young man with remarkable potential. Hearing and reading about the non-profit organization that he established-YES (Youth Engagement Services)-I reminisced about the time that Mr. Khan asked for advice on whether he should remain at work in his steady career, or leave his job to work on his own. Due to his confidence that he could do brilliant things if he worked independently, and his clear leadership skills, my advice to him was to 'burn all his ships' and pursue his dreams. This book is an endorsement of my faith in Ali's leadership capabilities.

The organization, and this book, are wonderful steps taken by a truly visionary young man to do his part in changing the world by employing one of Pakistan's most valuable, yet vastly untapped, resource: the youth. YES allows the youth of Pakistan to realize and take advantage of their full potential. This book provides deep insight into Ali's experience in engaging the youth and converting them into change agents; work that spans the last two decades. Ali, you are a role model and a great influencer for scores of young people. You have helped transform their passive lives into empowered and productive ones though your energy and passion. This book is truly reflective of your efforts. My best wishes are always with you."

Seemin Ashfaq
Director, Population Council

ACKNOWLEDGEMENTS

First and foremost, I would like to thank God for planting a desire in my heart to write a book on Youth-Led Changemaking. I also thank God for helping me to find a powerful vision in life. While writing this book, I felt that I was divinely guided and supported at every step.

The book is designed in a manner to offer key insights to teachers, policy makers, social workers, youth activists, and parents. This book provides facts and practical knowledge of unlocking the changemaking potential of young people. The seed of the book was the experimentation I did with the marginalized students of vocational training institutions. I am grateful to so many people and organizations that have helped me to write this book.

My mother, for instilling a positive belief system in me and for providing me with the greatest and most inspiring example of a changemaker. You are the true definition of a changemaker. You showed me what being a changemaker requires. Thank you for everything you have done for me. My father, for giving me the freedom to follow my ambition. You are a constant flow of encouragement. My brother, for his unconditional support and love. You are the best example of what a brother should be. My sister, for her constant prayers, encouragement, and support.

My wife, Rukhsana, for standing beside me throughout my journey. I feel totally blessed to have you as my life partner. Thank you for supporting me through all the challenges I took on in my youth-led changemaking work, which decreased the amount of time I spent with you and the children. My 3-year-old daughter, Khadija, for her patience and love, despite my frequent physical and emotional distance with her due to my work. My 9-year-old son, Omer, for asking me many intelligent questions while I was writing the book about the ways it is going to change the expectations of schools from children. I know at times you were not very happy with my high engagement in youth-led changemaking work. I remember one day, you said to me, "Baba, can you spend one hour without talking about youth-led changemaking?" I hope one day, both you and Khadija will read this book and understand why I have so much passion for youth-led changemaking.

All those young people that have participated in the changemaking projects and competitions to prove my thesis that every young person is born with changemaking abilities. I feel great pride and gratitude that I had the opportunity to help you start your changemaking journey. Thank you for showcasing your changemaking potential in such a short period of time. Thank you for helping me to challenge the way we work and look at the potential of young people. I firmly believe that your efforts will be instrumental in changing the role of young people in society. They will play a critical role in opening new doors for youth-led changemaking everywhere in society.

Words are powerless to express my gratitude to Sr. Martin, Principal, Sacred Heart Convent School and Mr. Maxwell Shanti, Principal, St. Anthony's High School and Sr. Victoria, Principal, St. Mary's Girls High School for their unconditional love, guidance and inspiration throughout my changemaking journey. I am grateful to all the principals of the Catholic Board of Education, Lahore for their support in engaging their several thousand students in changemaking.

I want to express my appreciation to Faisal Ijaz Khan, Chairman of the Punjab Vocational Training Council, for his trust, support, and partnership. My special thanks to several hundred heads of institutions and literally thousands of faculty members and adults who supported and joined me in testing my idea of youth-led changemaking. It would not have been possible for me to test this idea on a large scale otherwise. My thanks, also, to my team, who worked very hard with me to reach out to places and institutions across the country. Thank you for understanding and transmitting my vision to many people and organizations. Thank you for helping me to break down several barriers that hold young people back from unlocking their changemaking potential.

I want to express my sincere thanks to Susan Stroud, Chief Executive Officer of Innovations in Civic Participation for her matchless assistance, guidance, and encouragement throughout my journey.

I want to express my deepest gratitude to Ms. Seemin Ashfaq, Director of the Population Council for paving the way for me to embark upon a new and exciting journey.

I must confess the timely support of many international organizations that have shown trust in me and my work, such as Ashoka, Sauvé Foundation, British Council, Innovations in Civic Participation, International Association for National Youth Service, Waldzell Institute, Sumar Lakhani Foundation, KSB Pumps, and Global Knowledge Partnership.

My friend, Thomas, for inspiring me to write this book. Thank you for joining me on this beautiful journey. Thank you for your unflinching support, positive energy, and matchless commitment. Thank you for adding great perspectives to the book and assisting me with editing, designing, and publishing. Without your support, leadership, and cooperation, it would be very difficult for me to make this book a reality. Thank you for everything. You really are a changemaker.

I also want to thank the publisher.

Last but not least, I want to thank all those people who have supported me over the course of my changemaking journey, whose names I have failed to mention.

Ali Raza Khan

STRIKING FEATURES OF THE BOOK

This Youth-Led Changemaking book has all the new and invigorating ideas we need to end negativity against young people. The first purpose of the book is to provide compelling evidence for Youth-Led Changemaking. The second purpose of the book is to help the major stakeholders in designing, aligning, and delivering systems and structures that can support Youth-Led Changemaking. The third purpose of the book is to facilitate young people in starting their changemaking journey. The fourth purpose of the book is to provide conceptual knowledge and hands-on skills for advancing the concept of Youth-Led Changemaking. Another purpose of the book is to create awareness among readers as to how Youth-Led Changemaking can help achieve multiple developmental goals.

1. Personal Journey: The book shares a personal journey of the development of the idea of Youth-Led Changemaking.

2. Self-Study: This book provides detailed knowledge about Youth-Led Changemaking that is suitable for self-study. It does not only define the concept of Youth-Led Changemaking in detail, but also gives examples and comparisons to prove its uniqueness and effectiveness.

3. Changemaking Journey: This book provides step-by-step instructions to young people on how to begin their Changemaking journey.

4. Transforming: This book provides a step-by-step process to transform an average campus into a Changemaking campus. It provides guidelines and practical tips to break down traditional barriers of Youth-Led Changemaking.

5. Teaching: This book provides knowledge and insight to build Youth-Led Changemaking as a subject and field.

6. Engaging: The book provides step-by-step instructions and illustrations for teachers to engage young people in Changemaking.

7. Practical Examples: This book provides examples of many Changemaking projects to young people so that they may gain the confidence to unlock their Changemaking potential.

8. Inspiration: This book on Youth-Led Changemaking provides the right inspiration to donors and policy makers to move the field of youth development from seeing young people as problems to seeing young people as Changemakers.

9. Supplementary materials: A lot of supplementary material is provided in the book to help people and institutions to jumpstart the Youth-Led Changemaking process.

CONTENTS

Foreword xxvii
Introduction – The Entrepreneurial Spirit of the Marginalized Youth of Pakistan – The German Connection

PART 1

Chapter 1. Education Beyond the Numbers 3
Introduction – The Challenge – Education – A Broken Promise – A New Paradigm – Identifying Challenges in Building a Changemaking Culture – Changing Your Perception

Chapter 2. The History of the Youth Development Movement: Our Common Responses 29
The Prevention Approach – The Preparation Approach – A New Vision – Overhaul – A Top-to-Bottom Radical Change – Philosophy – Expectations – Attitudes – Practices

PART 2

Chapter 3. My Journey Towards My Vision: The YES Engagement Model 55
Launching of Youth Engagement Services (YES) Network Pakistan – Uniqueness of YES Network Pakistan – Shifting the Focus on Systems – Youth Engagement Spectrum

Chapter 4. Youth-Led Changemaking 92
Defining Youth – Defining Changemaking – Defining Youth-Led Changemaking – Core Purpose of Youth-Led Changemaking – Phases of Youth-Led Changemaking – Striking Features of Youth-Led Changemaking – Unique Features of Youth-Led Changemaking – Benefits of Youth-Led Changemaking – Domains of Youth-Led Changemaking – Changemaking Status – Conceptual Framework for Youth-Led Changemaking – Building A Scientific Foundation of Youth-Led Changemaking – Changing Times, Changing Definitions – Barriers of Youth-Led Changemaking

Chapter 5. Youth-Led Changemaking for Peace Building....124

Chapter 6. Youth-Led Changemaking: A Dream Into a Reality 129

The Results of YES Changemaking Competition – Twenty-Five Short Stories of the Changemakers – A Glimpse of Youth-led Changemaking Projects – Winners of Changemaking Competitions – A Glimpse of Changemaking Competitions

PART 3

Chapter 7. Become a Changemaker, Create Value, Give Abundantly, Discover the Giant Within, and Make a Living on the Way.............169

The Changemaking Kit – The Changemaking Journey – Value Creation – Share Your Gifts – Share Your Story – The Changemaking Paradigm – Decide to Act – Nurture Your Intention – Commit – Time and Resources – Changemaking Mindset and Changemaking Behavior – Thinking In Models: Blueprints, Frameworks, and Examples from Past Competitions

Chapter 8. Starting Your Own Changemaking Journey....254

Breaking the Myths About Changemaking – Key Steps to Begin a Changemaking Project – Build a Youth-Led Changemaking Team – Developing a Changemaking Plan – Setting-up a Changemaking Organization – How to Establish a Non-Profit Organization – How to Establish a For-Profit Organization/Company

Chapter 9. The Change Maker Workbook-Start Today and Jump Into Action! 279

Changemaking Self-Assessment and Belief System Check – Strengths and Weakness Self-Assessment – Revealing the Why – Creating an Empowering Outlook – Theory of Change Workspace

PART 4

Chapter 10. Support The Change-What it Means for Teachers, Facilitators, and Parents 295

Opening Hearts and Minds with Metaphors – What is Required for This Model to Work and Build an Enabling Environment – Integrating Youth-Led Changemaking in Educational and Vocational Institutions – Bringing Youth-Led Changemaking to the Classroom – All Failures Are Not Equal – Strategies to Encourage Young People to Become Changemakers – Design of Youth-Led Changemaking Program – Why Youth-Led Changemaking Should be a Top Priority – Financing Strategies for Youth-Led Changemaking

Chapter 11. Resources and Training for Facilitators and Institutions 337

The Role and Responsibilities of the Teacher/Focal Person – Changemaking Competition Forms for Use in Your Institution

PART 5

Chapter 12. The Long-Term Vision 345

The Changemaking School – World Youth Engagement Campaign – Gaining + Giving = Development

Appendices 357

Commonly Asked Questions – How This Book Was Made

FOREWORD

This is a book about change. It is a book about the greatness in every human being and the giant opportunity we have been missing all this time. It is about an overdue evolution, or revolution, if you will. And it is about a paradigm shift. A shift so huge that, if one thinks it through, in all finality, it will leave us with a vastly different world. A more just, beautiful world. A world in which everyone is empowered. A world in which the only limit is the limit of our creative imagination. And a world in which positive change will be an unstoppable, bottom-up process.

However, in order to seize the massive opportunity that is presenting itself, an investment must be made. But this is not an investment in new buildings or expensive infrastructure. In fact, we've got enough buildings already.

Instead, it is an investment that is much more meaningful. It is an investment primarily in the minds and souls of our youth. If you start telling someone they can, then sooner or later you will see this person doing what had been inconceivable to them before. If you tell someone that they hold the power often enough, they'll eventually feel it. If you inspire someone to be the change they want to see, and to act from abundance, they will become changemakers for life.

This kind of investment requires no money. Only a heartfelt love of life and a commitment to seeing the latent potential in our youth, just waiting to unfold. It is the commitment to see the oak in the acorn and the butterfly in the caterpillar.

We've been inadvertently projecting our own limiting beliefs onto our youth, and have thus passed on a belief system that is all but empowering. It is time to correct this error. It is time to change our expectations of the youth, and we shall be surprised at how our expectations will not just be met, but surpassed.

This book is about how to honor this commitment and how to create environments in which youth can discover the changemakers within them. But this book is also about the amazing results that young people have produced, and that our team has documented over the past years. It is a book about youth as citizens in action, instead of citizens in waiting; youth as service providers, instead of solely service seekers; and it is about the journey of young people as entrepreneurs and changemakers, creating value for themselves and others.

We hope you enjoy the read.

THE ENTREPRENEURIAL SPIRIT OF THE MARGINALIZED YOUTH OF PAKISTAN

by Ali Raza Khan

I have been pursuing a revolutionary idea for over 21 years – youth as a solution, not as a problem. I have seen through my work that when young people are encouraged and not looked down upon, positive change occurs in the lives of everyone. I have demonstrated again and again that when young people are provided structured opportunities, they show the ability to transform themselves from victims to leaders, from at-risk to at-strength, from sheltered to a shaper of society, and from service seekers to service providers.

During these many years, I have tested several ideas of working with young people successfully. Recently, I experimented with an idea that points to a new understanding of the entrepreneurial potential of the marginalized youth of this country.

I did this experiment with the most neglected, destitute, marginalized, and half-educated youth studying in the state-owned charity-based technical institutions in the Punjab province of Pakistan. I chose to test the idea with students of the technical institutions because they and their families are seriously struggling financially. They are living with little or no access to the basic amenities of life. What I wanted to prove is that these young people, despite living in the poorest families or neighborhoods and having very little or no education, can still turn their lives around if they are valued and trusted as equal partners in development.

It is not poverty, lack of education, or support that is blocking their progress, it is the paradigm, the collection of values, in which they live that creates the stumbling blocks in their progress. These young people are as gifted as any young people living in high or middle-income families.

I engaged 5,950 young people, both boys and girls, of 79 vocational technical institutions operating under the Punjab Vocational Training Council in a four-week Enterprise Development Competition. These institutions were nominated by the senior management of the Punjab Vocational Training Council after we sought an expression of interest from them. It was not compulsory for any institution to participate in the competition. The institutions were given the free will to decide whether they wanted to participate in the four-week competition. Twenty-two institutions were selected from the Southern Punjab, 32 from the Northern Punjab, and 25 from the Central Punjab.

Before engaging the young people in the four-week competition, I conducted a few workshops with the principals and teachers of the 79 technical institutions to build an ecosystem enabling young people to test their ideas freely. Young people were organized in small teams of 5 members. A total of 1,190 youth teams participated in the competition. 407 teams participated from the south, 466 teams from the north, and 317 teams from Central Punjab took part in the Emerging Entrepreneurship Competition.

Out of 1,190 teams, 523 teams were comprised of female youth, and 667 teams were comprised of male youth.

Each team was given a grant of Rs.2500, approximately US$25, on the condition that if the young people were able to generate a profit, it would be donated to YES, and in the case of a loss, YES alone would bear it. I designed this model because of the strong resistance from the parents and teachers to our offer of providing small loans without interest to young people, as they thought that the young people would not be able to pay back even a small amount of the loan if there was a loss in the business. They were of the viewpoint that, since young people have not received any formal training of enterprise development before, and they have no previous experience with running an enterprise, it would be virtually impossible for young people to start and run a business for four weeks successfully. Thus, I designed the idea in a manner to give a free hand to young people to do whatever they wanted to do without the fear of failure.

My organization invested US$34,900. After the completion of the competition, not to my surprise, the young people were able to generate a profit of US$29,000. The young people carried out a wide range of need-based projects in their communities and provided services to over 60,000 people of all ages.

Their projects included, but were not limited to: health and first aid projects; skill development projects; peace-building projects; handicraft projects; sports projects; cosmetic projects; child care projects; female empowerment projects; jewelry projects; information technology projects; and grocery selling projects. The top three teams, based on the triple bottom line of profit, positive social impact, and environmental stewardship, received cash awards and public encouragement. The top three winning teams earned US$1,026 (male youth team), US$1,021 (female youth team), and US$869 (female youth team) profit in four weeks, respectively.

The male youth winning team provided electrical appliance services to the people of their communities. They adopted a very aggressive field approach to reach out to masses. They mentioned during the award ceremony of the competition that the major reason for their success was the support and encouragement provided by their teacher. The first runner-up female youth team provided designing and stitching services to local industries. The female youth team mentioned that they decided to reach out to local industries instead of private customers. They established partnerships with more than 5 local industries in a short period of time. The second runner-up female youth team provided information technology training to the girls of "Madaris" at their institutions. The female youth team mentioned that they reached out to well-established "Madaris" and offered their services to equip the female students with computer education.

Out of 1,190 teams, 926 youth teams were able to generate a profit, while 130 teams stood with no profit and no loss, and 134 teams suffered a loss. Overall, 75% of male participating teams were successful in running a profitable business, and 81% of female participating teams were able to gather profits. Morever, a higher percentage of male teams experienced losses in comparison to female teams. 13.9% of male youth teams suffered loss, while 7.8% of female youth teams suffered loss. When the reason for these losses was investigated, it was found out that the dominating factor was the lack or complete absence of support from their teachers and parents.

The top-performing, or most entrepreneurial, region of the Punjab was south. Only 11 youth teams out of 407 youth teams suffered a loss. Overall, it generated 99% profit. It is important to note that Southern Punjab is under discussion and spotlighted for all the wrong reasons, including terrorism in recent times. This experiment further highlights the need and urgency to reach out to our marginalized youth and provide them with a better and more productive pathway to development.

My project proved the following hypotheses:

Hypothesis 1: We must not expect less of any young person. We should not consider marginalized young people as having no talents or abilities. Young people living in low-income communities possess enormous latent entrepreneurial potential, as much as is possessed by the young people who are educated and living in high-income communities.

Hypothesis 2: There is no pre-condition to becoming an entrepreneur or a social entrepreneur. The only thing which is required to unleash the entrepreneurial potential of young people is the support and encouragement of adults or youth-serving institutions. I learned that young people can succeed if they have a functional institution but a dysfunctional family. Young people can also succeed if they have a functional family but a dysfunctional institution. But young people are unlikely to succeed if they have both dysfunctional families and dysfunctional institutions.

Hypothesis 3: The outcome of the project reveals that education is not enough, skill is not enough, and financial assistance is not enough to become an entrepreneur or a social entrepreneur. It is the application of heart-and-mind intelligence that exceeds all other intelligence to become an entrepreneur or a social entrepreneur. Heart-and-mind intelligence flourishes in a culture of respect, love, and trust.

Hypothesis 4: The project seriously challenged and questioned the way in which entrepreneurship education is currently offered at colleges and universities based on the rational oriented educational system, which does not promote creativity, self-determination, or problem-solving abilities. The result of this project revealed that entrepreneurship can't just be taught as an intellectual discipline — it must be experienced. To become an entrepreneur, students need opportunities to experience the ups and downs of being an entrepreneur, including experiencing both success and failure.

Hypothesis 5: The project proved the fact that all young people can be changemakers if they are provided with the support and encouragement they need. Their success and failure depend on the paradigm in which young people live and operate. Degrees or skills do not control results, effectiveness, and productivity. When we change the paradigm of young people, we can change the results.

Hypothesis 6: The project has shown that a vast majority of young people are living their lives in a very restricted physical, intellectual, social, and moral circle of their potential being. They either do not explore their entrepreneurial potential or are not given the space to explore their talents and natural abilities.

According to the students, this competition has stimulated their innovative spirit and entrepreneurial desire. *This project changed the lives and thought processes of many young students ready to enter their professional adult lives.*

According to many female students, one of the most salient features of this competition was learning how to interact with customers and sell the product. Furthermore, a vast majority of the young people mentioned that, unexpectedly, the competition also taught them how a small amount of investment can help them generate multi-fold profits, alongside benefitting society in a positive manner. The youth were very happy with us for bringing such a competition to their institutes, as it taught them the nuts and bolts of conducting a business; something they could not have learned during their coursework.

At the end of the competition, YES organized an award ceremony to appreciate and acknowledge the contributions of the top-performing students, faculty members, principals, and regional heads. All the students, teachers, and principals who participated in the competition were given certificates of appreciation. The highest profit-making student team of the entire competition was given a cash reward of Rs. 100,000 (US$1000). The highest profit-making team of the winning Vocational Training Institute was also given a cash reward of Rs. 100,000 (US$1000). In addition to that, the teacher and principal of the winning VTI were also given a cash reward of Rs. 100,000 each.

Next Steps

At the Competition-Level: After the roaring success of the competition, we brought minor changes to the terms and conditions of other competitions we are currently running. YES is sharing 50% of profits with the student teams, and in the case of a loss in any student-led enterprise, YES will bear it alone. We have successfully tested this idea in several hundred institutes (vocational institutes, community institutes, and colleges/universities all over Pakistan) where the results are very identical, in terms of the social and economic value created by the students.

At the Country and Global-Level:

- **Traditional examinations** could be replaced by a changemaking project in the social sector, such as organizing a campaign on education, health, and environment, thus offering value to the community.

- **Existing youth internship programs** could be replaced with youth engagement programs. Under internship programs, young people are provided opportunities to get employment experience. It would be better if we encouraged and provided resources (such as an internship stipend) to young people to establish a community-based social enterprise, thus enabling them to create jobs, come up with solutions to social problems, and actually explore their potential.

- **Billions of dollars are being spent on poverty reduction programs** by providing nominal stipends to families without making any concerted effort to unleash the enormous entrepreneurial spirit present in human beings. The result is that, despite spending these enormous funds on poverty reduction or alleviation programs, people are unable to come out of poverty. These programs have further promoted a sense of dependency and sluggishness.

Conclusion

I cannot understand people, organizations, and donor agencies who work with youth and seem to refuse to surrender their long-held traditional views on working with young people. We could go so much further ahead if we changed our thinking and understood that marginalized youth is capable of much more than just crime and violence.

The youth-serving organizations have developed every kind of curriculum, and hired and engaged trained specialists to stem the tide, but without success. This long-held status quo is hurting the marginalized youth the most. A complete overhaul is required in thought, design, and practice.

We need a new way of thinking, as our old way has failed us miserably.

The time is ripe for a new idea which provides an alternative vision of what is desirable and possible — a vision which may truly reflect what is missing and needed. It is time to broaden responses and options.

We must provide at least one opportunity to every young person to explore their entrepreneurial potential. We must move away from crisis reduction programs to strength-based programs. We have a goldmine of talent in the shape of the young people in Pakistan.

They need not only education and skills, but also an opportunity to discover the champions within themselves. We must find new ways to nurture the entrepreneurial spirit, across the board, that include marginalized youth. The most important question today is not what we can do for the youth of the world, but what the youth can do for themselves, for the world, and for Pakistan.

We must be more innovative and thoughtful in our approach to engage marginalized youth, and avoid sending the message that we only care about them when they cause harm to others.

THE GERMAN CONNECTION

by Thomas G. Jakel

I am a great believer in destiny. I believe that everyone has a purpose in this lifetime and that, if we live from love and not from fear, and if we overcome doubt, trust our higher mind and intuition, and follow our hearts, only "good" things can come from it. Coming from the same line of thought and conviction, I believe that some people are supposed to meet.

The encounter I had in February of 2017 with Ali Raza Khan is one of these encounters that I believe was supposed to happen, and I want to tell you how it came about.

Shortly after I started my entrepreneurial journey as a 23-year-old, fresh out of college, I realized that there was an entire world out there that had thus far been completely hidden to me: The world of entrepreneurial endeavor. A world in which you decide how far you can go and how you contribute to your community. A world in which you decide when you get out of bed, how much you earn, and which ideas are translated into physical reality.

As obvious as this may seem to the veteran entrepreneur, it was exciting news to me.

Also, I learned that social entrepreneurs use the vehicle of business to create economic value AND tackle social and ecological challenges. Again, this was big for me, and a revolutionary idea. And as soon as I built my first company with my co-founder, automated the business by hiring a management team, and taken half a year off to celebrate my newfound freedom, I thought that more young people should know about this opportunity "hidden" in plain sight.

Formal education is not the be-all and end-all goal that it is made out to be.

You don't have to be a busy worker bee all your life, realizing someone else's dream instead of implementing your own ideas.

Everyone has the necessary toolkit to create and think.

And anyone can design their life in the way they want to, and become a changemaker and creator. As soon as we DECIDE, BELIEVE THAT WE CAN, and SET THE INTENTION that we ARE going to walk the path, success is already ours. If we trust the river, knowing that eventually we will learn and succeed in our efforts, that is exactly what is going to happen.

Why did no one ever talk about this in school? Why hadn't it even been mentioned in my business administration degree at college? And why is it that the only thing I ever heard about growing up was: "Be good at school, get a degree, and then get a job. Work all your life. Retire. Die." Tainted with the underlying message that if you are not good at getting acceptable grades, you'll be condemned to a life in poverty, relying on welfare or underpaid jobs. What an enticing outlook.

Why wasn't there a single mention that our ideas have value if we trust in our God-given ability to manifest them in the material world? To be changemakers?

And finally, why were we trained — systematically trained — to look to others for solutions to problems instead of creating practical solutions in the real world to problems and challenges, be they social, economic, spiritual or ecological?

From these contemplations came my desire to either change the education system or establish a parallel system, allowing young people to have the same entrepreneurial experiences that I did. We started hosting workshops and conferences that encouraged young people to start a business. Looking back, I barely knew what I was doing, but still, several "successful" businesses came forth from our workshops. However, a real change in the education system was nowhere in sight. Our model just wasn't the right one, considering the size of the challenge.

Additionally, the vision that I shared with my team members wasn't well-aligned. But my interest in the topic and the nagging feeling that it wasn't right to leave all these young people growing up in the dark about their opportunities, their latent potential, and their changemaking skills kept me investigating.

At first, my research approach was very haphazard; asking friends from different countries about projects on the ground that were trying to help young people start their changemaking journey. When my random searches and interviews didn't give me a clearer idea of where to get involved, I started ordering books about social entrepreneurship, hoping to find inspiration in them. And inspiration I found.

Although I never actually got to the real reading of the books, there was a book that made a big difference. Actually, that is imprecise. The *foreword* of the book is what made all the difference to me.

In it, Bill Drayton, the founder of the international Ashoka Network, wrote about a social entrepreneur from Pakistan named Ali Raza Khan who is changing thousands of young people's lives by telling them that they CAN. That they were born great and that they have all it takes to become changemakers. But not only that — he challenges them to start businesses and, unsurprisingly, the overwhelming majority of these kids that are regarded as "difficult cases" by the government succeed with flying colors, earning profits and challenging everyone's belief system about what young people are capable of if they are trusted enough and are met with high expectations. Wow.

After reading the foreword, I knew that I had to get in touch with Ali.

I sent him an email asking him for a video interview. His staff got back to me asking me for the interview questions, and said that he would deliver them in writing, as he was in Singapore at the time. I managed to postpone sending in the questions for about a week. Then I got an email from Ali, personally letting me know that he was back from Singapore and that he would be open to doing the interview at any time. We arranged the interview and got on the call for about an hour.

If you could have seen my face during that interview! I was brimming with inspiration.

Here, it seemed, I had finally found someone who had hacked the system and identified a systematic approach that helped young people start their changemaking journey. And he didn't do it by throwing money at the problem, building big infrastructure, setting up tech incubators, bringing on board investors, or looking for "fledgling potential" and all these other approaches that are nice, but are no scalable model to reach the hundreds of millions of young people at the "bottom of the pyramid" who need this experience and encouragement the most.

Not only did it seem that Ali had come across a workable, scalable model to give young people a practical entrepreneurship and changemaking experience, but he also managed to have stellar success rates AND have the majority of the kids and youth earning a profit on their projects. AND, on top of that, he manages to facilitate this experience within two to five weeks. This was insane.

I had more questions on my mind than we both had time for during the interview. So, I asked him whether I could go visit him in Pakistan and see the project for myself. I wanted to see every detail of how Ali's organization worked. "Sure, be my guest," he said. So, I booked my ticket to Pakistan on New Year's Eve 2016, and got the opportunity to accompany Ali for almost two weeks to different universities and vocational training institutes in the Punjab, speaking with hundreds of students, dozens of teachers and professors, and taking a bunch of random selfies with the students who wanted a picture with the brown-skinned German man that had come to see their enterprises. The trip was not only inspiring and fun, but also heartwarming, as I heard the stories of some of the students. I could literally pick up on how much this short experience had already changed their lives, their self-esteem, and their prospects for the future. At times, I had tears of gratitude in my eyes, for what I saw was way beyond what I could have hoped for. If it takes only two to five weeks to massively change a young person's life, mindset, and prospects for the future, and you even earn a return on the investment while facilitating them with the experience, why weren't more institutions and edupreneurs doing this?

The projects, and the results from the projects, in terms of monetary return and social impact, often blew my mind. Think about it: This was only the very first, minuscule, entrepreneurial experience that these youngsters had. Yet, it made a huge difference in their consciousness and how they saw themselves. Young girls who had never spoken to strangers had learned how to sell their products. Kids from poor families made a profit in two to five weeks that was beyond what many of their parents would earn in several months. And, as I have observed in myself and others: Once a changemaker, always a changemaker. This is a primary shift from victim mode to creator mode, and is likely to pay social dividends again and again, not only for the lives of these young boys and girls, but also for their communities, their country, and, finally, for all of humankind.

Imagine what will happen if this kind of experience is facilitated not only to the tens of thousands of young people that YES Network has reached thus far, but to the hundreds of millions of young people growing up all over the world. What if we could awaken *all* their latent potential? What if we allowed *everyone* to become citizens in constructive action? What if we *all* had practical experience using our natural capabilities of imagination, creativity, and empathy to create social and economic value? Not only as "passive" labor, but as changemakers, regardless of whether we are working for someone else or building our own businesses.

So, to make a long story short: I hope you will find the stories of the young people of Pakistan and the story of Ali's journey as encouraging and inspiring as I did when I first heard about them.

And I hope that even if all you do is read this foreword, you are now convinced that the youth is a huge, untapped goldmine, in terms of their size as a population and their untapped potential to create value and solutions for themselves and all of us.

I hope that getting an entrepreneurial and changemaker experience early in life will not be the exception, but the absolute standard, and that you will be a part of this development as a changemaker in your own right.

Part 1

Chapter 1

EDUCATION BEYOND THE NUMBERS

Introduction

In this part, we are calling for the major players in the field of youth development to move beyond the current state of "dueling approaches".

We need a new vision and effort that sees youth as changemakers *now*. This book reveals the method to help every young person become a changemaker. We have successfully tested this method with several thousand young people from different backgrounds.

I believe that this method should be shared with every young person to change their life, and with every adult to change the way they look at the potential of young people.

I have explained the method of establishing, growing, and restoring trust with young people many times in the book. If anyone is ready to trust the changemaking abilities of young people, this method will be revealed as you read on.

This method cannot be stolen. It cannot be searched. It cannot be purchased. It cannot be found in books. It cannot be found in educational and vocational institutions. In the end, it can only be experienced by those who are ready to trust the changemaking abilities of young people.

It is important to clarify here that this book presents facts, and not assumptions.

We have specialized in the failure analysis of young people. This book will provide a simple way to help young people become changemakers and explore their potential.

We have a record youth population today. Many of these young people are growing up in an environment where they are either not allowed to practice changemaking abilities or they are unaware that they have these abilities within them. Every year, millions of young people enter educational institutions to get a degree or diploma and find a path to become changemakers.

On the other hand, every year, millions of young people are completing their degrees without knowing what to do with them. They have no idea how to start their lives. This book will provide an inspiration to young people who are in schools or colleges, or out of schools or colleges, to get started as changemakers. Many of the stories covered in this book are of young people living in very low-income communities with very few tangible resources. Before participating in the process of self-discovery, many of these young people had no idea about their changemaking abilities.

Participation in the youth-led changemaking process proved to be a turning point in their lives.

Youth-led changemaking is an idea whose time has come to be realized. If this new vision has to occupy a powerful place in society, it has to reach out to a wide range of places, people, and organizations. Our efforts should not be narrowly focused. We must not limit our efforts to develop or strengthen only a single delivery system. We must engage *all* the stakeholders, such as parents, young people, schools, public and private organizations, and policy makers and researchers, as well as donor and philanthropic organizations, to advance the concept of youth-led changemaking. We must develop a structure within which all of us can identify and play our meaningful role in building the field of youth-led changemaking. We must develop clear performance measures for each of these players, and we must monitor progress on each of these fronts regularly. It will help us to become more collectively responsible for the new outcomes we seek for our young people. We must be strategic in our approach to facilitate young people to begin their changemaking journey. We cannot help young people become changemakers by accident. This book will increase the knowledge base of our major service providers about youth-led changemaking and equip them with tools to foster youth-led changemaking. Creating opportunities for young people to practice changemaking abilities will increase their chances to succeed. Introducing the concept of youth-led changemaking will also help shift the field of youth development away from prevention and preparation to engagement and community development. Youth-led changemaking requires an intentional, strategic, and wide-scale effort to create an ecosystem in society that supports and sustains opportunities that enable young people to become changemakers.

The Challenge

Have you heard these cries?

- My parents spent everything they had on my education. Now, I am unable to find a job.
- I am living my life in standby mode.
- I am tired of being rejected.
- I am jobless in spite of higher education.
- I am paid less despite being highly educated.
- I am rejected because I have no job experience.
- I am over my head in debt.
- I am unable to find a job in the area of my expertise.
- I am discarded and rejected by the society.
- I am unable to change my family circumstances.
- I have no one who values me.
- I have talent, but no opportunity.
- I am being micromanaged.
- I am sick and tired of waiting for a good job.
- I am not well equipped to meet the market demands.
- I am willing to do any job to get going.

I am sure you have heard these cries many times from our young people. Probably, you might relate to many of these cries yourself. The problem is that we have never tried to understand or answer theses cries of our young people. These are the devastating cries of literally millions of our young people.

Why do our parents, schools, and policy makers not listen to these cries? Why do they find themselves unable to do something about them?

Do we even understand the problem?

I have asked many parents, principals, educationists, politicians, policy makers, and young people a simple question: What do you think is the missing link in the education system?

I got very interesting and diverse answers. Here are a few responses:

- The curriculum is outdated.
- The teachers are not well-trained.
- The infrastructure is weak.
- There is a lack of parental support and supervision.
- Adequate funding is not available.
- There is low motivation on the side of the students.
- Poor teaching techniques are applied.

In short, everyone demands more: More education, more rigorous curriculum, more reading, more memorizing, more testing, more training, more monitoring, more accountability, and more investment in schools.

None of the discussion, criticism, and feedback on the education system has explored what the real "more" required in education is, in the light of massive evidence (what is happening with our graduates) and context (growing social, economic, and environmental changes and challenges) that real change is necessary.

It is, however, quite clear that we must stop defining success for our children in terms of high scores or grades. We believe that a new vision is required, which focuses on unlocking the inherent changemaking potential in every person.

The difference between what students are doing in the classrooms and what they are capable of doing outside the classrooms would solve many of our pressing problems.

The schools must realize that the quality of contributions, not the memorization of correct answers, should be the measure of the educative growth of our children.

It is very clear that increasing the size of the education budget will not solve our problems. Making our curriculum more rigorous will not help our kids succeed. Increasing the capacity of teachers in new areas or subjects will not change the future prospects of our kids. Increasing the number of graduates will not heal our system, and improving the infrastructure of the schools will not change the results.

Education-A Broken Promise

If we compare what schools promise versus what they offer at the end of a degree, it would not be very difficult to conclude that education is no longer a passport to a successful life.

A vast majority of schools in Pakistan are *for-profit entities*.

They don't measure their success by looking at the number of changemakers produced, but rather by looking at the number of graduates produced, which is directly linked to their financial bottom line. It wouldn't be wrong to say that a majority of our schools today compete in the quest for capital.

Despite daunting odds, we are letting schools get away with making broken promises to our kids.

What is quite strange here is not just that the schools make false promises, but how long those who suffer or know about it remain silent. I am willing to give the benefit of the doubt to a few schools, as I feel that they might have developed a kind of functional blindness to their own shortcomings.

But one thing that is clear: If schools continue to do what they have been doing, they will continue to get the same poor results.

We know that our educational institutions are seriously struggling; we know that our teachers are finding it difficult to help students succeed; we know that many students are stuck in a period of waithood. We know that the results of our efforts are not very hard to prove.

The time has arrived when we must stand up against this type of education where "winners" and "losers" are both struggling. How can we make sense of this education system? How can we justify this kind of education system where both "winners" and "losers" are playing a waiting game to turn around their lives as they are subjected to market conditions, as opposed to being proactively involved in creating *new* market conditions?

Some people might argue that the current education system has proved valuable to a few people. My answer to them is that you can find a piece of bread in a garbage bin if you search long enough. The tiny minority which is successful is progressing mostly due to the presence of a caring adult (parent or teacher), a good upbringing, the acquisition of a positive belief system, a strong personal drive, and sound moral training.

But didn't school's promise all students to be successful?

I am sure you have come across many lofty claims and messages advertised by educational institutions to attract parents and students. It is very sad to observe that our schools do not have their publicized effect. Schools show us the academic record of their students, and not the changemaking record of their students. There are so many young people out there who were promised high-quality jobs, but after completing their studies, found out that those jobs were not there.

Parents and students have been fooled by the schools when it comes to the promises they offered. Every year, we see how many promises were broken or proved wrong when we look at the number of young people that wasted their lives or potential.

We have been sold again and again on this idea that schools have been designed to bring out the best in our students, but unfortunately, results are showing that they are bringing out the worst in our students. Many of our children were better off before they entered school.

Before going to school	After going to school
Active	Passive
Create	Repeat
Imagine	Follow
Act	Wait
Ask	Quiet
Believe	Doubt
Trust	Mistrust
Respect	Disrespect
Humble	Proud
Cooperate	Compete
Conscious	Oblivious
Bold	Shy

Table 1: Impact of School on Children

Sadly, what is being offered in our schools does not help our children become changemakers. No one sends their children to school to become mediocre, or a follower, or to repeat the game.

If you doubt what I am saying, then try to spend some time observing what is going on in the schools and what happens when our children come out of the school system.

What is the most common feedback from employers about fresh graduates?

I have heard thousands of employers say that fresh graduates are not ready for the world of work. It is not a lack of education and skills which are missing, it is the inability of the students to apply their inherent changemaking abilities.

The most important question today is not what an average college student knows when he or she leaves the education system, but what an average college student gives back to society.

Schools must ask the question: What percentage of our students are changemakers?

A New Paradigm

We have a desperate need for new pathways to move into adulthood. The old model is to get a high GPA in order to find a job that is well-paid. But the evidence suggests that even the graduates of the highest-rated educational institutions find it difficult to find a valuable place in society.

The new model shows that changemaking is possible even without a professional degree. According to the new model, our kids should not wait for degrees to become changemakers. They can become changemakers at any age.

Every parent wants to see their child succeed after a long and painful educational experience. I have met many parents who have worked so hard to provide education to their kids. They worked like animals. They lived a miserable life. They sold everything. They took loans. They went to all this trouble with the hope that one day, their son or daughter would be able to turn around their circumstances.

In the end, what they get is a degree – a piece of paper, pompous in name but not in worth.

There is no shortage of data which validates that millions of students are graduating from colleges and universities unprepared to create value in society.

The idea of looking at educational institutions as places for preparing our children for the best paying jobs or for promising careers is one of the major reasons for the lackluster performance of our educational institutions. There are millions of young people who would never feel or experience what it takes to be a changemaker. Our educational institutions don't help our children admire their own inherent treasures.

Our schools are on auto-pilot. Many students, parents, and even teachers have started believing that education has become an entrapment, and is not worth it. The question is: What is going on inside the schools? Why are schools losing a staggering amount of credibility?

I believe it is due to the following reasons:

- Education is becoming overpriced.
- Knowledge repetition and skill repetition have become the routine.
- Learning is slow, boring, and passive.
- Individual accomplishment is glorified.
- Competition is pursued at all levels.
- Risk avoidance is the norm.
- Academic scores are considered enough.

Our schools are unable to unlock the inherent changemaking potential of our children. Why do our children, after spending 16 to 20 years in education, still find it difficult to change their paradigms?

Many of our children don't know what to do with what they know.

Our current education system is unable to change the belief system of young people. The belief system is developed by repetition and it is changed by repetition. When young people are continuously looked down upon, they develop a negative belief system. They start acting from a sense of scarcity and deprivation instead of abundance and having enough. I have seen in my work that when young people are provided with an opportunity to begin their changemaking journey, they begin the process of rewriting their belief system.

The problem is that our parents and educational institutions are not measuring the right things. Perhaps this is the major reason that we are not getting the right results. Our educational institutions are measuring the mastery of students in basic skills. We consider our students very bright and intelligent if they can memorize names of renowned leaders, capitals, formulas, and dates of history, or repeat knowledge, skills, and inventions. We never assess students against the application of their changemaking abilities.

If you doubt my observation, then simply ask yourself:

- How many of your teachers demanded that you create value in society?
- How often are you required to design and deliver solutions to the problems faced by your community?
- How frequently did you have the opportunity to create and innovate in your subject area?
- How often were you asked about or involved in creating new ideas, products, and services?

Many of our students and teachers have developed this mindset that worthwhile ideas are created and implemented by the most educated and skilled people, and everyone else is just a follower; taking orders; filling in the gaps; the small cog in the machine.

Every child is programmed for success by God. It is the family or educational paradigm which inhibits the ability of our children to become successful. We all are born with these miraculous changemaking abilities. Here are few of those miraculous changemaking abilities:

_	_
Explanation of Changemaking Abilities **How aware are you of your changemaking abilities?**	
Ability to Start	Everyone is blessed with the ability to initiate things and act independently with few constraints. Everyone can create something from nothing. We don't have to wait for someone else to help us begin. We can help others, improve things, do good, and make a difference.
Ability to Serve	Everyone is born with the ability to serve others. We don't have to have a school degree to serve. We can help people of different backgrounds, faiths, ages, and races. We can achieve greatness in life by serving others. The best way to achieve happiness and tranquility in life is to serve others. Everyone has something to offer to someone in pain, agony, or trouble.
The Ability to Imagine	God has blessed everyone with imaginative power. Everyone has the ability to imagine, to dream, and to bring the future in their hands. Everything we see in our world is a proof of imagination. Imagination leads to creativity and innovation. Our future is linked to our ability to imagine. When we do things, or repeat things without imagination, we waste our imaginative power, and face challenges and problems. When we use the power of imagination, we can bring magnificent change into our lives and the lives of others.

The Ability to Choose	Everyone has the ability to choose between right or wrong and good or bad. We are given the power to choose our actions. We make decisions every day. Our actions impact us and others. We can choose to live our lives in a waiting mode or we can choose to live our lives in a proactive mode. We can choose to wait for things to happen or we can choose to make things happen.
The Ability to Innovate	Everyone is born with the ability to create, invent, and innovate. Everyone has the ability to create new ideas that can save time and resources, and have a positive impact on others. The ability to innovate is often suppressed by our environment. It does not mean that you lose the ability to innovate. You can begin your innovation journey at your will and at any age or time.
The Ability to Alter	Everyone has the ability to alter his or her circumstances. No one is created to live a life of misery or poverty forever. Human beings are blessed with the ability to alter their direction whenever it is required to improve their lives. The power to alter our circumstances comes from within us.
The Ability to Express	Everyone is born with the ability to express themselves. No one can take this power from you. It is the most powerful ability to express our feelings, plans, and ideas to others. This ability can be used to highlight injustice and discrimination. It can be used to develop a shared vision and form alliances.
The Ability to Inspire	Everyone has the ability to create an impact or effect on the attitudes and opinions of others. There is no specific age or qualification required to inspire others. You can inspire others with your thoughts, words, and actions.

The Ability to Feel and Empathize	Everyone has the ability to demonstrate an understanding of the feeling and thoughts of others. We have the ability to walk in someone else's shoes. It has played a crucial role in stimulating innovation in society. We cannot solve the problems of the world without using our natural ability to feel the pain of others. Our ability to feel leads to problem solving and sound relationships.
The Ability to Collaborate	We all are born with the ability to work together towards common goals by sharing responsibility, authority, and accountability. Collaboration maximizes achievements.
The Ability to Care	Everyone has the ability to show care to others. Care cannot be downsized. Care does not require any funding. It requires a commitment to genuinely help others. There is no special requirement when it comes to caring. Care requires your attention and consideration to look after the needs of others.
The Ability to Appreciate	Everyone is given an amazing ability to appreciate others. Appreciation creates so much and costs nothing. It gives off great positive energy. It strengthens relationships. It improves team work. It produces great results.

Table 2: Inherent Changemaking Abilities

Our families and educational institutions always seek obedience and compliance from children and young people, so they get obedience and compliance from them. I promise that if they sought out innovation from children and young people, they would get innovation, too.

Changemaking Abilities	Consider the current teaching, curriculum, and testing in schools. Do they inspire students to become changemakers? Are they in accordance with the school's stated values or statements? How often do young people use these changemaking abilities in schools?				
	Always Used	**Often Used**	**Sometimes Used**	**Seldom Used**	**Never Used**
Ability to serve					
Ability to start					
Ability to imagine					
Ability to choose					
Ability to innovate					
Ability to alter					
Ability to express					
Ability to inspire					
Ability to feel					
Ability to collaborate					
Ability to care					
Ability to appreciate					

Table 3: Assessment Tool for Changemaking Abilities

I encourage you to go and visit the best institutions in your area or country and observe how many students are provided with an opportunity to practice their changemaking abilities. Our best schools and our worst schools are on the same page in terms of their inability to engage young people in changemaking. Our educational institutions are damaging the changemaking abilities of our children. The longer our children remain in schools, the more these abilities are drained.

I believe God has equipped us with everything we need to live a purposeful, successful, and contributing life. We were made to use these changemaking abilities. Why not use it to enrich our educational journey?

Our abundance is stored in the application of changemaking abilities. Students must realize that their current state is the result of their inability to practice changemaking abilities.

How can we rate any institution as high-quality or world-class if the students of that institution are deprived of any structured opportunity to create a value in the society? Getting young people from where they are to where they want to be represents a quantum leap.

A simple change of expectation can be the beginning of real change.

Identifying Challenges in Building a Changemaking Culture

Our educational institutions have never been designed to produce changemakers. There is no desire to facilitate children in becoming changemakers during their studies.

There is no agreement between parents and schools that students should practice changemaking abilities. There is no community of knowledge and practice in the field of youth-led changemaking.

Our teachers have not been trained in using their knowledge. They have been trained in *teaching* knowledge. And our schools have not yet developed the framework to measure the changemaking abilities of our children.

Measurement is the heart of a disciplined effort to produce changemakers, and to create social and economic impact. Defining performance measures is a major step towards creating a culture of changemaking. At the moment, there is no definition of changemaking. Therefore, there is no understanding of changemaking.

Our education system was engineered a century ago to develop and assess memorization skills. It was never designed to facilitate the development, application, and assessment of our changemaking abilities. We need a transition from the development and assessment of traditional knowledge and skills to the application and assessment of changemaking abilities.

What the real world cares about is not how much and how fast you can memorize, but how well you can use your changemaking abilities to serve others. In the real world, we are not judged by our grades, but by our ability to create and deliver value.

Grades are fine to enter a college or a job, but they do not guarantee success in real life. Real success, happiness, and prosperity comes from our ability to practice changemaking abilities.

History is replete with examples and stories of changemakers who had no professional degrees, but had the great ability to use their innate changemaking abilities. We live in a world where we are told again and again to "go and seek out" what is missing in our lives. We are never encouraged to "draw out" or "connect to" our inborn changemaking abilities. When you are involved in changemaking, many extraordinary things happen. Your mind goes beyond limitations. Your thoughts smash their boundaries. Your heart sends positive vibrations. Your spirit elevates. You find your power again.

How can we assess changemaking abilities in a classroom? Changemaking abilities are difficult to be objectified, but they can be assessed by the actions and contributions of students. The application of changemaking abilities cannot be judged through traditional examination systems, but they can be judged by their impact on society.

This will bring a massive shift in the mindset of our children. They will be encouraged to be changemakers by taking care of every form of life and the surrounding ecosystem. They will be assessed by their ability to act compassionately and fairly without excluding anyone. The impact of this kind of education would not only be on students, but also on the whole society.

Those students who display a higher degree of imagination, creation, and innovation in their given fields and solve the toughest problems of their society will be considered the winner.

This kind of winner would not be a winner for themselves, or for their family, but for the whole society. The great thing about this new kind of assessment would be that both schools and society will have no difficulty in recognizing the winner. This will encourage every student to build their identity and reputation around changemaking, and not around self-serving grades.

Parents and communities will not see changemaking as a side agenda, but as a part of life. This would be a huge turnaround of the focus of our education system from self-serving to other-serving, and from competition to compassion.

Students will be encouraged to arrive at school with ideas, thoughts, and plans for creating value in society. In this new era, students will be always on the move to identify and interact with the problems, rather than avoid or simply discuss problems. In this new era, changemaking will not be reserved for privileged young people, but for all young people. The most exciting thing about this new form of assessment would be that even those who fail will not be saddened, but they will wear their failure as a badge of honor.

Why do not even our best schools, best teachers, best parents, best policy makers, and best politicians understand the need to engage youth in changemaking? Why isn't there even a little bit of expectation raised or expressed by any quarter of our society to engage youth in changemaking during their studies?

Perhaps it is due to these three major reasons:

1. They are not conscious of it (awareness issue).
2. They do not have the capacity (capacity issue).
3. They do not want to do it (value issue).

I found out that it is easy to address awareness and capacity issues, but it is very difficult to address value issues.

People and institutions are often locked up in tradition. They tend to operate from their memories, and not from collective imagination. It is not comfortable for them to be uncomfortable by testing new ideas and thoughts that could challenge their own authority and influence. They have not imagined that their authority and influence could be increased manifold if they helped students to increase their influence on society at an early stage of their lives.

Our educational institutions have never been designed to treat our children as resources and equal partners in development, but they always treat our children as empty vessels into which we pour our wisdom. Hence, our institutions never allow our kids to use their changemaking abilities.

Recently, I saw a soap advertisement in which a child was suggesting to his friends that his mother advised him to wash his hands for at least 60 seconds. While he was giving a practical demonstration of washing hands, he was singing, "Keep washing, keep washing, and keep washing". One of his friends came and asked him, "Is your soap so slow that it takes 60 seconds to wash your hands?"

This advertisement can be related very well to our education systems. It seems that our education systems are following the same mantra of *keep educating* children for such a long period of time without unlocking their inherent potential for changemaking.

Changemaking abilities play a greater role in our success than basic reading, writing, and arithmetic skills. Many of our kids are not even aware that they possess these changemaking abilities because they have never applied them or gotten in touch with them.

Our institutions have never even provided them the space to explore these abilities. In short, our institutions have never been designed to produce changemakers. They are designed to produce good employees who carry out orders. Dreaming, strategizing and changemaking are considered a "sin" in many of our educational institutions.

Young people	Schools	Society
Young people will serve rather than be served.	Schools will re-connect with communities as places for public good.	Youth-led changemaking will accelerate the social and economic development process.
Young people will establish a new identity.	Schools will develop new partnerships.	Youth-led changemaking will create an innovative service delivery mechanism for poor people.
Young people will develop or rewrite a positive belief system.	Schools will attract more students and funding.	Youth-led changemaking will provide new and innovative ideas to society.
Young people will build social capital and strategic partnerships.	Youth-led changemaking will improve the quality of teaching and learning.	Youth-led changemaking will reduce youth unemployment.
Young people will become self-reliant and contributing members of society.	Youth-led changemaking will provide millions of students with hands-on competence in their chosen fields.	Youth-led changemaking will reduce the incidence of crime and drug abuse.

Table 4: How Will Youth-Led Changemaking Help Young People, Schools, and Society?

Changemaking abilities are God-gifted and not society-gifted. Without practicing changemaking abilities, the human body becomes a physical machine without a soul. Societies develop and grow when people master changemaking abilities.

One major reason of growing poverty among young people is the inability of young people to recognize that they are blessed with countless changemaking abilities. It is the lack of use of their changemaking abilities that causes poverty.

Poverty is never indispensable or inevitable. Playing the victim all the time does not help you.

No one is created to live a life of misery. We are born to be changemakers. Changemaking is the real purpose of life. We take our changemaking abilities for granted. Every person has to see themselves as a changemaker and must strive for changemaking. Changemaking begins with your ability to see the difference between right and wrong and good and bad. All Prophets Peace Be Upon Them (PBUT) aimed at enabling people to become changemakers. They tried to spark a flame in the hearts of their followers to become changemakers.

The spirit of changemaking has been weakening in young people due to their love of an easy life. Parents and teachers have failed to transmit positive impulses to young people to become changemakers.

When you inherit a weak belief system, your changemaking abilities become a victim of your belief system. How can we change a weak belief system? It can be changed by practice. How is it developed? It is developed by practice. Your changemaking abilities have come to you as a gift from God. We often take these abilities for granted, and thus, ignore them, but we must use them for our own advantage, and the advantage of others.

Poem: You-led by Ali Raza Khan

You have read so much
You haven't read yourself
You have talked to so many people
You haven't talked to yourself
You go and seek help from others
You never seek help from yourself
You are quick to admire others
You never admire yourself
You celebrate others
You never celebrate yourself
You have created many things for others
You have forgotten to create yourself
You have helped others to succeed
You never try to succeed yourself
You have sunk in the river of doubts about yourself
You have not tried to believe in yourself
You blame others for your failures
You never blame yourself
You have taken a passenger seat in your life
You never try to drive your life yourself
God gives you a chance every day
You never give a second chance to yourself

Changing Your Perception

It is my firm belief that when we change the way we view young people, we change the results for young people. When we honor young people as equal partners in development, when we seek innovation from young people, when we approach young people optimistically, then we help young people unlock their inherent changemaking potential.

On the contrary, when we see young people as a problem, when we treat young people uncaringly, when we seek compliance from young people, when we approach young people pessimistically, when we consider young people as consumers, and when we handle youth with no expectations, we are manufacturing a risk.

It's time to change the way we look at children and young people, and their potential. Changing the way we look at young people is the first step to activating young people as changemakers.

Far too often, we use negative vocabulary to define young people. Parents, policy makers, and youth development practitioners measure their efforts against the reduction of problem behaviors and improvement in academic performance of young people. Many youth development initiatives believe in the philosophy that young people must be "fixed" before they can be developed. There is a growing body of evidence that shows that the characterization of young people as problems to be fixed leads to negative outcomes. No one feels inspired when someone walks in the door and says, "*We are here to fix you.*"

It is very unfortunate that young people are treated as passive beneficiaries in many of our adult-led and adult-supervised programs. Teachers continue to treat young people as empty vessels into which they try to pour their wisdom. Policy makers continue to design and deliver policies and programs that are aimed at repairing and punishing young people who are involved in risky behaviors. Parents continue to believe that their children are weak and not ready to become changemakers. What kind of message are we sending to young people? When we examine the results of these traditional and long-held attitudes towards young people, we witness poor results everywhere.

It is interesting to observe that the vocabulary for defining youth as "changemakers" is not as rich as the vocabulary available for defining young people as problems to be managed.

Why are young people not viewed as changemakers? The simple answer: Because their assets are ignored and their changemaking abilities are not utilized and trusted. By changing the way we treat young people, we can impact upon the lives of everyone positively.

Without looking at young people as a "solution", one cannot start anything. Without providing a changemaking practice opportunity to every young person, one cannot finish anything. We cannot deliver success to young people. Every young person has to experience it and feel it. The young person who learns the art of using their changemaking abilities early in life will never wait and seek approval. One of the greatest things I have learned in life is that when we treat young people negatively, they are going to act negatively. When we treat young people with respect, they will show us their greatness.

I have observed that even our best parents and teachers are involved in inflicting "micro-damages" to young people on a regular basis. These micro-damages have devalued and disempowered so many young people already. These micro-damages have proved to be major stumbling blocks on the way to helping young people become changemakers. These micro-damages send subtle messages to young people that they are not capable of changemaking yet, that they are too young to create and innovate, and that they are too lacking, limited, and weak to begin their changemaking journey.

These messages are conveyed through gestures, word selection, tone of voice, and actions. Repeatedly sending "micro-damages" often results in serious consequences for everyone.

On the contrary, micro-affirmations can have a reverse impact on young people. Micro-affirmations are little appreciations of young people's value. I use micro-affirmations as a tool to tell young people that they are strong, blessed, empowered, equipped, and wonderfully made to live an impactful life. In my work, I conveyed this message to young people again and again: that they have to recognize what they are blessed with and that they have everything they need to be a changemaker. They should not wait and pray for something that they already possess. These micro-affirmations open the doors to changemaking.

I found out that impressing upon young people that they can set a course and reach whatever destination they choose has proved to be very effective. When I go and talk to young people, I tell young people explicitly that I don't care what their story of the past or present is, what their education and skill level is, what their economic condition is, what their family circumstances are, or what they have or have not accomplished in the past. But what I do care about, and what I know, is that each and every one of them is fully capable of becoming a changemaker. My work has proved again and again that ALL young people, and not just a FEW, are capable of creating social and economic value in society.

Their success and failure depend on the paradigm that young people are growing up with. Many of us believe that degrees, diplomas, and skills produce desired results. But getting young people from where they are to where they should be requires a simple change in the way that we look at young people.

When we engage young people in changemaking, we don't have to tell young people what to do, when to do it, how to do it, or where to do it; they will always surprise you with their creativity.

When young people start using their changemaking abilities, they find endless opportunities. No special knowledge and skills are required to begin a changemaking journey. A simple realization of *"I have everything I need"* is enough to begin their journey. The good news is that young people can switch paths anytime. One of the most exciting changemaking abilities is to start something from nothing. The "wait until told" strategy does not help young people to become a changemaker. When we look at the lives of young people today, we find many similarities between educated and uneducated young people. Both are failing to realize that they have everything they need to live a purposeful life. To become a changemaker, both need to uninstall their negative belief system. Their minds need a reason to replace what they believed for so many years. These beliefs are entrenched deep in their minds. The good news is that they can change their belief system. They need to be involved in changemaking to develop a new belief system or to rewrite their current belief system.

When I was in college, I used to be very shy and timid. I developed the negative belief system that I can't speak in public. When I started my first job, I was soon sent to attend an international conference on youth in Nepal. During the conference, the moderator asked me to share my thoughts and experiences with the delegates after the tea break. I remember my heart started beating so loud and swiftly. I ran into the washroom to gather myself. I did not listen to my subconscious mind. I decided to give it a try. I came out and spoke at the conference. I got very positive feedback from the delegates. This was the time when I was able to change my limiting belief system and replace it with a positive belief system. At that time, I felt most fulfilled in life. Another important thing that happened after that experience was that all the negative thoughts that were previously limiting my options in life worked in reverse to help me move forward in life. I strongly believe that there is only one thing which can lift youth living in poverty out of their situation of learned helplessness, and that is to start practicing their changemaking abilities.

Well-intentioned, BUT…

This is the first time in the history of the world that young people have been recognized as a priority. Every country is drifting into a "what should be" policy stance towards its young people. It is indeed very encouraging to see the increased interest in young people. There are many reasons behind this increased interest in young people.

- According to UNFAP, the world has a record youth population of 1.8 billion between the ages of 10 and 24. About 9 out of 10 young people are living in less developed countries, where the social and physical infrastructure needed to foster positive development of young people is being eroded.
- The unprecedented increase in youth-led terrorism incidents have acted as a wake-up call to all of us. The young people involved in carrying out these deadly attacks were not uneducated, poor, or backward.

- Our past efforts to empower young people have not been able to produce the desired results. We have seen that short-term interventions brought only short-term results.
- Our current efforts lack comprehensive vision, as they focus either on problem reduction or future preparation.
- The growing number of young people presents a great opportunity to accelerate the development process in many countries.

Chapter 2

THE HISTORY OF THE YOUTH DEVELOPMENT MOVEMENT: OUR COMMON RESPONSES

The history of the youth development movement can be described as fragmented, inadequate, misguided, problem-oriented, and charity-driven. No single country has ever tried to help youth get started as changemakers intentionally.

There is no encouragement and mechanism available to encourage and engage young people in changemaking, even in the best families and schools. If we examine the basic data collection and measurement systems of youth in developed and developing countries, we will find that there is no focus on youth-led changemaking, only on youth problems and youth preparation.

Ask this simple question to parents, teachers, youth development workers, and policy makers: How do we know that young people are doing well in life?

Their answers will give you a good idea of the state of knowledge about youth development. I am pretty sure you will get the following answers:

- If young people are staying away from problems.
- If young people are obedient.
- If young people are performing well in academics.
- If young people are skilled.
- If young people are behaving politely.

My more than 20 years of personal experience of working with young people has helped me to understand that:

- Innocence is not enough.
- Compliance is not enough.
- Academic performance is not enough.
- Skill development is not enough.
- Politeness is not enough.

I have met so many young people in life who are innocent, obedient, educated, skilled, and polite, but they are seriously struggling to find a place in society. What is stopping young people from living the life of their dreams? It is their weak belief system.

A vast majority of young people are struggling, not because of their genes or deficits, but due to their weak belief system. They have enormous changemaking abilities, but no empowering belief system. Hence, their changemaking abilities become a victim of their poor belief system. Parents, teachers, and policy makers believe that the problems encountered by young people are out *there*. They don't realize that the problem is inside, and not outside.

Not surprisingly, when we examine the work that is being done in the field of youth development, we will find out that the whole youth development field centers around two major themes: prevention and preparation. Let's examine each approach.

The Prevention Approach

The prevention approach focuses on addressing the individual risk level. It emphasizes protecting young people from problematic behaviors. According to this approach, youth problems are the main barrier of sound youth development and growth. This approach puts its complete focus on designing and delivering surgical interventions for young people who are troublemakers.

This approach has condensed the challenges of youth development to a set of problems that need to be addressed. This approach views young people as passive recipients who receive services to resolve a problem. This approach is considered effective when the youth problem is eliminated. It is interesting to note that many of the prevention-related programs were not the result of sound research and evaluation.

There are many reasons why the prevention approach is not helpful and should be replaced:

- It restricts the scope of youth development work to troubled youth only.
- It focuses on quick-fixes.
- It focuses on addressing a single problem behavior.
- It focuses on avoidance of youth problems only.
- It is about delivering services to young people as passive beneficiaries/recipients.
- It labels youth as problems.
- It does not consider the person-in-environmental perspective.
- It assumes that youth development happens in the absence of youth problems.
- It does not recognize and treat youth as changemakers.
- It defines youth development in terms of what it is not, rather than what it is.

It is fundamentally wrong to define everything in terms of a problem. We don't assess people in terms of problems. "Innocence" does not represent the only goal that most parents and teachers want from young people. More importantly, it does not reflect the goals that young people want for themselves.

We have enough longitudinal studies available that show our prevention programs have not delivered the desired results. Our prevention programs have not helped young people stay away from drugs, and they have not reduced incidents of suicide, juvenile crime, risky sexual and reproductive health behaviors, conduct disorders, or delinquent and antisocial behaviors.

Drivers of Problematic Youth Behavior

I personally believe that there are three main factors that influence young people to get involved in problematic behavior(s):

- The absence of a caring adult or institution.
- A weak belief system.
- The inability to practice changemaking abilities.

Let me explain each of these factors briefly.

Absence of a caring adult or institution

The presence of a caring adult or institution in the life of a young person serves as a principal barrier of getting involved in risky behaviors. The presence of a caring adult or institution will help the individual develop a desire to become a changemaker in life. The presence of a caring adult or institution is a prerequisite to engage in positive behavior. It is important to understand that it is not poverty and deprivation that hurts young people, but the loss of respect from others, self-respect, and dignity that hurts our youth the most.

Weak belief system

I have observed that many times, unconsciously, our families and institutions breed a weak belief system which brings out the worst in young people. Negative beliefs hurt more than the absence of education and skills. Our beliefs play a huge invisible role in our lives. Although science and technology have made huge progress in the current century, they have not reduced the amount of time required to raise a child with a positive belief system. The results we get in our lives are the reflection of our belief system, and not the reflection of our potential.

Inability to practice changemaking abilities

The other major reason why young people get involved in risky behaviors is their inability to recognize and use their changemaking abilities. Many young people have become unaware of the fact that they were born with greatness. They all have greatness within them, and they don't need anything else to be great. God has given them so many natural gifts and abilities. They simply need to draw it out or tap into their greatness. The best thing about human beings is that they have the ability to alter their circumstances anytime in their lives, simply by using their changemaking abilities. Many young people today want to have everything without using their changemaking abilities. If you ask an average young person in the street, *"Are you aware of your changemaking abilities?"*, you will notice that most young people don't know. When young people start recognizing and using these changemaking abilities, they start changing the results in their lives.

There is a clear-cut understanding that young people require more than the avoidance of problems to become changemakers. We need a broader and more positive vision for every young person. Prevention programs have failed to generate the belief among young people that they are valuable human beings. They have also failed to realize that young people do not grow up in activities, projects, and programs. They grow up in environments, such as their family environment, their school environment, and their community environment, all of which offer pathways and roadblocks to becoming changemakers.

The Preparation Approach

The preparation approach is characterized by the social, emotional, behavioral, cognitive, and vocational development of young people. Its emphasis is on providing young people with the education and skills they need to succeed in life. The philosophy behind the preparation approach is that the absence of problems is not equivalent to the acquisition of knowledge and skills.

The preparation approach focuses on creating social settings that are supportive of young people. It tries to move beyond a perspective that focuses on the disturbances in the lives of young people, and instead focuses on context. The focus on social context provides a new direction for policy makers and youth development practitioners.

Now, they want to know where and how young people interact with their families, friends, teachers, and other community members. The most appealing thing about this approach is that it has recognized young people as "resources to be developed" and as a "good investment" for the future.

Gaps in the preparation approach are:

- The preparation approach takes a futuristic approach. It does not take into account how the changemaking abilities of students can be used in the present.
- It predicts that young people have great potential to serve only after acquiring knowledge and skills.
- It focuses only on the provision. It does not focus on providing opportunities to young people for engagement.
- It sees young people as assets to be developed. It does not recognize that young people are a resource to meet the social and economic needs of society *right now*.
- It does not offer ownership to young people to decide what is good for them. Youth preparation programs are developed and executed by experts.
- It sees young people as consumers of services.
- It manipulates young people to follow a particular view or agenda.

Academic qualifications and vocational skills are not enough. We have seen that academic and vocational skills have not made a difference in the lives of many young people. Failure to clarify the real needs of young people has already cost us a lot.

We have seen that academic qualifications and vocational skills often go unused or underused. It is interesting to observe that some young people who are involved in antisocial activities are successful in achieving their goals and targets, while young people with knowledge and skills struggle to create an impact.

Young people involved in gangs often did not go to any educational and vocational school, but they show extraordinary competence to use their changemaking abilities for the wrong purposes.

These young people show more confidence and self-determination than young people in school. The question is, how can they show so much confidence, self-determination, and competence in carrying out their destructive ideas?

The reason is that they often find someone in their lives that trusts their potential and gives them a sense of purpose and ownership. Since these young people often grow up in low-trust environments and want better lives for themselves, they respond to this blind trust enthusiastically by misusing their innate changemaking abilities without considering the consequences of their actions.

Imagine what would have happened if all these young people who are involved in gangs and have committed suicide attacks were engaged in positive activities. Imagine what would have happened if these young people had used their changemaking abilities to address issues like education, female empowerment, health, and the environment, instead of blowing themselves up.

I am not making these statements to undermine the importance of academic qualifications and vocational skills. Academic qualifications and vocational skills are vital, but not sufficient. The best preparation for the future is the engagement of young people as changemakers today.

A New Vision

The field of youth development has reached an important crossroads in terms of its focus, achieved results, and future directions. It is clear that we need a "change in approach", as both prevention and preparation approaches have struggled to achieve the desired results.

Time is ripe for a new vision. It is time to surrender our long-held traditional approaches of working with young people. Our current vision is restricted to problem reduction and meeting the needs of young people objectively.

We must provide an alternative vision to broaden the range of our expectations and responses. We need a positive vision for every young person, and not only for a few troubled or well-prepared (educated and skilled) young people. We have a record population of young people today. We must not move slowly to broaden our response. Providing a new vision can have a powerful impact on the world.

So, what is the missing dimension in the current vision?

The missing dimension from the current vision is to view young people as changemakers, and as a solution instead of a problem.

It is very unfair that young people are cut off completely from changemaking on false premises. I have shown through my work that ALL young people are capable of changemaking. We are missing out so much every day because of our weak and wrong belief system regarding young people.

It's time for us to be open and brave. Our old way of working with young people has not been effective.

We have already lost so many precious lives. We have led so many young people to live miserable lives by passing on incorrect belief systems. We have forced so many young people to set up small goals instead of big goals for themselves.

History is full of examples of people who achieved big goals in life. Many of them were not raised in rich and educated families. They did not go to the best schools. They did not bring their needs and deprivations into the market. They decided to use their changemaking abilities to make a difference in the society.

Imagine what the world would be like if every young person was seen as a changemaker and was provided with an opportunity to practice changemaking abilities. Our present and future depends upon the ways in which youth are treated. It is time to see young people as a part of the solution, rather than as a part of the problem, and as a major force to bring positive change in our communities. Their enthusiasm, energies, and changemaking abilities are the best resources available to us to create a meaningful impact on the socio-economic development of the world. Young people must be intentionally given the space to become changemakers and constructive forces of positive change.

We have more young people in less developed countries than in developed countries. These young people, if trusted as equal partners in development, can speed up the development process. Currently, they lack the trust of society. They are living disconnected lives. They are often trusted by "bad" people to carry out "bad" actions. We have already seen that when young people turn to violence and crime, they become the biggest threat to peace and prosperity. However, if these young people are turning to changemaking, they could become the biggest ambassadors of peace and prosperity.

Everything that young people need for changemaking has already been given to them. All they have to do is use it. It is sad to observe that very few young people use it. Many young people might be thinking that it would be very expensive to use their changemaking toolkit. But the opposite is true; it is free to use your changemaking abilities, and it can bring great returns for society and the individual.

Overhaul-A Top-to-Bottom Radical Change

Philosophy

Changemaking is a choice. Every day, when we interact with young people, we can choose what kind of expectation we have from them. We can choose compliance, or we can choose changemaking. *My purpose of writing this book on youth-led changemaking is to help parents, teachers, policy makers, youth development practitioners, and young people change their mindset so that they can choose changemaking every day.* We must challenge every young person every day to become a changemaker. We must provide space to young people to practice changemaking abilities every day, not just when there is a natural calamity or a disaster.

The best way to choose a constructive philosophy for young people is to reflect on our current philosophy. We have gathered a considerable amount of data and knowledge. This data and knowledge can help us to reach an objective review of the conclusions we have drawn about young people. We know what is not working for young people. We know that an overwhelming majority of our parents and teachers do not operate from a sound philosophy when it comes to measuring the progress of children and young people.

They have no idea what they have missed out on and left undone. The question, then, is why do parents, teachers, and policy makers continue to enshrine the old way of assessing young people every day? The simple answer is because *they don't know* that their children and young people can become changemakers *during* their studies. If we have not provided a single opportunity to young people to practice changemaking abilities during their educational journey of 16 to 20 years, then chances are that they are going to repeat the same misjudgment for the next 20 years.

It is time for everyone to change their philosophy towards young people by adding new knowledge. *I know it is difficult to give up long-held beliefs without new information and evidence.*

Parents and teachers should not wait for 16 to 20 years to see if young people can become changemakers after their education. Progress must be assessed on a regular basis. The intentional checking on the changemaking abilities of every young person can serve as a great barometer of responsible thinking. The longer we wait to see the impact, the harder it will be for young people to become changemakers.

The lack of data on youth-led changemaking has made the job very difficult in the past. Our current tools to measure the performance and development of young people are so misleading and flawed. There is an urgent need to change or improve our philosophy. A new philosophy can lead to the creation of new indicators to measure the performance of young people. There is a need to develop common indicators that can be used by parents, teachers, policy makers, and youth development practitioners. This book on youth-led changemaking is written to provide a new philosophy to parents, teachers, policy makers, and youth development practitioners after testing it with several thousand young people.

Expectations

Expectations play a significant role in shaping young people's lives. Our expectations from children and young people have remained unchanged for a very long period of time. These expectations are based on our beliefs and customs. These expectations are to be obedient, intelligent, polite, and problem-free.

These expectations are communicated to children and young people again and again by several stakeholders, such as families, schools, politicians, policy makers, and youth development workers, and they have not served children and young people very well. The schedule provided to children and young people to achieve these expectations is lengthy, and yet, it still leaves young people without a consciousness of their changemaking abilities.

It is time to have different expectations for children and young people. It is time to expect every child and young person to become a changemaker by creating a social and economic value in society. It is time to see youth-led changemaking as the main expectation to be met every day, rather than in the future, or on some sunny day that will never come. This expectation should not be judged against a long-term framework. It is the responsibility of parents and teachers to help children and young people see themselves as changemakers. It is time for parents and teachers to redefine childhood and adolescence as the best time for changemaking.

We must spread this expectation in every part of the world to help children and young people switch to a more empowering path. I believe that the best time to begin your changemaking journey is when you are a child. Every child must receive the message early in life that there is no fixed age for changemaking. Every child is born with changemaking abilities. They just need a single opportunity or an individual who shows trust in their changemaking abilities to get started on their changemaking journey.

People who see themselves as changemakers early in life are more likely to be successful, well-educated, and self-reliant. We must have high expectations for every child and young person. It is distressing to see that our expectations from children and young people who are educated and from higher social economic backgrounds are very high, whereas our expectations from children and young people living in low-income families and communities are very low. We must not forget that *everyone* is gifted with changemaking abilities.

How can we help ALL young people to become changemakers?

- By believing that every child is born with changemaking abilities.
- By communicating our expectations to children and young people on a regular basis.
- By taking responsibility to facilitate children and young people to become changemakers.
- By measuring the performance of every child and young person as a changemaker on a regular basis.

Taking young people from where they are to where they should be requires a simple change in expectation. When a young person looks into our eyes and feels that we trust their changemaking abilities, the new paradigm for growing up is established.

Attitudes

"Young people are always like that," is an often-spoken phrase by adults. It reflects the adult's attitudes towards young people. It is a harsh reality that young people in our society are seen in a bad light. They are not treated as people, but rather as a problem. They are seen as a demographic challenge.

There is a persistent high level of fear of young people among many adults. They are seen as a potential threat. Their talents and changemaking abilities are often going unnoticed by society. They are not trusted. Parents and teachers are suspicious of young people. They are often subjected to unfair treatment. They are micromanaged. Widespread prejudice against young people is recognized in many studies.

Young people living in low-income families and communities with little to no education experience a harsher treatment than young people from high-income families and communities with degrees and skills. During the last twenty years of my work with young people, there were thousands of young people that shared with me that they were seen as "criminals", "useless", "a burden", "disrespectful", "lazy", "trouble", "bad", "rude", "rebellious", "drug dealers", "insensitive", "careless", "undisciplined", and "unmotivated". It is no wonder, then, that so many young people are struggling to find a place in our society, as our society has failed them.

It is interesting to note that attitudes towards young people in academic literature are associated with problems. It would be rare to find positive attitudes towards young people in academic literature. There are so many research studies and articles available on the market that deal with young people's attitudes towards violence, smoking, drugs, HIV/

AIDS, terrorism, and their parents. The major theme emerging from this literature is that young people are a "lost" generation.

The electronic and print media love to report the violent behavior of young people. Youth is visible in the media only when they pose a threat. Young people who are involved in carrying out criminal activities get widely covered.

Negative portrayals of young people are doing a serious disservice to young people. The media hardly talks about young people who are making a difference in the lives of others. The adults' negative perception of young people has to do with how they were raised. The problem comes when they paint every young person with the same brush. The negative views of adults are based on fear, rather than objective reality.

Specific examples of adults' attitudes towards young people are given below:

- *Parents:* They insist that young people pursue a particular direction or career. They don't give freedom for young people to decide. They define boundaries. They define the roadmap to success. They are in charge. They seek obedience. Parents put a lot of pressure and expectations on young people.

- *Teachers:* They believe that young people cannot think and create for themselves. They force young people to memorize things. They try to control young people. They treat young people like lesser human beings. They are always ready to fix young people. They don't see their gifts. They tend to discipline young people. They burden young people with unwanted work. They judge young people against their academic performance.

- *Elderly People:* They doubt the capabilities of young people. They misjudge young people. They talk at young people, not to them. If they see young people in the street alone, they might grab their mobile phones or bags firmly so that young people can't snatch them.

- *Policy Makers:* They don't listen to young people. They do not create a space for young people. They see young people as inferior. They are quick to punish young people. They treat them as victims or sinners.

- *Politicians:* They manipulate young people. They break promises with young people. They value young people only when they need their votes or support to organize a political gathering. They do not show any sense of accountability towards young people.

- *Youth-Serving Organizations:* They treat young people as passive beneficiaries. They are interested in numbers, and not in real change. They represent young people's problems. They use the hammer as a main strategy to solve the problems of young people.

- *Donors:* They have failed to take into account the changemaking potential of young people. They are interested in supporting crisis intervention programs, rather than youth-led changemaking programs. They are targeting primarily at-risk or socially excluded young people, as opposed to all young people.

- *Police:* They mistreat young people. They are always suspicious of young people. They treat young people like criminals. If a bunch of young people are walking up the street, they might be searched. They treat young people as being guilty of something.

The impact of these attitudes on young people is damaging and far-reaching. Young people feel devalued. They believe they are seriously lacking and limited. They act from a sense of scarcity in life. They lose control over their lives and feel vulnerable. Their changemaking spirit is broken. Their changemaking abilities are frozen.

It is interesting to observe that adults develop their attitudes and opinions about young people by looking at a small number of young people who are involved in risky behaviors.

Adults tend to ignore a vast majority of young people that are not causing any trouble. They are in communities and in schools. Yet, many adults don't see them, and only focus on the *bad* behavior of a few young people.

Adults also send the message again and again to young people that they are superior to young people, or of greater value, and young people, by default, have less value and worth. This attitude views young people as objects, and not as a group of people that can also create value in society.

It is interesting to observe that no adult recognizes youth as an ideal time for changemaking. They define success for young people as getting a degree and staying out of trouble. Most adults are unable to imagine that young people can serve as changemakers *now*. Therefore, there is no expectation from parents, teachers, and policy makers for young people to become changemakers at a younger age. They keep telling young people that they should put their complete focus on education for getting a well-paying job in the future. Why can't young people use what they learn in classrooms now? The time has come when we need to see every young person as a changemaker. We should stop seeing young people as either saints or sinners. We should stop mistrusting young people. We must establish and restore trust with young people. As a society, we need to reassess our attitudes towards young people. We must abandon this saying that "young people are the best investment in our future". Schools must provide the space to all young people to practice changemaking abilities now. Parents must expect young people to become changemakers during their studies, and policy makers must recognize young people as a huge untapped resource to drive change in their communities.

We must remember that young people are not always future-driven. They are often passion-driven and activity-driven. Providing a changemaking opportunity to young people sooner will have a positive impact on both young people and the communities they serve.

Practices

Youth development concepts and approaches are introduced all the time. The concept of youth-led changemaking emerged as a counterbalance to the overemphasis on youth prevention and youth preparation programs. Youth-led changemaking represents an important new lens through which to view the potential of young people. There are many people and institutions around the world that have started exploring new alternatives to promote youth development. It is a very good time to advance the concept of youth-led changemaking, as the concept is gaining momentum internationally. We need to find out the kind of scientific work needed to advance the field of youth-led changemaking. Youth-led changemaking cannot become a top priority without making it happen in a variety of settings. There are four main settings that need to be involved in nurturing an environment of youth-led changemaking. These four settings are: families, educational and vocational institutions, communities, and organizations.

Families

Youth development work is mostly taking place around schools and organizational dimensions. But learning changemaking begins at home. One of the most exciting gifts that parents can give to their children is to provide space and encouragement to their children to practice changemaking abilities. It is essential that parents get involved early in encouraging children to embark on a journey of changemaking. It is important that parents accord sufficient time, energy, resources, and commitment to inspire children to practice changemaking abilities. It is time that we see inculcating the changemaking spirit as a part of basic parenting. If parents do not practice changemaking abilities, there are very little chances that their children will practice them. If the parents practice changemaking abilities and encourage children from the day of their birth, it makes it possible for the children to practice changemaking. If the family does not lay the psychological foundation for children to become changemakers, it would be very difficult for children to practice changemaking abilities later on. Family is the first major unit that needs to be oriented and engaged if the changemaking spirit is to be made a top priority in our society. There is no better place to set patterns for changemaking than within the family. The degeneration of the changemaking spirit is done at an early age. How can we start the regeneration of the changemaking spirit? There are many ways that parents can instill a changemaking spirit in their children.

- Create a book about changemaking for your children.
- Encourage children to think and share ideas during family meetings.
- Promote teamwork among children.
- Encourage problem solving in children by encouraging them to share their ideas about how to solve a family or societal problem.
- Reward changemaking actions of your children instantly.
- Give your children the chance to take the lead when completing a family task.
- Share stories of young changemakers.
- Take your children to places where less privileged children are living.
- Celebrate a changemaking day or week with your children.
- Ask your children regularly whether they are using their changemaking abilities in school or in the community.
- Practice changemaking abilities so that your children can see what happens when you use your changemaking abilities.
- Show them how happy it makes you when your children practice changemaking abilities.

A changemaking attitude is a natural outcome of a family environment. The drive for changemaking stems from moral training and moral responsibility. Good moral training automatically leads to changemaking.

Educational and Vocational Institutions

Educational and vocational institutions need to stimulate the changemaking abilities of young people. The importance of educational and vocational institutions in advancing the concept of youth-led changemaking is widely recognized. These institutions can offer so much in the shape of human resources, intellectual resources, physical resources, and social networks to build the momentum for youth-led changemaking.

Our educational and technical institutions have started to recognize their failure to help young people to become changemakers. Educational and vocational institutions can play a vital role in developing a desire among young people to become changemakers, creating opportunities and mechanisms to engage young people in changemaking, and integrating youth-led changemaking into the culture and curriculum.

Currently, there are no opportunities provided to young people to practice changemaking abilities. There is a serious shortage of staff for promoting youth-led changemaking. There is no funding available for youth-led changemaking. Faculty members are not trained and do not have experience in the field of youth-led changemaking. And there is no obligation or reward for students to embrace changemaking. There is no space provided for students to build a career in changemaking.

There are many ways that youth-led changemaking can be introduced and institutionalized in educational and vocational institutions:

- Create a changemaking center which would serve as a changemaking hub within the institution.
- Offer academic credit for carrying out a changemaking project.
- Offer rewards to motivate faculty members and students to begin their changemaking journey.
- Create a trust-based model, like the *YES Model*, to inspire young people to become changemakers.

- Build the capacity of faculty members and students in the field of changemaking.
- Develop a network of changemakers.
- Build connections with changemaking organizations.
- Launch changemaking competitions.
- Celebrate a changemaking day or week in the institution.

Youth-led changemaking will elevate the quality of teaching and learning. It will enable educational institutions to shift their focus from memorizing to changemaking. It is high time to open the doors for youth-led changemaking in educational and vocational institutions to revolutionize the entire educational and skill-building system.

Communities

Communities provide an important setting for youth-led changemaking promotion. Communities can serve as the most powerful vehicle to promote youth-led changemaking. Today, young people are growing up in communities that present tremendous opportunities and challenges. Young people's development processes are heavily influenced by many factors, such as family expectations, community expectations, educational institution's expectations, and other stakeholder's expectations.

It is, therefore, necessary to focus on social settings so that we can move beyond a perspective that focuses on the problems of young people and the preparation of young people for the future, to the creation of settings that are supportive of youth-led changemaking. The emphasis on youth-led changemaking will stimulate a new agenda in our communities, one that focuses on knowing how each player in the community can contribute to creating multiple opportunities for young people to unlock their changemaking potential, practice changemaking abilities, and gain a sense of hope, connection, and usefulness.

I believe that what is missing in our communities is the vision to see and engage young people as changemakers *now*. The vision of safer, stronger, more peaceful, and more prosperous communities cannot be realized without the meaningful involvement of young people in the changemaking process.

A strong and united commitment to promote youth-led changemaking at the community level is needed. The early involvement of young people as changemakers in our communities offers the best solution to the threats and deficits facing our communities.

The best way to advance the concept of youth-led changemaking at a community level is to encourage the creation of a *Changemaking Charter* in each community. The Changemaking Charter will include the principles and plans of action that each community should pursue to facilitate young people to begin their changemaking journey. *The main purpose of this charter should be to make sure that every young person is entitled to be treated as a changemaker.*

This Changemaking Charter should bring together key stakeholders, such as government representatives, religious leaders, teachers, parents, business leaders, and young people to establish strategic partnerships to mainstream youth-led changemaking in the local service delivery systems. The Changemaking Charter will provide an opportunity to unlock young people's inherent changemaking potential and community goals simultaneously. *It will also offer young people an opportunity to build a positive relationship with adults that is based on trust and respect. Serving as changemakers in communities will open multiple paths for young people to live a life of purpose.*

In conclusion, I must say that engaging young people in changemaking is an investment in the richness of our communities, both today and tomorrow.

Organizations

Organizations hold remarkable but untapped potential as sources for promoting youth-led changemaking in the society. It is a sad reality that a large number of youth-serving organizations have not recognized young people as part of the solution.

It is very difficult to create a culture of youth-led changemaking without the support of local and international organizations. Our efforts to build a culture of youth-led changemaking requires broadening the youth development agenda of organizations.

Organizations have to be aligned to have any chance of implementing the vision of youth as changemakers. Organizations must support all areas of youth-led changemaking programs to create new opportunities in all settings. If organizations are unable to move beyond addressing the problems of young people, or training and educating young people, they will continue to waste an enormous opportunity to benefit from the changemaking potential of our young people.

Their failure to recognize what is missing will only lead to the distrust of donors in the youth development field and will make future investments more challenging to get ahold of. There is a desperate need for realignment towards a new youth development vision and a replacement of old, outdated practices. *It is understandable that many organizations will find it very difficult to make new choices, as they might lack knowledge and expertise of the youth-led changemaking process. Therefore, this book can be a source of great inspiration for those organizations that have decided to embark upon a new territory.*

How can organizations play a role in advancing the concept of youth-led changemaking?

- Adopt a youth-led changemaking approach that recognizes youth as changemakers *now*, and not only in the future.
- Assess the capacity of existing players when testing and implementing this new approach.
- Forge new strategic partnerships to offer the full range of support that society needs to support their young people in becoming changemakers.
- Create new programs and projects that can help young people become changemakers.

- Transmit this new vision to communities so that other stakeholders can also become major players in the field.
- Provide technical and financial resources to strengthen existing service delivery mechanisms and to create new local intermediaries that will act as champions in the field of youth-led changemaking.
- Invest in the documentation and evaluation of youth-led changemaking programs.
- Develop assessment tools to track the progress of youth-led changemaking projects.

These recommendations are meant to build the capacity of organizations to implement the youth-led changemaking approach.

There is a serious shortage of vocabulary for the promotion of youth as changemakers. It may even be the key challenge while developing and evaluating youth engagement policies and programs.

Families, schools, communities, organizations, and policy makers cannot measure what they cannot imagine and explain.

The daunting challenge in front of us is to provide an alternative vision and vocabulary to all of them. We have created a kind of society where it requires serious efforts to create conducive conditions that inspire all stakeholders to revisit their philosophy, expectations, attitudes, and practices.

This book is written to create a sense of urgency among all stakeholders that something we have been following has failed to produce the desired results, and that it is time to be more daring and unorthodox in our approach to make it right.

Stakeholders must understand that this new vision of seeing "youth as changemakers now" is already happening. There are already thousands of stories available. They must be circulated and read to further the advancement of our new belief system.

It is time for all stakeholders to change expectations and practices pertaining to young people. They must realize that there is a huge gap between where we wanted our children to be and where they are. They must realize that even our best efforts have not produced results.

Stakeholders who touch the lives of young people every day and are in the position of investing time, effort, and resources must recognize the gap and create a sense of urgency. We must realize that business as usual will continue to hurt not only young people, but all of us. It is time to launch a new generation of initiatives at all levels of society to help every young person become a changemaker now.

Conclusion

Human beings have the remarkable Changemaking ability; they can turn weeds into gardens. We must do everything to help every young person discover the changemaker within.

I firmly believe that unlocking the changemaking potential of young people can prove to be a game changer for everyone. I believe that the longer our children are in school, the fewer chances they have of becoming changemakers.

Enabling young people to practice changemaking skills can make a huge difference in the lives of young people.

It is not what changemaking will cost our schools; it is what it has already cost us.

Deep inside, each one of us wants to become a changemaker. We may doubt our abilities to do so, but I believe that each one of us can live the life of a changemaker.

Part 2

Chapter 3

MY JOURNEY TOWARDS MY VISION: THE YES ENGAGEMENT MODEL

I wanted to begin by sharing my story about my vision. I wanted to share how circumstances led me to launch the first-ever "Youth as a Solution" movement in Pakistan to help young people get started as changemakers.

I did not arrive at this vision overnight. I developed this vision slowly and gradually. It was not an instant thought. It was the outcome of my intensive engagement and interaction with young people. It was the result of the constant frustration I experienced while implementing deficit-based youth development programs. It was a response to the growing deprivations faced by young people. It was the result of the reflection on my experiences of working with young people. The only asset that helped me to pursue and eventually prove my thesis was the positive and strong belief system which I inherited from my mother.

Here is my story.

I believe everything in life happens for a reason. Every experience in your life helps you to reform you, prepare you, direct you, and shape you. I entered the youth development field by accident. Youth development work was never on my radar. The story goes that my elder brother applied for a job in the Family Planning Association of Pakistan. He got shortlisted. In the meantime, he passed the civil services examination of Pakistan. He encouraged me to apply for the job.

Since I was free after completing my post-graduation exams in political science, I decided to apply for the job to get some experience. I got selected instantly. I never wanted to stay in this field. I wanted to become a civil servant, as it was seen as the most respectable job in our culture and country.

I was given the responsibility to assist the youth and female development section with designing, implementing, and evaluating sexual reproductive health programs. Since it was my first job, I was working very hard to learn, grow, and contribute.

Very soon, I was given the responsibility to conduct and monitor the sexual reproductive health awareness sessions for young people across the country. I was traveling extensively. I had the opportunity to interact with many young people living in the rural and most deprived communities of Pakistan.

I received first-hand knowledge of the difficulties and tragedies faced by young people. I heard countless cries of young people saying *no one cares about us, no one trust us, no one values us, no one respect us, and no one really wants to help us.*

At that time, I was so consumed by the delivery of my sexual reproductive health messages that I could not realize that the young people who were attending my sessions had a very weak and limiting belief system. They were growing up in an environment of little to no trust. They had so many problems in their lives. They were rejected by society and they had very low self-esteem. Their attention was taken up by serious concerns. They were worried about the unmet needs of their families. They were looking for someone to believe in them. I had only a very superficial understanding of their deprivations. I wanted to resolve all their problems with a dose of information about sexual reproductive health.

Try to imagine the scenario: Young people that are humiliated and degraded by society were asked to participate in sexual reproductive health programs that offer nothing about how to uninstall a negative belief system and change their lives. To have all those needs-to yearn to be trusted, valued, respected, cared for, and positively engaged, and then to be spoken to about sexual reproductive health. Imagine their frustration.

It was quite amazing that, despite my inability to understand what was missing in the lives of young people, I was constantly getting great evaluations. Young people were mutely trying to follow the model of success that I defined for them. They did not vent their feelings and frustrations to me. They showed me a great deal of respect. They were hoping against hope that one day, I might be able to offer them something that could turn their lives around.

My career was growing at a great speed. I was continuously getting a boost in my perks and privileges. On the other hand, the sufferings of young people were also increasing at a great speed. Every time I went back to those communities, I would hear some terrible and heartbreaking stories of young people that had destroyed their lives. I used to get very upset.

As my level of interaction was increasing, I started feeling like there was something seriously missing in my work. I started shifting my focus from myself to young people. I started accepting my inability to improve the condition of young people. I started realizing that simply providing youth with sexual reproductive health information would not change their situation.

I realized that our response to the serious situation facing young people had completely gone wrong. I started feeling very frustrated in my efforts to address the tragedies of young people. I realized that it is not poverty or deprivation in an absolute sense that hurts youth. It is not the lack of material goods or services that truly holds them back, but the loss of self-belief, trust, dignity, and self-respect. I realized that our families, educational institutions, communities, and organizations were producing and nourishing a psychology which brings out the lowest, most base part of human beings.

When I was going through this depressing and tough phase of my career, I was assigned the task of conducting an awareness-raising session on reproductive health with the displaced people who migrated from Bangladesh in Lahore. When I went to the community to conduct a training session on sexual reproductive health, I saw a huge crowd of children, young people, adults, women, and elderly people had gathered to welcome me. They were hoping that I would make some big announcement to them. They did not realize that I came to conduct an awareness session on reproductive health with young people in that community. The community organized a ceremony to honor me. I was very perplexed deep inside.

I was thinking that my field supervisor who arranged the session had not communicated the purpose of the meeting clearly. My confusion heightened when a young man called Samiullah Khan, who was conducting the ceremony, mentioned in the opening address very passionately that many government representatives and organizations had come here before, only to deliver what was not needed to them, and that everyone had exploited their troubles and made false promises.

As tension was creeping into my mind, I decided that I would not conduct the session on reproductive health. When I was invited onto the stage to share my views, I spoke briefly and said, *"Today I have come here to listen to you and find ways to work with you, to harness local resources to deal with your challenges"*. Although the community members were slightly disappointed to hear all this, as they were expecting a big announcement, they offered complete support to work with me to overcome their challenges. I was deeply impressed by the passion and commitment shown by a young person to contribute to the development of his community. I decided to work with Samiullah. He became my primary source of communication with this community.

I left the community without conducting a session and discussed the situation with my supervisors. I was told that since their needs are beyond the scope of our work, we cannot offer any assistance. Since I promised the community members that I would work with them to find a way to help children and young people grow in a safe environment, I decided to visit that community after my office hours, as my office was not very happy to see my increasing engagement in that community. I decided to challenge the status quo. I decided to go beyond my job description. I decided to stop doing things that have very little or no impact on young people.

I had several meetings with Samiullah to decide what needed to be done, and how it should be done in the absence of financial resources. The community had many unmet service needs. Samiullah wanted to start a project for children, as they were the most vulnerable to multiple forms of maltreatment. He wanted to set up a school to provide a wide range of services to children. I liked the idea. Since we had no financial resources to hire a building and staff members, *we decided to engage local young people, especially young girls between the ages of 12-16, to set up a school.* These girls were half-educated. They served as teachers, counselors, and administrators. We decided to engage girls, as they were available. It was difficult to engage boys in the daytime, as they were away for work. Since we had no proper place to start the school, we started using empty spaces without a roof in that community.

My Journey Towards My Vision: The YES Engagement Model

In a short period of time, we were able to enroll over 400 children, and the school became very popular among the masses. Parents started sending their children in the morning and evening to get an education. They were willing to pay a nominal fee. I was surprised to see the level of commitment and leadership shown by the young people of that community. Young girls who started serving as teachers also resumed their education. Later on, they attained graduate and post-graduate degrees. Many of them found good jobs in different companies.

This *youth-led school* has not only transformed the lives of many children, but has also inspired many people and organizations to invest in that community in the field of education and health. This whole experience really changed my life and helped me to find a new vision. Now, I wanted to change the role of young people in the society. I wanted to challenge traditional and outdated ideas pertaining to young people. I wanted everyone to see young people in a different light. I wanted to engage young people as problem solvers. I wanted to create and mobilize the support that young people need to embark upon a changemaking journey. I wanted everyone to honor young people.

By simply honoring young people, we can help them to transform themselves from victims to leaders.

I realized that there are so many young people who had no opportunity to realize their changemaking potential. They may never know what it is like to use these changemaking abilities to benefit themselves, their families, and their communities. I learned that our programs should help to improve the belief system of young people. Our programs should not be based on fear and mistrust. Trust-based programs that enable young people to unlock their changemaking potential can create a climate of hopefulness, allowing everyone to believe that all things are possible.

I realized that we are making a serious mistake by thinking that young people are ignorant, and that all we need to do is to educate them and protect them.

Of course, information and education are important for our kids, but it does not uninstall limiting belief systems in our youth. I found out that the most effective contraceptive is activated when you improve the belief system of young people and help them see themselves as changemakers, and not the victims of circumstances. I decided to develop a new vocabulary to define young people.

I arrived at three major conclusions from that experience:

1. Every young person is born with changemaking abilities.
2. It takes only one person or experience to become a changemaker.
3. When young people begin their changemaking journey, they rewrite their belief system.

This experience set me up for the rest of my life to bring a paradigm shift in the field of youth development; from seeing young people as a problem to seeing young people as a solution, from seeing young people as passive beneficiaries to seeing young people as the shapers of society, and from seeing young people as future leaders to seeing young people as changemakers *now*.

I resigned from my job and decided to embark upon a new and unchartered journey. I realized that the time was right to make a major leap forward. I launched the first-ever "Youth as a Solution, Not as a Problem" movement in Pakistan in 2002.

LAUNCHING OF YOUTH ENGAGEMENT SERVICES (YES) NETWORK PAKISTAN

Walking away from my current path was not very difficult for me. I did not want to continue with something that I believed was not making a real difference in the lives of young people. I was super excited, and not even slightly scared to start a new journey. I knew that I had set up an audacious goal, and I kept my eyes on my vision. I did not allow negative thoughts to distract me.

The example of my mother was right in front of me; how she stood firm in the worst of times to move forward with her vision to set up a school for children forty years ago. My mother displayed extraordinary commitment and courage to make a difference in the lives of several thousand children. My mother taught me a very important lesson in life: *that when we expand our vision in life, we expand our possibilities in life, and we are guided divinely.*

I laid out 5 core principles upon which I founded my organization:

1. We must focus on ALL YOUNG PEOPLE.
2. We must give every young person AT LEAST ONE CHANCE to practice changemaking abilities.
3. We must go BEYOND QUICK-FIX PROGRAMS.

4. We must SEE every young person as a potential changemaker NOW to build our society.
5. We must focus on young people's STRENGTHS, rather than on their deficits.

The next step was to choose the name of the organization. I decided to choose "Youth Engagement Services (YES) Network Pakistan" as the name of my organization. "Youth Engagement Services" defined exactly what I wanted to achieve and offer. I wanted everyone to recognize Youth Engagement as a vital force in achieving peace, prosperity, and stability.

I realized that young people represent a massive proportion of the population that is disengaged and overlooked when catalyzing positive change socially and economically. I came to the conclusion that the major reason for the mounting tragedies faced by young people is disengagement. Youth disengagement was not visible to people and institutions. It was, however, experienced by ALL (troubled and prepared) young people.

I thought it was important to define the term Youth Engagement, as it can be misinterpreted in many ways. I found out that many people and organizations were defining the term Youth Engagement differently, and it was very important to deal with the definitional dispute.

Since it was a new term for many people and organizations at that time, I decided to focus on defining Youth Engagement in a way that would increase clarity.

I began by thinking about how my definition of Youth Engagement is different from other youth development initiatives.

Here is how YES Network Pakistan differs:

1. It is more than an act of showing up.
2. It is more than youth participation in the political process or voting.

3. It is more than occasional volunteering.
4. It is more than the participation of young people in training programs.
5. It is more than the participation of young people as beneficiaries.
6. It is more than the participation of young people in adult-led and adult-supervised programs.
7. It is more than seeking advice or consulting young people.
8. It is more than organizing young people.
9. It is more than caring for young people.
10. It is more than the limited participation of young people in crisis situations.
11. It is more than providing basic services to young people.
12. It is more than the participation of young people in co-curricular activities.
13. It is more than the participation of young people in meetings, conferences, and talk shows.
14. It is more than the episodic engagement of young people in protests.
15. It is more than the participation of self-selected young people in community development work.
16. It is not meant for male youth only.

My definition of Youth Engagement is:

"It is an intentional and intensive process where young people are engaged in problem-solving that benefits everyone."

Let's take a look at the different parts of that definition:

- *Intentional:* This means that Youth Engagement is seen as an organized activity where young people are provided well-structured space, support, value, and recognition from an institution or community to carry out missions that are left unattended or unresolved.

- *Intensive:* This means that Youth Engagement is not seen as a side agenda, or something to be done on one sunny morning, or during free hours by young people. It is seen as a deliberate process to mainstream young people in all phases of programming to address a critical need. It means young people are not asked to simply plug into pre-determined programs.

- *Process:* Youth Engagement is a dynamic process where young people establish a positive and reciprocal relationship with others. This process is based on mutual respect and trust. It is not like other traditional concepts of relationships with youth, where young people are seen as "lesser" or "weak". In this process, young people and adults form a partnership to make a difference in their community.

- *Young People:* This means that ALL young people should be engaged in problem-solving. It does not focus on troubled or prepared young people only. It does not exclude young people on the basis of education, background, skill, gender, or setting. It views every young person as a vital resource to drive change in the society.

- *Problem-Solving:* Youth Engagement brings a massive shift in the field of youth development, as it challenges young people to serve rather than be served. It does not perceive young people as a problem to be fixed, but as people with a lot of potential to solve problems. The most exciting thing about this approach is that by engaging young people in problem-solving, we help young people stay away from problems and grow in profound ways.

- *Benefits Everyone:* Youth Engagement has a positive impact on everyone. It helps young people grow in profound ways. It provides the most viable and cost-effective ways for a community to meet its challenges and lay the foundation for a bright future.

In light of the existing realities faced by young people, and my experience working with young people, I developed a vision statement that described what I want to accomplish:

"YES strives for a world in which young people are not treated as empty vessels into which we pour our wisdom, and instead we treat all (troubled and prepared) young people as the most promising resource available to us in developing a new societal structure and meeting the high service needs of our communities; a world in which all young people are provided at least one practical changemaking experience; a world in which all young people are viewed as equal partners in collective efforts to improve civic life, rather than consumers, constituents, or foot soldiers for adult-supervised programs."

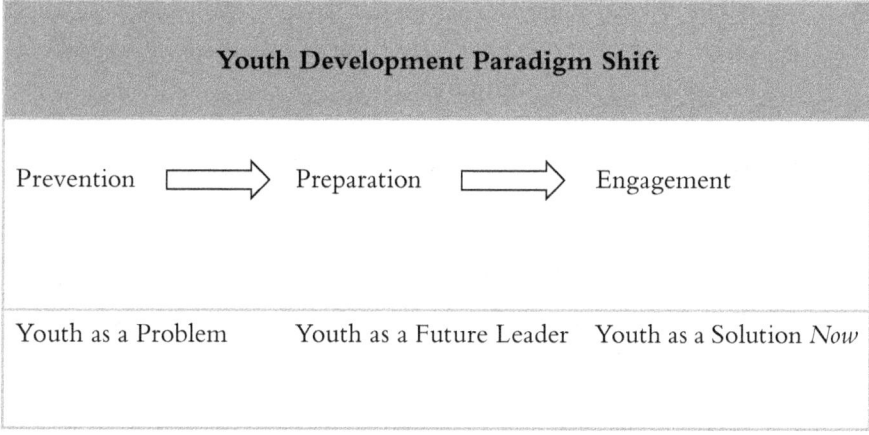

Table 5: Youth Development Paradigm Shift

It is indeed very distressing that society holds young people back without any concrete reason. If young people can serve effectively in military service, and if young people can achieve milestones in sports, fashion design, and information technology fields so early in their lives, then why can't they be engaged in carrying out important tasks to improve society?

I firmly believe that today, the biggest missing link in the lives of all young people is "engagement" in problem-solving. A vast majority of young people want everything without doing anything. Young people must understand that real life begins only when we do something. I wanted young people to act and lead, not just to be ready to act and lead. I see no reason to delay youth engagement in real problem-solving.

Uniqueness of YES Network Pakistan

In order to really understand how different the YES approach is, I wanted to contrast our way of seeing the world and engaging young people with the approach of existing players.

Existing Players	YES Network Pakistan
Serves Youth	Youth Serves
Focus on Problems of Youth	Focus on Engagement of Youth
Single-Domain Youth Development Programs	Multi-Domain Youth Development Programs
Single Value Creation	Multiple Value Creation Programs
Programs Designed for Young People	Programs Designed by Youth
High-Cost Programs	Low-Cost Programs
Short-Lived Programs	Long-Lived Programs
Focus on Limited Outcomes for Youth	Focus on Broader Outcomes
Focus on Limited Role of Youth	Focus on Broader Role of Youth
Focus on Troubled Young People	Focus on All Young People
Focus on Academics and Skill Development of Youth	Focus on All-Around Development of Youth Through Engagement
Focus on Reactive Programs	Focus on Youth-Led Changemaking

Table 6: Difference between Existing Players and YES Network Pakistan

Shifting the Focus on Systems

I started my journey from one community. After the validation of my idea, I decided to take my idea to many communities which are deprived and suffered due to natural calamities. I started working with a large number of young people across the country.

I was very happy to see the impact of my work on young people. Young people showed again and again how fast they respond when their changemaking abilities are trusted and valued. Now, I wanted to increase the impact of my work.

I realized that I might not be able to reach millions of young people in my country directly. I also felt the need to create a permanent mechanism to reintegrate youth into the society as changemakers. *I learned that young people do not grow up in projects and programs, but they grow up in paradigms.* I realized that if I am able to change the paradigms, I may be able to impact the lives of many young people quickly.

I realized that if I wanted to make quantum and tangible changes in the way we treat our young people, I would have to change the paradigms. I was thinking that putting youth-led changemaking at the center of educational and vocational institutions would be an easy job.

But very soon, I realized that I would have to overcome several attitudinal, structural, and cultural barriers to begin this process. I was surprised to find out that the major challenges were coming from those who were entrusted to empower children and young people.

I felt the need to do two things to move towards the creation of favorable paradigms for youth-led changemaking.

1. I realized that it is imperative to bring the top leadership of educational and vocational institutions on board.
2. I felt that I needed to win the support of credible people and organizations for my way of thinking.

My direct work with young people won the support of many international influential figures and organizations. The Jeanne Sauvé Foundation of Canada was the first to recognize my work with young people in 2004.

Ashoka, a US-based organization and a global leader in the field of social entrepreneurship, was the second organization that gave me the kind of social proof and validity that I needed at that time. I could not believe that there was an organization in the world that invested in changemakers.

Later on, the British Council joined me in my work, and supported my ideas and work graciously. It opened the doors to teamwork, collaboration and partnership-building for me.

This sort of social proof within and outside the country came at the right time for my work. My work continued to attract many international partners to invest in the field of youth-led changemaking.

I began my efforts to build a sound ecosystem for young people. Without building a supportive infrastructure for young people, I knew I would never be able to prove my thesis that every young person is born with enormous changemaking abilities. Being a sportsman, I realized the significance of an infrastructure to achieve your dreams. I knew that I did not have to build a new infrastructure; I had to simply transform the existing infrastructure to enable young people to showcase their changemaking abilities to society.

I began my journey to introduce the idea of youth-led changemaking in the educational and vocational institutions in 2007. I found out that the challenge is very complex. I thought I would get permission from the top leadership of educational and vocational institutions to start youth-led changemaking projects at their campus quickly. I came to know very soon that it was like climbing a mountain. Even though the destination was clear to me, the path to reach that mountain was full of obstacles. Every time I thought that I was very close to my destination, I encountered serious setbacks. I felt that I was fighting against an institutional oppression against young people.

In my climb, I met and found many positive people who understood the significance of my work in the lives of young people. They candidly and honestly reflected on the outcomes of their efforts. They accepted wholeheartedly that the current crisis faced by the young people had been manufactured by the institutions. These people gave me the confidence and courage to continue my journey with zeal and vigor. Each time I held an open session with the representatives of institutions, I assigned my team the task of identifying people in the group who showed passion and commitment to advance the field of youth-led changemaking. Each person that agreed to test the idea made my dream so much more attainable and the journey so much more endurable. I felt so happy inside with these small victories. I was very happy with each and every victory. I mobilized a large number of educational and vocational institutions, brick by brick, laying the foundation for the realization of my vision.

I also met many people who opposed the idea uselessly. I was surprised to see their passion to defeat something they did not try yet. I used to feel very emotionally disturbed when they passed on negativity about young people in open forums. A few of the sentences which I often heard from them were the following:

- Our students can't pay the fee. How can they become changemakers?
- Our students are from poor families. They only need jobs.
- We are here to teach students, not engage them.
- Students have no capability to drive change.
- Students have no training to start a changemaking project.
- Students will waste their time on such projects.
- We are already over-burdened.
- Parents of the students will not allow us to engage their children.
- The security situation is not good enough to engage students.
- Only students of high-income families should be engaged.
- Only students of business studies should be engaged.
- It is the beyond the scope of our work.
- It requires a lot of money to start a project.
- You are going to waste your time and resources by engaging young people in changemaking activities.

I used to feel very frustrated inside; I used to calm myself down by saying to myself that if I ever got an opportunity to give one piece of advice to the students of these people, I would tell them, *"When you plan to begin your changemaking journey, don't listen to the advice of those who have not taken the journey"*. I did not vent my feelings.

Apart from my frustration, I was actually grateful to all those people who resented my idea. It gave me a chance to learn the reason for their rejection. I was able to look at the way they were wired. I started preparing myself accordingly. I realized that I could not go with the same preparation all the time. I would have to prepare for every encounter with the representatives of educational and vocational institutions carefully and wisely. I would have to make sure that the information I was going to provide was relevant and truthful. It would have a strong effect on them.

I collected many case studies from the field. I invited young changemakers who won local and international competitions to share their experiences with the representatives of educational and vocational institutions. I started engaging professors and instructors of schools and colleges to share their experiences with others. I made sure that the information was presented in an easy-to-understand way. I was very hopeful that people would be inspired to join the field when they saw other people doing it. I used to carry a lot of social proof with me to inspire people to act urgently. I realized that I had to quickly show proof that their students were capable of driving social and economic value.

I designed a unique trust-based methodology (shared in the beginning) to unlock the changemaking potential of young people. Looking back, I must say it has been an incredible journey. At the beginning, I did not realize that it would be a physically and emotionally exhausting journey. I went through hardship of mind and body. I reached out to every nook and corner of the country. My car became my office, eating, meeting, and sleeping place. I tried to reach out to places with my small team where no one wanted to go. I wanted to prove that *all* young people, regardless of their location and background, have the latent changemaking abilities needed to drive change in their communities.

I was very happy when I launched the youth-led changemaking program in the Azad Jammu Kashmir (AJK), Federally Administered Tribal Area (FATA), and Gilgit regions. I engaged institutions and young people of AJK, FATA, and Gilgit to open doors for youth-led changemaking. The young people of AJK, FATA, and Gilgit showed incredible changemaking potential in a short period of time.

I remember one incident when I had to travel from Azad Kashmir to Multan to lead a session with the top leadership of the Punjab Vocational Training Council (PVTC). One day, I received a call from Mr. Faisal Ijaz Khan, Chairman of the PVTC. He requested that I hold a session with his management team and principals during his trip to Multan. I checked my schedule. I found out that I would be in Muzaffarabad-the capital of Azad Kashmir-for a session with the principals of the technical and vocational colleges a day before. It would be virtually impossible to reach Multan on the same day in order to conduct the session the next day. I did not tell the chairman that I would be coming from Azad Kashmir to Multan. I did not cancel the invitation. I realized that I may not get the opportunity to conduct the session in his presence again. I knew that his presence would send a strong message to his team to take the idea of youth-led changemaking seriously. I knew that if it went well, I would have access to over 150 vocational training institutions operating under PVTC.

I confirmed the session immediately. I asked my office team to prepare the material and folders for the session in my absence. I finished the session in Azad Kashmir around 3pm. We left for Multan. I asked my team to bring and hand over the material and folders to us on the road as we entered Lahore city. We reached Lahore around 9:30pm. My staff was waiting for us at a certain point in Lahore. We were very tired. We were sitting in the car when my staff put the material in the trunk of the car. When they were finished storing the material, we left Lahore city. The road from Lahore to Multan at that time was mostly smooth with occasional bumps. As we were about to enter Multan city, the road got worse. After a short time, we entered Multan. It was now 1:30am. I asked my team member to inquire about the address of the guest house. When he went out of the car, he noticed that the trunk of the car was open.

When he told us, we all jumped out of the car and started counting the folders and material for the next day session. We found out that we had lost almost half of the folders. Since it was midnight, there was not a lot of traffic. We decided to go back and see if we could find a few folders.

We only found three folders. It was a big session. We were expecting more than 60 people. We were very worried as all the photocopy shops were closed, so we decided to first check in at the guest house and asked the management of the guest house to help us. It was almost 2:30am when we checked in. The first thing we asked the person who helped us check-in was about the photocopy machine, and luckily, he informed us that they did have a photocopy machine. We were so happy to hear it. When we went into the photocopy room, we found out that there weren't many pages available. We hardly made a couple of folders.

We made a plan. We divided the team into two. I assigned one team to make photocopies of the folders in the morning as quickly as possible. In the meantime, the second team comprising of 3 people would go and engage the participants.

The session was planned to begin at 9am. That night, I did not sleep well. I was under a lot of stress. As per the plan, the next morning, I went to conduct the session with my team. The other team went to get photo copies from the market. When the chairman of the PVTC arrived at the session, I told the participants that we would be sharing the material on youth-led changemaking shortly for discussion, but before that, I would like to brief you about the concept of youth-led changemaking and its relevance to your work. I had a very interactive session with the participants. The chairman also participated in the discussion actively.

This session proved very useful to build consensus among participants to engage the students in changemaking. During the session, my team was constantly following-up with the other team on the cell. They were telling me constantly about the progress. When I was told that the folders were ready and had arrived, we took a tea break at 11am. During the tea break, we put the folders on the tables of all the participants. The session went very well. We could not believe that we did it. The session opened the doors of youth-led changemaking for several thousand young people later on.

I conducted several hundred sessions and meetings with the top leadership and faculty members of educational and vocational institutions to create a favorable environment for young people to practice their changemaking abilities. I wanted to use their physical and social infrastructure to inspire and engage young people in changemaking projects. I trained and engaged several thousand faculty members of these institutions as facilitators and mentors.

While doing all this work with the top leadership and faculty members of educational and technical institutions, I was hoping that when I would go and present a changemaking opportunity to their students, they would immediately latch onto it. Surprisingly, I found out that the road I traveled to reach the hearts of young people is badly broken. It is broken because whoever came before me made young people feel very inferior and treated them like objects. I was surprised to see that young people have no awareness of their changemaking potential. I realized that young people have developed a strong mental framework that does not allow them to think beyond what is already prescribed to them.

Young people have been subjected to operate in a certain fashion in the society. A single track is offered to them. They are not allowed or given the space to think of switching that track. Any deviation from the track is dealt with an iron hand. I came to know about the stories of many young people who tried to switch the track and faced serious consequences.

I realized why so many young people gave up their lives because they were not able to meet the academic or other expectations of their parents and the society. I understood why young people pursued their dreams clandestinely. I recall many interviews with young people that have done something extraordinary in sports. Many of them mentioned one common thing in their interviews after attaining tremendous success: That they were often scolded and beaten by their parents and teachers for following their dreams. They mentioned that they did not disclose their dreams to play for the country to their parents and teachers until they were able to achieve some serious milestones. Once they achieved the milestones and demonstrated their talents at a very young age, they started getting different treatment from their parents and society. These young people were lucky that they were able to find people, places, and institutions to pursue their dreams. Many young people do not have the privilege to nurture any desire for a longer period of time in their areas of interest, due to an absence of supportive people, places, and institutions.

The question is: If a young person can achieve whatever they want in sports so early in life, then why do other young people have to wait for ages to achieve their dreams in the area of creating value through changemaking? Why do they have to take such a slow and long route? Why can't they begin their changemaking journey while still in school? Why does society not try to benefit from their abilities during the many years that young people attend school? Why are the majority of our young people not provided with the physical, social, financial, and legal infrastructure to begin their changemaking journey now?

After creating a supporting environment for youth-led changemaking in educational and vocational institutions, I wanted to provide a practice opportunity to young people to find their real power, or to reconnect with their lost power. Every time I met young people, I realized how serious the damage that had been done to them was. I found out that young people are not thriving in our educational institutions. They are not excited about what they are learning. They don't have the belief system that they can turn their lives around. As I interacted with young people, I noticed the following:

YES! Youth-Led Changemaking

- **Young people are living in a low-trust environment.** It is a sad reality that a large number of young people today are growing up in low-trust environments. No one is trying to reach out and trust young people and their changemaking abilities. As a result, we are missing significant opportunities and facing serious consequences. I believe that the illiterate of the 21st century are not those who cannot read and write, but those who cannot trust young people. *The changemaking potential is latent in all young people. It is the paradigm of mistrust which veils it.* When the paradigm of mistrust is shredded, the changemaking potential of young people surprises everyone. I knew that when we trust young people to lead a changemaking project, their minds forget all limitations and harsh treatment by the society. Their passion expands in new directions. They feel that they are living in a different world. We must ask ourselves why child labor and youth-led terrorism is on the rise. It is on the rise because selfish people trust and tap into the changemaking potential of our children and young people. We must understand that if our children can use their changemaking abilities in difficult conditions for others to succeed, they can certainly use their changemaking abilities to turn around their own lives. I found out that when we do not trust young people, they look for people outside their close circles who trust them.

- **Young people are in receiving mode.** I found out that a majority of young people were operating in receiving mode.

They got into this mode so early in their lives. They were convinced that they cannot move forward in life without the support of others. They have accepted what others think of them. They have submitted to the views and judgments of others. They accepted that they were only created to serve the interests, needs, and conveniences of others. I realized that it would be extremely challenging to change their mental framework. I realized lectures, training, and workshops would not be enough to change their mode from gaining to giving. They needed a practice opportunity to recover their lost confidence.

- **Young people have a narrow vision.** Young people, especially those who are living in low-income families, are micromanaged to the extent that they have developed a very narrow vision in life. I found out that a vast majority of young people approach every situation by first looking at what is in it for them. They wanted to achieve success without doing anything. They wanted instant success. Their definition of success was all about having a lot of money and material possessions. They missed many opportunities in life due to their narrow vision and desire to achieve everything instantly. They were mistreated to the extent that they forgot to realize that they could bring a positive change in the lives of others. In short, they had very little realization that they can actually contribute to the society. I realized that I will not be able to help young people until I am able to expand their vision. I knew that when they expanded their vision, they would increase their possibilities.

- **Young people represent deprivations.** During my conversations with young people, I found out that a vast majority of young people brought their needs and deprivations to the market. They didn't bring their ideas to the market. They believed that they were underachievers. They didn't represent hope, possibilities, or solution. They represented problems, hopelessness, and helplessness. They thought the best way to attract the attention of others was to share their problems.

- **Young people are very vulnerable.** The vulnerability of young people emerges from the mistreatment through society. Young people are treated like things. Things have no power to move and decide. They are strictly controlled. They are separated from the society. They wait for approval all the time. They carry out orders. They are not given any space to act freely. They are not given any credit. It increases their chances to be exploited and victimized. They forgot completely that they are gifted and blessed with changemaking abilities. They feel that success is all about power, status, and position. Since they don't have these things, they must wait for orders. These young people present a silent risk, either through their own wrong choices and actions, or at the hands of extremists. There is no data available in any country to show the number of young people feeling vulnerable. The bad news is that the numbers are not decreasing, but increasing, because of the growing demands from young people by society.

- **Young people showed little capacity to distinguish between right and wrong.** I was quite surprised to observe that a large number of young people, especially those living in low-income families, showed very little capacity to distinguish between right and wrong. Since these young people are not trusted and involved in decision making, they feel their voices and actions are irrelevant. They don't calculate the costs of their impulsive actions. They prefer short-term impulsive fulfillment to escape from their deprivations. They feel humiliated, and thus, show very little value for their lives and the lives of others. They prefer to learn the hard way. We must remember that youth development is about developing a positive identity, a sense of purpose, and a value in society. The social, emotional, and financial marginalization can push them to a point of despair. When we see young people pursue wrong and short-term choices, we must try to imagine the emotional environment in which they are being raised.

- **Young people are living their lives in restricted circles.** I learned that a vast majority of young people are living their lives in a very restricted physical, intellectual, social, and moral circle of their potential being. They either do not explore their changemaking potential or are not given the space to explore their talents and inherent changemaking abilities. Most of the marginalized young people feel they have no talents or abilities. They are liabilities. My work has shown that young people living in low-income communities have enormous resilience and latent changemaking potential; as much as is possessed by the young people who are educated and living in high-income communities. The success and failure depend on the paradigm in which young people live and operate. The degrees or skills do not control results, effectiveness, and productivity. When we change the paradigm of young people, we can change the results.

- **Young people are disappointed by stakeholders.** It is interesting to work with the stakeholders that are given the responsibility to empower young people. They all want to see young people succeed. Unfortunately, they have developed or inherited a mental model from society which is no longer working and applicable. They are following systems and structures that restrict young people from becoming changemakers. These stakeholders are not trying to understand why young people are not responding and meeting their expectations. They lack the capacity to refine systems and structures to get the desired results. They don't know or realize that they are not on the right track. They blame young people for their weaknesses. It has created a deep sense of disappointment among young people about the role of stakeholders in their lives. They believe that they are only interested in numbers.

- **Young people have poor social capital.** It was interesting to observe that young people tend to rely on the social capital of their parents and less on building their own social capital. The interaction of young people is limited to like-minded young people. It leads to a very static nature of social capital. Young people have very restricted interaction with the environment. Hence, they do not develop the ability to accumulate social capital beyond the influences of their family, school, and geographical location. I found out that many young people living in low-income communities often have a traumatic experience of diversity. They are either reluctant or fearful to establish a connection with someone who has more knowledge, experience, resources, and wisdom. This lack of ability reduces the possibilities of growth, improvement, and civic participation.

I realized that I had my work cut out for me, and that I had to establish a positive relationship with young people immediately to activate the renewal process. I wanted to invoke positive emotions in young people, and I saw every young person through the eyes of compassion. I tried to pull young people out from a negative emotional state into a positive emotional state. I wanted to help young people see that they are capable of becoming a changemaker. I tried to make them feel positive and hopeful. I focused on young people, and not on what people think about them. I treated every young person as the very important person that they are. I made them feel special. I reminded them again and again that they were born with the God-given changemaking potential to drive change in their communities. I told them that they have great changemaking abilities locked up within them and that they can choose to live a life of happiness simply by using their inherent changemaking abilities. I told them that I didn't care what their report cards said about them or what their teachers, their parents, or society thought about them. All I tried to do was to make them realize that they are the architects of their destiny. I shared with them that the only thing which separated them from other changemakers is their inability to use their changemaking potential. I gave them many examples of changemakers who achieved so much without power, position, and status. Therefore, they must focus on using their inner resources instead of waiting for things that are beyond their control.

I tried to make them realize that God has not made them for failure. God designed them for changemaking. I was fully aware of the fact that many young people who were sitting in front of me had not met many people in their lives that trust and honor them. I knew that simply providing knowledge and skills would not change the way they saw themselves. I wanted to develop a desire among young people to lead, and not to wait.

I found out that when we are able to meet the emotional needs of young people, we help them find their power. I wanted them to change the way they think, feel, and act. I knew that many of them did not have quality relationships in their lives. I see every interaction with young people as an opportunity to build trust and a high-quality connection. I wanted to go beyond empathy and understanding to compassion.

After establishing a positive connection with young people, I provided an opportunity for young people to discover their changemaking abilities by designing and disseminating an idea that produces social and economic benefits. I felt that I had to find a way to validate my point of view quickly. Otherwise, I might not be able to sustain the relationship with these institutions. *So, I designed a methodology to show how youth-led changemaking might work. I launched small-scale youth-led changemaking projects to show quick wins and success. Not to my surprise, young people responded to my trust in them amazingly.*

The data we have collected during the last few years from the field showed that 88% of young people were able to create a social and economic impact. Only 8% of the student teams suffered some kind of financial loss, and only the very tiny minority of 4% quit the competition. Those young people who struggled to create a social and economic impact were mostly due to poor support and guidance from the faculty members, as well as pressure from parents to concentrate on their studies only. I demonstrated that every young person has changemaking potential, regardless of his or her background. I also showed that young people thrive on trust.

I found out that our initiatives have failed to extend trust to young people. I learned that our initial task is to restore trust with young people and to deconstruct all the negative constructs, negative attitudes, expectations, and beliefs that have been built over the years. My experimentation makes it clear that no matter what a young person's past or present, no matter what they did or thought, they are fully capable of succeeding. My work also helped young people to realize that they are fully capable of achieving many things for themselves and for society. *I learned that instilling a positive belief system in young people requires a positive experience. A limiting belief system is the single most critical challenge when working with young people, and it has a crippling effect.* It hurts me to see that our institutions and policy makers have failed to imagine the cost of failing to engage the passion, inherent changemaking talent, and abilities of young people. A vast majority of parents, teachers, and policy makers continue to think in the same manner. They believe that by teaching young people what they don't know, or equipping young people with skills they don't have, or by hunting and punishing young people involved in risky behaviors, they will prepare them for the future. This belief is flawed.

Due to mistrust and humiliation, a large number of young people are acting from a sense of scarcity, rather than a sense of abundance and having enough.

Young people who have been mistrusted during their development generally have a difficult time demonstrating the kind of behaviors that adults love to see. These young people have imposed unwanted self-deprivation upon themselves. They have inherited a weak belief system. For many reasons, they did not receive the trust, support, encouragement, affection, and generosity. There is a dire need to get their mental framework right and help them understand that they are the architects of their reality, and that they are not the victims of circumstances, but they are equipped to create favorable circumstances for themselves and others.

In the span of 5 years, we were able to reach out to and engage 1200 educational and technical institutions. The British Council carried out a third-party evaluation of our work with technical and vocational institutions. The evaluation reported that 93% of the respondents believed that the project had benefited them by developing their entrepreneurial skills, enabling them to start their own businesses, improving their confidence level, and enhancing their team-building skills.

The findings showed that:

- **71.4 %** young people got employed after one year of participation in the changemaking competition.

- **21.4%** young people got employed after two years of participation in the changemaking competition.

- **7.1%** young people got employed after three years of participation in the changemaking competition.

In addition to that, we were able to embed the concept of youth-led changemaking (social entrepreneurship) in the curriculum of 225 vocational institutions.

The presence of a large youth population can have a serious effect on any country. It's up to any government to decide whether this effect should be positive or negative. Governments can decide to see their growing numbers of young people as problems to be fixed, or as opportunities and blessings. By bringing change in our attitudes, expectations, and policies towards young people, we can facilitate millions of young people to drive change *now* by instigating potential solutions to problems.

My youth engagement programs showed very positive results immediately. I started building credibility among youth-serving institutions, and was able to attract many local and international partners to invest in the field of youth-led changemaking. I assisted several international organizations of the world to design or deliver youth-led changemaking projects. I have recently launched the first-ever "Changemaker Institute" program in over 80 universities in Pakistan, in partnership with the British Council to align their structures for youth-led changemaking through a variety of exciting and innovative projects.

Youth Engagement Spectrum

It would be useful to define the Youth Engagement Spectrum to identify where we are currently standing and where we would like to go.

In my opinion, the Youth Engagement Spectrum consists of five levels.

Disengagement level

Youth disengagement means that young people are not valued as equal partners in development. They are detached physically, socially and mentally from any constructive activity. They are rejected by society from participation in any organized effort to improvesociety.

This rejection is both unspoken and flat-out. Youth disengagement is being experienced by both in-school and out-of-school youth. It is interesting to observe that in-school young people are deprived of meaningful engagement in problem-solving on the plea that they are getting prepared for future leadership roles.

Young people who are out-of-school feel rejection more deeply than those who are in-school. Our best schools and best parents have failed to realize that young people are fully capable of driving change today.

I found out that disengagement of youth leads to higher engagement in socially sanctioned forms of engagement. I believe that youth disengagement is our biggest threat, biggest loss, and greatest failure. It threatens everyone. It carries a very high social and economic cost, and threatens the fabric of our society. One of the major reasons for the growing deterioration in the security situation in many countries is the growing disengagement of young people.

The greatest threat to the world is not coming from terrorist groups but it is coming from the increasing number of disengaged children and young people. Despite the fact that the world has the largest cohort of children and young people in its history, there is no public cry to reach out and engage young people. Terrorist groups target the youth of those areas where the deprivation and disconnection level between youth and the society is high.

Pakistan is one of the unfortunate countries in the world where young people are disconnected from society. The numbers of disengaged and vulnerable young people are increasing tremendously.

These numbers are never lit on the billboards of the city so that everyone can see how quickly they are increasing. There is no shortage of evidence reflecting the costs of neglecting young people in Pakistan. Almost all the terrorist attacks carried out in Pakistan are committed by young people between the ages of 12-30.

These young people are telling us through their behaviors what is missing in the society, and it is our responsibility to listen to their voices and understand their needs. We need to ask ourselves why extremists and terrorist groups find it so easy to mobilize and engage youth in self-destructive activities.

What do they offer to young people?

Why do young people listen to them?

Why do young people give up their lives so easily?

We must understand our vulnerabilities. These extremist groups offer everything that is missing in the lives of young people. *They give hope, desire, and most importantly, a sense of purpose and a sense of usefulness to young people.*

Our politicians, policy makers, and practitioners have very little to no understanding about the consequences of ignoring young people. If there are any efforts underway, they are limited to discussion and manipulation. It is the need of the hour that we must recognize young people as partners in development. How can we even think of any development, prosperity, and progress without the engagement and contributions of young people?

Episodic engagement level

This level refers to the short-term engagement of young people in crisis situations. Young people are inspired and encouraged to help in rebuilding communities following a disaster. There are many examples of youth engagement in crisis situations such as the 2004 tsunami, the 2005 Hurricane Katrina, the 2005 earthquake in Pakistan, the 2007 cyclone in Bangladesh, the 2008 floods in Algeria, the 2015 earthquake of Nepal, and the 2016 earthquake of Ecuador.

These examples show how young people can contribute to saving lives and rebuilding communities.

Unfortunately, youth engagement was limited to responding to the immediate needs of the people, families, and communities, as it did not go beyond these crisis situations. This level of engagement is not sustained over time, despite the fact that it produced remarkable results both for young people and their communities.

Under-engaged level

This level refers to engagement of young people in pre-determined and pre-structured programs. It is driven by an expert or organization. It pursues social value creation. It inspires young people to implement a solution or hold a particular view or agenda. It does not go beyond organizing, training, educating, protecting, defending, volunteering, and voting. It does not engage young people as changemakers.

It sees young people as human resources to carry out the work of an organization or state. A number of countries engage their young people in carrying out developmental activities. These countries believe that young people have the potential to serve society.

In this level, young people carry out initiatives that are adult-led and adult-controlled. Young people wait for instructions, rather than initiating things on their own.

Young people are viewed as a major resource to implement a change, rather than to design and deliver social innovation ideas to revolutionize a whole field. It is an important level of youth engagement, but it is still only a subcategory of youth engagement.

Short-term engagement level

Young people are trusted and valued as equal partners in development. They are given the opportunity to design and deliver innovative solutions for a short period of time.

There are some organizations that aim at engaging young people in changemaking, but due to the absence of a proper ecosystem for youth-led changemaking, young people find it very difficult to sustain their interventions.

Structural and legal barriers, such as setting-up organizations, getting registered, accessing financial resources, opening bank accounts, and applying for patents, serve as principal barriers to extend the youth engagement in changemaking. In short, young people lack social, legal, political, emotional, and practical support in driving a change in their community.

Young people are not well supported by the external environment or other players. Young people encounter unsupportive institutional environments at every step. Young people are not provided enough time, space, or opportunities to innovate by parents and teachers.

Large-scale engagement level

This happens when every young person is seen as a changemaker and offered environments that help them become changemakers. Youth-led changemaking is viewed as a top priority by community institutions.

Young people are encouraged to develop and deliver innovative solutions.

Young people are inspired to lead a change, rather than follow a change. Youth-led changemaking pursues a triple bottom-line (social, economic, and environmental). Young people are provided structured support and the opportunity to experiment with new ideas in the real world.

It is valued and supported by people and organizations. Youth-led changemaking is embedded in the social, political, economic, educational, and cultural aspects. It is valued by major stakeholders of society. All types of institutions, such as families, educational, vocational, businesses, religious, and government agencies are engaged in creating opportunities for youth-led changemaking.

Young people are viewed by everyone as changemakers. Spaces for youth-led changemaking are created at all levels of the society to enhance the ability of young people to practice changemaking skills. Parents, teachers, and policy makers encourage and reward young people for changemaking. The large-scale engagement level moves beyond the outputs (number of people served by young people) to the process of youth-led changemaking, which puts all young people in the position to take complete responsibility to solve the problems of everyday life.

It is very important that countries understand the need to move toward the large-scale engagement of young people. In each country, societal needs are increasing at a very fast speed. I believe young people can meet these needs by designing and delivering innovative solutions.

	Episodic	Under Engagement	Short-term Engagement	Large-Scale Engagement
Objective	Meet emergency needs	Appeal to goodwill	Unleash changemaking potential of young people	Mainstream youth-led changemaking in the systems- Focus on process

Nature	Individual-driven agenda	Core agenda of charity based organizations	Core agenda of a few non-profit organizations	Core agenda of state (including educational and vocational institutions) and private institutions
Support	No permanent support or mechanism.	Single-service delivery- Adult-supervised.	Single-service delivery. Young people lead the process. Not well-supported by the environment.	Multiple service delivery mechanisms. Well-supported by public and private institutions. Young people lead the process.
Focus	Social value creation	Social value creation	Social and economic value creation	Social, economic, and environmental value creation
Identity Formation	Not a priority	Not a priority	Leads to a short-term new identity development	Leads to a long-term new identity development
Measurement	Number of lives saved. Infrastructure restored.	Number of people served.	Impact on youth and communities.	Impact on youth, communities, and society.
Financial Reliance	Self-Supported. No earned income.	Donor Support. No earned income.	Organization-supported- Earned income.	Multiple institutions supported- Earned income.
Sustainability	Self-funding	Donor funding	Mix of grants and income generation	Self-sustainability

Table 7: Summary of Youth Engagement Spectrum

Chapter 4

YOUTH-LED CHANGEMAKING

"The most exciting breakthroughs of the twenty-first century will not occur because of technology, but because of an expanding concept of what it means to be human."-John Naisbitt

It has been almost 21 years that I have been trying to light a fire under the feet of everyone to see young people as changemakers. I have given enough evidence through my work that all young people are capable of driving change when trusted. I have developed a blueprint for unlocking the changemaking potential of young people.

I believe that the greatest discovery of the 21st century is the discovery of young people as changemakers. In the past, changemaking was considered as the job of big, powerful, highly educated, experienced, and skilled people. There is now increasing evidence that changemaking is possible by everyone. There is no age restriction. There is no education restriction. There is no gender restriction. There is no economic restriction.

Technology and social media are making changemaking easier for everyone. There is so much focus on creating new sources of changemaking. Many countries are making serious efforts to unlock the changemaking potential of their people.

I have developed and tested a new youth-led changemaking model with several thousand young people. The results are amazing. The model I developed is based on extending and restoring trust with young people.

I will explain the model and results later in the chapter. Now, I would like to explain the phrase *Youth-Led Changemaking* in detail.

Words have great power. We have a rich vocabulary of negative words to describe young people. But words can also be used to inspire and uplift young people, rather than tear them down. Words can be used to open the hearts and minds of people. Let's examine each word that is used in the phrase "Youth-Led Changemaking".

Defining Youth

The term *youth* is a bit fuzzy. It is not a fixed term, rather it is fluid. Youth can be defined in many ways:

- It is a period of pleasure and joy.
- It is a period between childhood and adulthood.
- It is a period when you are moving out from the dependence of childhood and entering into the independence of adulthood.
- It is a period of physical, emotional, and psychological growth and development.
- It is a preparation period.
- It is a period of forming a new identity.
- It is a period of vulnerability.
- It is a period of experimentation.
- It is a period of strength.
- It is a period of risk-taking.
- It is a period of storm and stress.
- It is a period of disturbance due to sudden mood swings, family, and peer relationships.
- It is a period of the transfer of influence from parents to peers.
- It is a period of changemaking.

In short, youth is a socially constructed category defined by societal attitudes, expectations, and responsibilities. We must not forget that young people begin their lives in families and expand to multiple institutions and settings that can either offer pathways or roadblocks to their development.

The role of natural actors, such as parents, teachers, peers, neighbors, and community institutions, cannot be ignored. The difficulties we witness while working with young people are the results of the environmental factors. It is not the gender, color, or gene pool of young people that makes our work with young people so challenging.

It is the social, economic, and political marginalization that leads young people to a point of helplessness and despair. If young people are not civically engaged, valued, and treated equally, and are dropping out, disillusioned and hopeless, I warn you, we've got a time bomb.

Age is the easiest way to define youth. Many countries and organizations define youth statistically to understand the needs of young people and develop policies and programs to meet those needs.

- *"Youth is defined as those persons between the ages of 15 and 24 years."*-United Nations General Assembly
- *"Youth comprises persons between the age of 15 and 24."*-World Bank
- The Commonwealth Youth Programme works with *"young people (aged 15-29)"*.
- In Pakistan, *youth* is defined as the population in the age group of 15 to 29 years.
- The Government of India officially defines *youth* as persons between the ages of 13 and 35 years.
- In Malaysia, *youth* is defined as the population in the age group of 15 to 40 years.
- *Youth* is defined in Nepal as those aged between 16 and 40 years.
- In Bangladesh, *youth* is defined as the population in the age group of 15 to 40 years.
- In Singapore, **youth** is defined as the population in the age group of 15 to 30 years.

The definition of youth varies in different countries around the world. Youth should be seen as the most exciting period of life, rather than a biological life stage. From this position, the starting point is to look at young people as assets. Our future is based on our ability to tap into the changemaking potential of young people.

So how do we differentiate between programs that are youth-led and programs that are adult-led?

Adult-led	Youth-led
Pre-determined	Youth-driven
Well-structured	Loosely-structured
Compliance	Innovate
Consumers	Creators
Control	Unlock
Victims	Leaders
Closed-ended	Open-ended
Problem-oriented	Solution-oriented
Narrowly focused	Broadly focused
Incomprehensive	Comprehensive

Table 8: Difference Between Adult-Led and Youth-Led Programs

In comparing the two program types, we can see a very different approach and vastly different paradigms and worldviews at work.

Defining Changemaking

In the dictionary, changemaking is defined as a noun or a verb.

- Noun: A process through which something becomes different. Example: The change from a citizen-in-waiting to a citizen-in-action.

- Verb: Become different. Example: A young person becomes a service provider instead of a service seeker.

Defining Youth-Led Changemaking

It is a conscious effort of young people to discover their inherent changemaking potential by initiating an idea or activity that produces social and economic dividends.

Youth-led changemaking refers to the inherent truth that all young people are capable of giving birth to new ideas and activities that can create social and economic value and change.

Youth-led changemaking is a process by which we move away from deficit thinking and victim mentality toward the discovery that we have everything we need to transform our life and the lives of others.

During the changemaking process, young people take complete responsibility to identify, develop, market, sell, and evaluate their projects in the market. Youth-led changemaking may lead to the testing of new ideas, or improvement in an implementation process, or both.

YES Youth-Led Changemaking Model	Existing Players (Educational Institutions and Organizations)
It follows a bottom-up approach. Everyone can join and participate in it.	It follows a top-down approach. Best ideas are rewarded and supported.
Complete autonomy is provided to decide the nature of changemaking project.	Ideas are subjected to the approval of authorities.
No plan is required to begin the changemaking journey. The desire to participate is the only major condition.	Detailed plans are required for consideration before funding.
No need to pitch the idea to anyone. The focus is on doing.	Ideas need to be pitched before implementation.

Focus is on the person and the application of their changemaking abilities.	Focus is on presentation and their research and communication skills.
The focus is on starting early by taking feedback from the buyers.	Focus on starting late after doing a lot of research.
Pursue a "get out of the building" approach to test their ideas.	Focus on elaborate planning.
Focus on using personal knowledge and experience.	Focus on gaining insights from experts.
No need to wait for initial investment to begin the changemaking journey.	Has to wait and sell the idea before getting any financial assistance.
It is open for every young person. It follows an inclusive model.	It follows an exclusive model. Young people enrolled in economic/business studies and projects can participate only.
Young people have the opportunity to experience the whole changemaking process from start to finish.	Young people's ideas are subjected to the approval of experts.
Customer feedback is preferred right from the beginning over detailed planning.	Intuition is used to design the project.
Instant access to risk-free funding.	Inaccessibility to risk-free funding. Banks don't even talk to young people who want to borrow small funding.
Build an ecosystem first to support youth-led changemaking.	Has to operate in difficult and unfavorable conditions.

Table 9: The Difference Between YES and the Old Model-A Comparison

Core Purpose of Youth-Led Changemaking

The core purpose of youth-led changemaking is to engage young people in the creation of values. I believe every value has four components: Social, Spiritual, Economic, and Environmental.

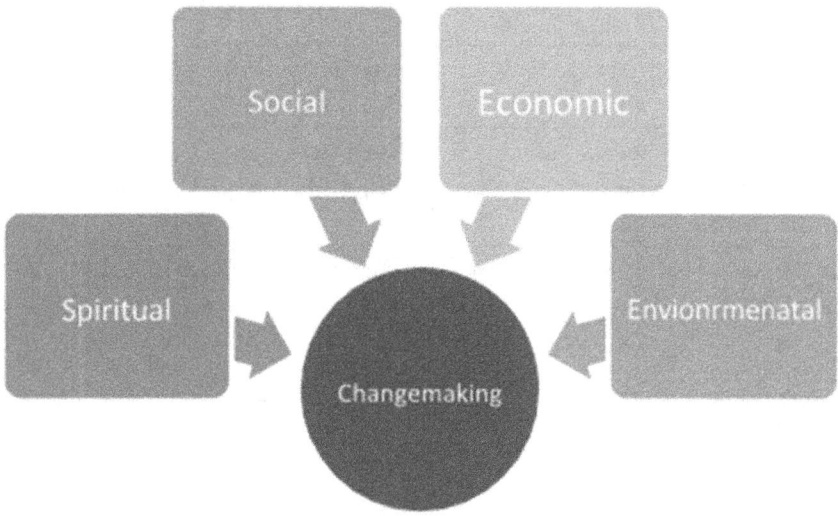

Figure 1: Components of Value

Apart from the economic component, all other components are difficult to measure. The desire for people-centered changemaking often originates from a social and spiritual vision. Social and spiritual values inspire and encourage us for changemaking. When we study history, we find out that:

- Spiritual considerations rank very high among religious leaders.
- Social considerations rank very high among non-profit and political leaders.
- Economic considerations rank very high among businessmen.
- Environmental considerations rank very high among nature lovers.

In my work, I encourage young people to design and deliver an idea or activity that transcends traditional non-profit ways.

I encourage young people to set up an enterprise to meet social needs and generate funds. Youth-led changemaking must be driven by two forces:

First, the desire to bring change in society, and *second,* the sustainability of the idea or enterprise and its services.

I encourage young people from the start to integrate commercial methods to support their enterprises. In developing countries, it would be very difficult for young people to attain grants, as the markets are shrinking, and the legal environment often creates obstacles. Therefore, the focus on mission and money is important.

Running a youth-led changemaking enterprise is a balancing act which requires a clear understanding of what the ultimate impact the youth-led enterprise wants to achieve, and how much money it needs to generate. Generating money is seen as an evil act by many people in my culture, rather than what it should be seen as-a way to promote self-reliance among young people and create sustainable social value.

It is interesting to observe that a large number of young people prefer to begin their changemaking journey by offering ready-made or popular products or services to peers. Many young people often prefer to provide services in the areas of their expertise.

Changemaking competitions help young people with:

- Introducing new ideas.
- Meeting unmet service needs.
- Enhancing accessibility.
- Improving the quality of a product or service.
- Stimulating the demand for proven innovative products.
- Adding innovation to an existing product.
- Utilizing their gained knowledge and skills.

The participation of young people in changemaking activities enables young people to use their learned knowledge and skills in the field.

A very small number of young people begin their changemaking journey with something very innovative. Opportunities to participate in changemaking activities help young people break down traditional barriers and patterns, and once old paradigms are broken, it becomes easier for them to create something new and pursue endless possibilities.

Young people's participation in changemaking early in their lives increases young people's likelihood to excel in changemaking in the future. The example of youth-led changemaking is visible in many fields, such as sports, music, IT, and fashion.

There are very few examples of young people involved in changemaking in the field of social development. Youth-led changemaking can be advanced through educational and vocational institutions.

These institutions can provide spaces to young people to find innovative solutions to social, economic, political, and environmental problems. Young people show a higher capacity to innovate when they work in teams. *Creating a youth-led changemaking culture requires a cultural shift from seeing young people as resources to be developed to seeing young people as resources to be engaged.*

It requires creating spaces outside formal education to engage young people in value creation.

Phases of Youth-Led Changemaking Journey

In my work, I found out that young people go through different phases to become changemakers. Before I explain, I must say that it is not necessary that all young people go through the same phases:

a) Desperation and Inspiration Phase
b) Experimentation Phase

c) Reflection Phase
d) Decision Phase

a) Desperation and Inspiration Phase

This is the first phase in the life of a changemaker. Many young people often find themselves with their backs against the wall. They feel a desperate need to change their lives or the lives of others. Desperation has proved to be an important ingredient in the lives of changemakers. Desperation can lead to the creation of something new. It pushes young people to get ahead in the game. When many young people experience or see inequality, injustice, humiliation, hopelessness, helplessness, pain, and agony, they decide to overcome it. They decide to take risks and be bold.

Similarly, inspiration plays an important role in activating young people as changemakers. Young people are often inspired when they see someone doing something special and extraordinary. Inspiration leads to a new understanding and perspective about our talents, capabilities, and possibilities. In my work, I define inspiration as our ability to inspire young people to appreciate the idea of changemaking and decide to participate in it. I try to inspire young people by showing complete trust in their natural abilities to drive change. I don't have any condition for the participation of young people in changemaking activities.

I make every young person feel special through my behavior. I share the stories of young people who have already begun their changemaking journey. I try to build an ecosystem first within the institution and community before engaging young people in changemaking.

b) Experimentation Phase

During the experimentation phase, young people are provided practical opportunity to participate in the changemaking activities or competitions by countering underlying psychological, social, and economic barriers that limit their ability to become changemakers. The duration of the opportunity varies from two days or two weeks, to up to four weeks to develop and execute an idea or activity. Young people are provided with complete social, financial, emotional, and infrastructural support.

c) Reflection Phase

During the reflection stage, young people reflect on what happened. How was their experience? What was the best thing that happened to them? What was the worst thing that happened to them? Did they benefit from the changemaking experience? What did they learn about themselves from the changemaking experience?

d) Decision Phase

Young people decide whether they should continue to work on their ideas or discontinue in order to work on their weaknesses, or to gain more knowledge, skills, and experience. Young people ask themselves whether they are good enough to continue. The decision to continue or to discontinue does not necessarily represent failure.

Striking Features of Youth-Led Changemaking

The characteristics of Youth-led Changemaking are:

- It is youth-led.
- It pursues an open-ended civic process.
- It is comprehensive. Young people would have the opportunity to lead the process from start to finish.
- It takes an organic and bottom-up approach.
- It represents a solution.
- It aims at efficient problem-solving.
- It creates double or multiple bottom-lines.
- It has an enterprise orientation.

Unique Features of Youth-Led Changemaking Model

The unique features of the Youth-Led Changemaking model are:

- Youth-Led: It assists youth to lead rather than be led.
- Self-Reliance: It helps youth become self-reliant and contributing members of society.
- Workforce: It provides society with a large number of workers at a very little expense, or even no expense at all.
- Social Exclusion: It combats social exclusion by mainstreaming left-out youth to drive change in their communities.
- Training Ground: It provides an excellent training ground for producing changemakers.
- Service Delivery: It develops an indigenous service delivery mechanism for the poor and left-out.
- Employment Policy: It contributes to employment policy by providing the first-ever full-time work experience to young people.
- Head-Off Terrorism: It is an effective way to reduce the incidence of neighborhood crime, poverty, drug abuse, and terrorism by engaging young people in constructive activities.
- Education in Action: It is the most effective way to counterbalance the years of largely passive education received by students in the classroom.

Benefits of Youth-Led Changemaking for Young People

The benefits of Youth-Led Changemaking for Young People include, but are not limited to:

- It helps young people develop a sense of bonding and connection with society.
- It develops a sense of ownership among young people to solve unresolved problems.
- It develops a sense of purpose among young people to value their lives.
- It builds a sense of usefulness among young people that they are capable of driving change in their communities.

- It leads to the development of strong resilience among young people to stay firm in the face of risk.
- It fosters self-determination among young people to chart their own course.
- It develops self-efficacy among young people to achieve their goals through proactive action.
- It breeds a positive identity among young people to avoid risk factors.
- It develops a sense of achievement among young people.
- It fosters a positive sense of belief in the future among young people for a productive adult life.

Domains of Youth-Led Changemaking

Youth-led changemaking covers multiple domains, which are as follows:

- Self: The youth-led changemaking model builds the competency of young people. It brings change in the youth's self-belief, image, self-esteem, confidence, and attitudes.
- Peers: It has a very positive impact on other young people. It inspires young people to take action and work shoulder-to-shoulder to execute their ideas.
- Teachers: It helps teachers enrich the learning process of students. It helps teachers improve the academic performance of students.
- Communities: It helps young people establish a positive connection and relationship with their community or society. Young people become changemakers by adding value in society while developing themselves. Often, young people develop and disseminate unique products or services that improve the status quo.

Changemaking Status

It is interesting to observe that those who drive change and those who follow, manage, advocate, and replicate change have a huge compensation difference. Those who drive change not only transform their lives, but they transform the lives of many other people. Those who follow change live a life of mediocrity. Every young person can live the life of their dreams by simply practicing changemaking abilities.

Sadly, many young people decide to become only buyers and consumers very early on in their lives.

Changemaking Status	Explanation	Your Personal Status
Driving Change	Are you driving change?	Yes: No
Following Change	Are you following change?	Yes: No
Managing Change	Are you managing change?	Yes: No
Advocating Change	Are you advocating change?	Yes: No
Replicating Change	Are you replicating change?	Yes: No

Table 10: What is Your Changemaking Status?

We were originally created for changemaking. God has created man and woman in the best conformation. God has not created human beings to live a life of misery, pain, and helplessness.

It is we who have decided to reduce ourselves to the lowest of low. We are born with a complete changemaking kit. The heart is the most vital component of that kit. If your heart works well, you are bound to live the life of a changemaker. The heart directs the brain, eyes, and ears to act compassionately. Sometimes our changemaking abilities die when we live in an environment where changemaking is not practiced.

Good and positive actions strengthen your changemaking abilities. Similarly, bad actions weaken the changemaking spirit.

Sometimes, we use changemaking abilities to fulfill our personal desires. In changemaking, value appropriation is desirable, though not a goal in itself. Sometimes, we use changemaking abilities to bring change in the lives of others.

We have miraculous changemaking abilities. It is important to remind yourself that biologically, every human being is equally powerful.

The question is, then, how some people become very powerful and successful, and others remain in learned helplessness. The simple reason is that successful people practice their changemaking abilities.

We focus on education. We focus on skills. But we often forget our changemaking abilities. We develop the skill-set without developing the proper mindset.

A vast majority of young people today spend their time on waiting or entertainment.

How can you become a changemaker when you are not practicing your changemaking abilities?

Everyone is born with tremendous changemaking abilities. When we study the lives of changemakers in the past and present, we will find that they were not necessarily very educated and skilled. Many of them had no formal education. The question is, how could they become changemakers? It is simply due to the application of their changemaking abilities. They showed us that success is not what you get, it is what you apply.

It is important for young people to understand that your report card does not say anything about what you are capable of accomplishing in your life. A large number of young people are not aware of the fact that they are blessed with changemaking abilities.

It is no wonder, then, that so many brilliant and intelligent young people continue to have difficulties all throughout their adult life. On the other hand, you have people that are functionally illiterate but become millionaires because they practice their changemaking abilities.

Young people have historically left their greatest abilities largely untapped. Why are so many young people stuck? So many young people have degrees, but they are struggling. How can someone know so much and still suffer? Why do so many young people have degrees in economics, business administration, or management, and are still broke?

Young people go through an extensive education system and learn absolutely nothing about their changemaking abilities. Changemaking has nothing to do with age, gender, position, education, skills, and geography. It is the application of changemaking abilities that counts. Action is the biggest measurement of knowledge.

Everyone and everything created by God is so perfect. Birds, animals, trees, fruits, vegetables, flowers, and mountains are a perfect example that whatever is given to us is perfect.

We have many crises. The biggest crisis is that most people are unable to know what they are capable of. Many people have no sense of their changemaking abilities. Many young people have concluded that they don't have it. There is nothing special about them.

But the truth is that if you are a human being, it comes to you automatically. If you deny your changemaking abilities, you actually deny God. Parents spend millions of dollars on the education of their children, but they don't get results.

Similarly, many organizations spend millions of dollars on the training of employees, but they don't get results. The reason people give for this failure is not the true reason. The failure to get results has nothing to do with knowledge and skills. It is your ability to apply your changemaking abilities that counts. Every year, there are so many young people graduating from colleges and universities, and they have no idea what to do with their degrees. They are often broke. They live in poverty. They wait for so long. Report cards say that they are very intelligent and brilliant, but in real life, they are struggling. Report cards say they are exceptional, but in real life, they are not very smart and bright.

On the other hand, there are some young people who have no degrees and they earn millions of dollars. Have we ever asked why? It is mainly due to the application of changemaking abilities.

Conceptual Framework for Youth-Led Changemaking

Youth-Led Changemaking generates professionals, programs, social settings, organizations, and communities to unlock the changemaking abilities of young people for the benefit of everyone.

Generates ⟹	To Unlock Changemaking Abilities ⟹	To Benefit Everyone
Professionals Programs Social Settings Organizations Communities	Start Imagine Serve Inspire Choose Alter Innovate Express Feel Care Appreciate Collaborate	It offers substantial benefits to young people. It includes reintegration into the society as active citizens, career exploration, work experience, positive belief system, skills acquired, new identity formation, social maturity, and a sense of connection and usefulness. Impact on Society *Youth-led changemaking will result in:* - Meeting unmet service needs - Developing and disseminating new solutions - Peace-building - Transcending traditional social divides - Decreasing dependence

Table 11: Conceptual Framework for Youth-Led Changemaking

The *multidimensionality, integration, and sustainability* are three useful lenses for strategic decision making about the youth-led changemaking framework. It is a sad reality that the data we have gathered over the last few decades provides us with misleading information about young people. It focuses too much on finding what is wrong with young people. When we intend to generate professionals, programs, social settings, organizations, and communities, we are faced with several challenges. These challenges include restoring trust with young people, showing quick wins, building a team of knowledge and practice, developing new performance measures, establishing new pipelines, and developing new theoretical frameworks.

Building a Scientific Foundation of Youth-led Changemaking

I believe that building a scientific foundation of youth-led changemaking is imperative to advance this field. We need to make a collective effort to develop and advance a science of youth-led changemaking. By advancing the field of youth-led changemaking as a science, we will be able to continuously monitor and improve the effectiveness of our initiatives. The biggest challenge today is that there are very few people and organizations involved advancing the field in an organized manner.

The potential of youth-led changemaking is not matched by professional programs and social settings. Educational settings provide us with an incredible route for testing, advancing, and strengthening the youth-led changemaking field. The boundaries of youth-led changemaking are very broad and multidisciplinary.

I would like to propose the following framework for developing the scientific foundation of youth-led changemaking:

The Conceptual Agenda	• Definition (difference with the old definitions of youth development) • Territory of Inputs (people, places, and opportunities for youth-led changemaking) • Territory Outputs (benefits to young people and society) • Develop Theory of Change for Multiple Partners
The Baseline Agenda	• Current Level and Nature of Youth Engagement • Cost of Youth Disengagement • Degree of Use of Existing Knowledge and Skills by Young People • Job Possibilities (present and future) for Young People • Youth Involvement in Crime, Violence, and Terrorism
The Evaluation Agenda	• Social Returns for Youth, Institution, and Community • Economic Returns for Youth, Institution, and Community • Environmental Returns for Youth, institution, and Community
The Contextual Agenda	• Level of Understanding Among Key Stakeholders • Level of Funding Available • Level of Technical Support Available • Level of Initiatives Undertaken • Level of Human Capital, Social Capital, and Political Capital
The Program Agenda	• Type of Engagement (compulsory or voluntary) • Duration of Engagement (episodic or permanent) • Nature of Activities (single, double, or triple bottom-line) • Incorporation of Youth-Led Changemaking in Culture and Curriculum
The Community Agenda	• Level of Acceptance of Youth as Changemakers • Type of Support Offered by the Communities • Level of Stakeholders Involvement • Unmet Service Needs of Communities • Possible Outcomes of Youth-Led Changemaking for Communities

Table 12: Developing the Scientific Agenda of Youth-Led Changemaking Changing Times, Changing Definitions

It would be not wrong to say that earlier generations' definition of success is no longer working. It's time to redefine.

Defining	From	To
Academic Success	Scoring good marks	Changing lives
Good Parents	Meeting the needs of children	Inspiring and enabling children to become changemakers
Good Teachers	Helping students to acquire new knowledge and skills in the classroom	Unlocking the changemaking potential of young people in the real field
Good Schools	Number of graduates produced	Number of changemakers produced
Good Policy Makers	Making policies and programs for troubled kids	Enabling and encouraging all young people to become changemakers
Good Politicians	Seeing young people as resources to be developed	Seeing young people as changemakers now
Good Donors	Training and capacity building of young people	Enabling young people to drive change
Religious Leaders	Teaching children about goodness	Inspiring children to act and lead

Table 13: Changing Times, Changing Definitions

Barriers of Youth-Led Changemaking

There are many barriers of promoting and supporting youth-led changemaking. They include:

a) Limiting Belief System;
b) Excessive Focus on Prevention;
c) Passive Education;
d) Financial Constraints;

e) Legal Constraints;
f) Shortage of Human Resources; and
g) Poor Media Coverage of Youth-Led Changemaking.

In the following lines, we will cover the barriers of Youth-Led Changemaking individually and deepen our understanding of them and how to overcome them.

a) Limiting belief system

Our beliefs are everything. Our belief system plays the most important role in our lives. But how is our belief system developed? Who plays the most important role in the development of our belief system?

Most of our beliefs are influenced by others. Parents play a major role in developing a positive or negative belief system. TV, movies, peers, and teachers also play an important role in the development of our belief system.

Many young people today have developed a very rigid mindset. They believe that everything in their lives is pre-determined and pre-decided. On the other hand, there are young people who have a growth mindset. They believe that everything is possible with hard work and commitment. Many of our beliefs are passed down to us. Most of the beliefs of young people are not based on their personal experiences and judgment. This, then, is the reason that so many young people are suffering today. Many young people are living their lives in a self-created invisible prison.

Let me explain this. I have two kids. My son is 9 years old and my daughter is 3 years old. They watch us, observe us, and often copy us. Every time I watch a cricket match, my son asks me a question: Which team are you supporting and why? When I tell him the name of the team and the reason why I like the team, he immediately starts supporting that team. Similarly, if we start telling our kids that they are lacking, limited, and worthless, they will start believing that they are indeed lacking, limited, and worthless. Beliefs can liberate us, and beliefs can imprison us.

The results we get in our lives are linked to our belief system. I believe that our belief system controls our success, our productivity, our happiness, and the results we see in life. I have met many talented, educated, and skilled young people in my life who are seriously struggling to live a happy life. I used to wonder why this person with so much knowledge and skill is struggling to find a job, build a relationship, and create an impact. I used to think it could be due to bad luck. As my level of interaction was increasing with young people, I had the opportunity to learn more about their views, philosophies, and perspectives. I came to know that many young people are growing up with a limiting belief system. They think that life is a *do it for me* project. They think that success is all about getting a degree. They think that academic skills are enough to achieve success in life, they think success is getting a high-paid job and they define success in terms of finding a government job. Young people spend so many years in schools and do nothing to change their belief system. Schools have not realized the importance of changing the belief system of students.

Often, students come to school with limiting belief systems and they leave school with limiting belief systems. Yet, our schools are unable to figure out what is happening to young people. Schools don't realize that serious damage has already been done to a large number of young people by the environment they were raised in. Young people have started believing everything that is said about them, about their capabilities, and about the way to achieve success. They believe everything that was said to them by someone close to them. After repeatedly hearing that they are good for nothing, and they are lacking, limited, and worthless, young people started looking down at their innate changemaking abilities and talents.

While I am writing this book, I have come to know the story of a man who committed suicide in order to provide a government job to his son. This man was a government servant and wanted his son to be employed in the government department after his retirement. He came to know that the only way to get a government job for his son was if he died during service. He went to the sixth floor of his office building and jumped off. He ended his life. It seems to me that he and his family defined success in terms of getting a government job. They blindly followed a wrong belief system. His family did not realize that they were following a wrong belief system. They did not realize that this is not the way life works. That this was only their belief about how life works.

I learned through my own experiences that there is an incredible power within us, a power that can change our lives and the lives of many people around us, and a power that nobody can take away. The name of this incredible power is a belief system. Our beliefs are everything.

If you are lucky to be born in a family where you see your parent(s) modeling a positive belief system, the chances are that you will become what you observe. If you are born into a family where your parents are following a limiting belief system, the chances are that you will become what you observe.

When I looked back at my life, I realized that I inherited a very positive belief system from my mother. My mother decided to set-up a school about forty years ago, and against family traditions, to provide an education to children, especially to those who couldn't afford it. At that time, my grandfather was serving at a very important position in a government department. We had a big house of almost 1200 square yards. The ground floor of the building was mostly rented out.

In between, there used to be a time when the property was not vacant. During one of those times, my mother requested that my grandfather to allow her to open the school on the ground floor. Initially, my grandfather and the entire family showed strong resentment to her idea.

My mother refused to accept the limitations that were passed on to her politely. My mother promised my grandfather that she would run the school in a culturally appropriate manner. Finally, my grandfather allowed my mother to establish the school. We shifted to the ground floor of the building. My mother decided to have only two rooms for su to live in, while the rest of the rooms would be used for the school. At that time, my father was working abroad. I have one brother and one sister. As kids, we were not very happy with the decision of our mother to occupy only two rooms to live in.

My mother started the school. She did not use any marketing strategy to attract kids and families. Her only marketing strategy was her passion for teaching and helping young people. She passionately started teaching the kids of domestic workers. My mother was very focused and determined. She turned the families of the children she taught into advocates.

Everyone in my extended family was convinced that my mother would not be able to succeed. But slowly and gradually, my mother was able to attract many families to send their children to her school. Everyone was quite surprised to see the results. My grandfather was also very impressed by the commitment of my mother and the way she ran the school.

I remember that my mother put a big board in front of the main gate of the school that "men are not allowed in school, and if they want to talk to teachers or the principal, they must talk from outside".

My mother showed extraordinary commitment, coming from a positive belief system. Her day used to start very early, around 3am. She used to prepare food for us, iron our clothes, and organize our bags, in addition to her assignments as a principal of the school. The school was open from morning to evening. Many children of the working-class parents used to come in the evening. She used to get free around 5:30 pm.

After that, she used to teach us and help us with our homework. This was her daily routine. My mother ran the school very successfully for 27 years. She educated several thousand children. She helped us to get an education, too.

My grandfather, before his death, used to help my mother with her assignments. My father came back from abroad knowing the success of my mother. My mother did not buy into the belief of others telling her that she would never be able to run a school. When I examined the life of my mother, I found that the single most powerful factor in her success was her positive belief system.

My mother inherited a powerful belief system from her mother. My mother lost her father when she was only one. Her mother took the responsibility of raising 7 kids. I realized that my mother inherited a very strong and positive belief system from my grandmother. I believe that beliefs are passed on from one generation to another. If these beliefs are positive, they can change your life. If these beliefs are negative, they can destroy your life.

All it takes is one person to help you to develop a positive belief system or rewrite your belief system. In doing so, that person not only empowers you, but also empowers generations to come. My mother showed how much power one person has to overcome limiting belief systems. I believe that from observing my mother, I started becoming part of what I was observing. My mother instilled a very positive belief system in us through her actions and commitment. I did not learn anything close to what I learned from my mother from any other educational institution.

Today, I use the same place and office where my mother used to work to help young people become changemakers.

b) Excessive focus on prevention

We live in a culture which is dominated by deficit thinking. It inspires the creation of programs and policies that describe the positive development of young people in regard to the absence of negative behaviors. Our definition of a successful young person includes the avoidance of problems. In reality, there are millions of young people who are not involved in crime, drugs, abuse, robbery, and other risky behaviors. Many of these young people are well-educated and skilled. This does not mean that these young people are not struggling.

They are also facing serious challenges for a smooth transition into adulthood. It is a sad reality that problem behaviors of young people are tracked more often than their ability to drive a change in their communities. It is good to provide services to young people in the areas of their greatest need, but we should also avoid sending the wrong message to young people that we only care about young people when they do harm.

Our current efforts focus much of their attention on young people that are troublemakers. We must not forget that all young people have phenomenal changemaking potential locked up in them. As a society, we can do a better job of creating, activating, and multiplying places for youth-led changemaking. We must send the message to young people as early as possible that we trust them, their abilities, and their potential to drive change in society. We must offer young people the opportunities to practice their natural changemaking abilities. We need a collective effort to replace the vocabulary used to define young people. We need a new vision and a new vocabulary to define young people. The new vision must see every young person as a changemaker. Importantly, this new vision must engage all stakeholders in devising strategies to translate our new vision into solid actions.

c) Passive education

The culture of educational institutions is at odds with the culture of youth-led changemaking. There is no space provided by the schools for students to think, create, and innovate. Students are forced to memorize names and contributions of past changemakers, but they have no opportunity to drive change themselves.

Changemaking is seen as a future agenda. Our schools have never been designed to produce changemakers. Our schools force students to memorize a wide range of names, stories, and scientific facts, but they never encourage students to use classroom learnings to drive change in their communities.

Our curriculums are not designed to assess the changemaking potential of young people. If you have any doubt about what I am saying, then those of you who are in schools, and those of you who are out of schools, ask yourself: How many of your teachers encouraged you to drive change in communities? How often were you given an opportunity to develop potential solutions to the problems being faced by our communities? How many of you were appreciated because you created social and economic value in the society?

It would not be wrong to say that our current education methods do not correlate well with helping students to become changemakers. My simple question to schools and families is what we expect our children to become. Our schools are given the responsibility to produce better human beings who can contribute to making this world a better place. In other words, we want every child to become a changemaker.

It is strange that our expectations from our schools are not well-aligned with the structures to produce these results. If you go to any school today, how many of the changemaking abilities mentioned above would you see the teachers use to analyze the performance of students?

Our best schools and teachers have failed to realize the significance of practicing changemaking abilities during studies. My definition of a great teacher is someone that facilitates students to discover their natural changemaking abilities and helps them to turn their ideas into reality for the greater good.

I think that the time has come when we should move beyond labeling our children and young people as gifted and talented to creating structured opportunities for them to practice their changemaking abilities. There are many ways we can transform our education system. We can replace traditional exams by a changemaking project in the community. Such a project would be a win-win situation for everyone, such as students, communities, schools, and society. Instead of sitting in the examination hall for exams, students would be required to organize a changemaking celebration in the community to showcase their impact on the community members. Students should be encouraged to form small teams to carry out their changemaking projects.

The culture of youth-led changemaking can be cultivated by encouraging schools to develop a changemaking center at their premises to bring together schools and communities in a common strategy. Through this, students of all classes and disciplines are encouraged to practice changemaking abilities.

We can also establish a steering committee to facilitate and determine how changemaking can be incorporated into the school system across primary, secondary, and higher education. We can develop an accreditation system to validate courses and activities that support youth-led changemaking. We can offer credits to students for their changemaking projects. We can start changemaking award programs for schools and teachers that promote great examples of changemaking.

d) Financial constraints

There is no permanent funding available for youth-led changemaking. If there is any funding available, it does not flow to young people at the bottom of the pyramid. It is available only for privileged young people. The financial services offered by the banks do not fit the needs of young people involved in changemaking. They impose unrealistic and troublesome conditions on young people. No field can survive without stable funding. The funding should be available in multiple forms, such as grants, loans, investments, and equity.

One of the striking differences between traditional youth engagement programs and youth-led changemaking programs is the focus of youth-led changemaking programs to generate income from both earned and unearned income strategies. Youth-led changemaking provides a better option to donors, banks, and philanthropists for investment. Youth-led changemaking projects create a fine balance between grants and income-generating activities. They make sure that the pendulum does not move too much in either direction.

There is a need to develop a sound ecosystem for youth-led changemaking. Developing a financial market for youth-led changemaking can play a very instrumental role in strengthening the ecosystem. There are many ways to foster a youth-led changemaking culture in society.

Government, donors, and private enterprises should focus less on providing high-profile grants and investments to well-established enterprises, and more on providing small grants and investments to young people interested in changemaking.

The government should use the development sector budget wisely by spending less on projects that consume enormous resources, and more on youth-led projects that generate resources.

Internship programs for young people should be replaced with changemaking programs to help young people to create and disseminate new products, ideas, and services that produce social and economic benefits. Donors should revisit their funding priorities and try to create funding mechanisms for youth-led changemaking. Schools should allocate a small fee for changemaking. Schools should not see it as a burden, but rather as an opportunity to be able to invest in new ideas for social and economic change.

Private companies can play a leadership role in encouraging youth-led changemaking by enabling young people to engage in changemaking and innovation by creating new products and services. These companies can provide a space to young people to improve their products and generate new product ideas.

e) Legal constraints

There are serious legal obstacles in the way of helping young people become changemakers. These barriers include setting up companies, getting registration, opening bank accounts, applying for patents, and getting financial assistance.

The current laws do not allow anyone under the age of 18 to become a changemaker. In some developed countries, the age to set up a company is slightly lower. The current legal system in many countries can be described as a suppressor of youth-led changemaking.

Many great ideas of young people are often copied and stolen because of the inability of the legal system to provide space to young people to protect and expand those ideas.

The legal structure in many countries is inhibiting genuine youth-led changemaking by putting many restrictions on the participation of young people. It is vital to review the existing policies and programs for the purpose of improving and developing new legal structures that can support youth-led changemaking inclusively.

f) Shortage of human resources

There is a serious shortage of people for promoting youth-led changemaking. There are hardly any teachers, workers, and volunteers in the field of youth-led changemaking. There is a dire need to create a community of knowledge and practice in the field of youth-led changemaking to advance this field. There are no incentives to inspire people to get involved in the spreading of youth-led changemaking.

Without an active community of knowledge and practice, the field of youth-led changemaking cannot spread effectively. The community of knowledge and practice is comprised of people who have a shared vision and a strong desire to expand their knowledge and skills in the field of youth-led changemaking. This is the best time to take strategic steps towards creating a community of knowledge and practice at all levels of the society to benefit from the natural changemaking abilities of young people.

There is a dire need to re-position young people as changemakers who can initiate an idea or activity in the areas of greatest need, such as health, education, poverty, and agriculture.

Youth-led changemaking extends the very familiar idea of volunteerism and civic engagement by enabling young people to actively participate in finding new and innovative solutions. Youth-led changemaking is likely to capture the attention and imagination of many people and organizations, because it sounds like an exciting approach to view the potential of young people.

The idea of youth-led changemaking can prove to be paradigm-shattering, with the potential to transform the way we look at young people. And when we change the way we look at young people, we change the results that they produce. The success of this youth-led changemaking field depends on the creation of a community of knowledge and practice that has the vision, strength, resources, and patience to move forward in the field.

g) Poor media coverage of youth-led changemaking

Why is there so little media coverage of youth-led changemaking in our society? There are many reasons for it:

1. The concept of youth-led changemaking is a new concept and many people are not aware of it;
2. Advertisers are not interested in youth-led changemaking news;
3. News reporters are not well aware of the places where youth-led changemaking projects are happening;
4. Young people involved in changemaking underestimate the value of media; and
5. Negative coverage and attitudes towards young people.

There are many ways that the use of media and the interaction with the media could be improved to advance Youth-lLed Changemaking: Here a few examples:

- Engage young people in the development and dissemination of TV shows and radio programs on youth-led changemaking.
- Create a permanent space for youth-led changemaking programs.

- Highlight the case studies of young people involved in changemaking to improve the lives of underprivileged people.
- Help schools develop their own media programs to showcase the work and ideas of young people involved in changemaking.
- Highlight and reward people and organizations that are involved in youth-led changemaking programs.
- Sensitize and orient media personnel on the concept of youth-led changemaking for effective reporting.

Chapter 5

YOUTH-LED CHANGEMAKING FOR PEACE BUILDING

Youth-Led Changemaking has the potential to become a top national interest in many countries in the light of growing youth-led incidents of violence and terrorism.

Many developing and developed countries are facing unprecedented internal challenges to maintain peace and stability. These challenges stem from the inability of these countries to engage young people in positive and constructive activities. It is important for all countries to immediately set up mechanisms to reintegrate young people into the society as changemakers.

Young people are both the biggest tools and the biggest victims of terrorism. Terrorist groups are recruiting disengaged and disconnected young people into their ranks. Young people are the primary target of recruitment, both forced and voluntary, by terrorist groups. We cannot win any war against terrorism without the meaningful engagement of young people in peace building and rebuilding our communities. Young people have an enormous capacity to either build or destroy.

We have countless examples of young people that have been involved with terrorist groups to implement their agendas. Terrorist groups are nourishing terrorism with the blood of our young people. When we reject, devalue, and disengage young people, we open the doors for violence, crime, and terrorism in our society. There is no peace and stability possible without the engagement of young people in problem-solving. If you take a look at the countries which are seriously affected by the conflict, you will find that young people represent more than half of the total population.

A vast majority of these young people are growing-up in humiliating environments where they are deprived of their basic human rights. Terrorist groups offer exactly what is missing in the lives of these young people: a sense of connection, a sense of purpose, a sense of ownership, a sense of usefulness, and a sense of belonging.

Since 2001, the nature of the threat has changed in many countries. The major threat is no longer coming from outside. It is coming from inside. The war tactics have altered tremendously. The enemies of peace operate from the shadows. They misguide and misuse young people to declare war against their own people. The professional armies cannot fight this war alone. They need the support of civil government and civil society to counter these efforts. We know governments in many countries are not in a position to respond to these internal challenges.

The governments in many countries have just started to realize that the major threat is coming from their inability to match the extremists' capabilities to influence young people. There is an urgent need to fill the huge youth engagement vacuum that is being exploited by the extremists by trusting them to achieve their hidden agendas.

The recent youth-led incidents have shown that this vacuum cannot be filled by only providing education and job opportunities to young people. Many of the recent terrorist attacks have been made by well-educated and well-bred young people. There is not a single reason for why young people get radicalized. There are many factors which are contributing to youth radicalization. Disengagement, disconnection, humiliation, exclusion, ignorance, weak familial ties, deprivation, hopelessness, helplessness, humanitarian sufferings, misinterpretation of religion, marginalization, and unemployment are the factors that have created environments conducive to radicalization and recruitment of young people by extremist groups.

It is virtually impossible for any government or army to fight with all these factors alone. They need the support of the entire society. More inclusive societies are needed to prevent this from happening. If young people can become easy targets of radicalization, they can also be engaged to combat terrorism.

The key question is how to change the scenario from a world in which young people are portrayed in an overwhelmingly negative light to a world in which everyone is aware of young people involved in changemaking. The best way to do this is to advance Youth-Led Changemaking at all levels of the society to create a more inclusive society. Youth-Led Changemaking sends a strong message to young people that society values and honors them.

Families, educational institutions, and communities must be engaged in creating, activating, and multiplying spaces for Youth-Led Changemaking. If young people can become easy targets of radicalization, they are also capable of creating a strong force to reject radicalization. The best thing about Youth-Led Changemaking is that it harnesses the passion and risk-taking abilities of young people for the greater good. Youth-Led Changemaking offers an exciting opportunity for young people to discover their inherent changemaking potential by doing something impactful. We must understand that unless we develop a strong counter-narrative which provides young people living in humiliation with a substantive and appealing reason to reconnect with society as useful citizens, it would be very difficult to stop the impact of extremist ideology on their hearts and minds. Youth-Led Changemaking offers multiple outcomes to society.

It is time to give Youth-Led Changemaking the same kind of public recognition and acceptance that is accorded to military service in many countries of the world. The demand for peace and prosperity is increasing. The traditional family system is being eroded due to the desire for more. The technological revolution has changed everything. The Internet has removed distances. The unmet service needs of society are increasing. Young people are exposed to a new world.

Youth-led violent extremism is on the rise. Young people have developed a strong sense of exclusion. The time is ripe for a new vision. We have already seen that young people in military service carry out humanitarian tasks successfully in the most difficult conditions. Is there a way in which an average young person can be engaged in promoting peace and prosperity in society? The answer is YES.

Youth-Led Changemaking provides the most effective mechanism for every young person to contribute positively to society. At a time when many countries are threatened by terrorists, there is a dire need to create an alternative mechanism in society to overcome terrorism and other social, economic, and environmental problems. Youth-Led Changemaking provides us with the most cost-effective mechanism to reduce internal threats to peace and security.

We have a remarkable opportunity to speed up the peace efforts in many conflict-affected countries by creating a space for Youth-Led Changemaking. We need to move fast to stop the recruitment of young people into the ranks of extremist terrorist groups. Policy makers and politicians must realize that fire-fighting is not the only option when it comes to young people. It is very important to hunt down terrorists. It is more important, however, to stop our children and young people from *becoming* terrorists. Young people have a lot of latent changemaking potential, but governments in many countries are unable to develop a plan to benefit from it. On the other hand, youth-led terrorism incidents are happening consistently. It is a wake-up call for all of us.

Our policies and plans are incomplete without viewing our youth as equal partners in counterterrorism and development. I believe that the primary purpose of any policy or plan is not to restrict action, but to promote action. I personally believe that Youth-Led Changemaking will help many governments mobilize and engage millions of young people against terrorism at a very low cost. We need the active contributions of young people in many fields, especially in our efforts against terrorism.

Like military service, Youth-Led Changemaking should be seen as a national service. In many countries, including Pakistan, military organizations have become excessively involved in dealing with domestic terrorism threats and humanitarian missions. This shows that we need more than a military solution to combat terrorism. As armies are overburdened with carrying out counter-terrorism operations within the country, more young people are needed for civic service initiatives.

There is an urgent need for a recruitment of the whole youthful population to drive change in communities on an emergency basis. The present situation calls for a Youth-Led Changemaking movement that would serve as a bridge between military and civilian sectors of society to fight against terrorism. Youth-Led Changemaking will provide a human resource program that could work at every level of society.

Chapter 6

YOUTH-LED CHANGEMAKING: A DREAM INTO A REALITY

The Results of the YES Changemaking Competition

I have found that a large number of young people today are living their lives with a limiting belief system.

They don't know that that they are following a limiting belief system. Our education systems are not designed to change the belief system of young people in a way that truly empowers and engages them.

I found out that our education systems do not change anything inside of us. Our belief system remains the same. Our outcomes in life are directly linked to our belief system.

I knew that I would not be able to help young people without changing their belief system. Young people feel helpless when it comes to changing their circumstances. They are living their lives in standby mode. They have false assumptions. They have imposed limitations upon themselves.

I used to ask myself several questions: How do we help young people find out whether they have a positive or negative belief system? How can we help young people change their belief system? How can we help young people discover that they were born with great changemaking abilities? Such a discovery will always drastically change everything for them.

I created a very simple model of youth-led changemaking. I followed six steps to transform young people from victims to changemakers. Here are these steps:

- **Step 1:** Build an echo system for the support of youth-led changemaking.

- **Step 2:** Use the existing infrastructure (schools, colleges, communities, organizations) to deliver.

- **Step 3:** Open a trust account in young people. Invoke positive energy among young people by treating them as changemakers/gifted and valuable (help young people release the negative energy they are holding on to from past experiences).

- **Step 4:** Offer trust-based (risk-free) funding to young people to practice changemaking abilities. I provide small risk-free funding (US$1 to US$50) to activate young people as changemakers. Risk-free funding means that if there is a loss, I will bear it, and if there is a profit, it will be distributed equally. The data below gives you an idea of what happened when we offered trust-based funding to young people.

- **Step 5:** Reward and celebrate young people and adults (teachers, principals, workers) publicly.

- **Step 6:** Repeat these steps and embed this ideology in the culture and curriculum.

I found out that providing changemaking opportunities to young people can help them let go of the limiting ideas they have been told about themselves, about their "limited" capabilities, about their "limited" relationships, and about the "limited" success that is possible for them.

I often start my conversations or sessions with young people by asking a few questions. These questions are the following:

- Are you a changemaker?
- Do you want to become a changemaker?
- Why do you want to become a changemaker?
- How will you become a changemaker?

In response to the first question, "Are you a changemaker?" young people's most common response is, "No".

In response to my second question, "Do you want to become a changemaker?", young people often say a big, "Yes!" There is hardly anyone in the room saying no to this question. This response from young people provides me with a great opportunity to lay the foundation of my work in their minds, and develop or strengthen the desire among young people to become changemakers.

When I ask my third question, "Why do you want to become a changemaker?", most of the young people say it is because they want to serve society. The desire to serve and improve society was found in almost all young people. After that, I ask my final question, "How will you become a changemaker?", and young people give interesting answers, such as after getting a degree, diploma, skill, job, or opportunity.

It is interesting to observe that a vast majority of young people do not give a real answer to this question. One major challenge stands in their way: Young people desire to become changemakers, but they are left up to chance. They show desire, but have no method or strategy to achieve their desire.

They have developed a mental model about their success which is not proving useful. They have built this model of success even without knowing about it. They have developed this model from their interactions with society.

My role is often to make them aware of this "unsuccessful but blindly pursued" model, in order to deconstruct it.

The problem with this model is that it defines changemaking as something to be done at the end of your degree. This mental model does not activate young people to become changemakers *during* their academic journey.

This mental model says to them: "hold on until you achieve personal milestones". My work has proved again and again that there is no right age for changemaking. You are designed by God in a manner that you can become a changemaker at a very young age.

My youth-led changemaking model has shown that there is no reason to wait for a degree to begin your changemaking journey. During my sessions with young people, I also tried to make a clear distinction between personal accomplishment and changemaking.

Accomplishment refers to the personal milestones that we desire to achieve during our journey to become a changemaker. Personal accomplishments are good for the person who achieves them. However, they should not be mixed with our efforts to bring change in the lives of others. Changemaking is the positive consequence of our efforts, experienced by others *and* ourselves.

Personal accomplishments can be seen as "enablers" to become a changemaker, and with every accomplishment in your academic career or life, you prepare yourself for changemaking. Sometimes, personal experiences also serve as strong "enablers" to live a life of changemaking.

The YES Changemaking Competitions offer a new source of innovation in society. These competitions give complete freedom to young people to discover their inherent changemaking potential in the real world. The Changemaking Competitions provide an opportunity to young people to develop and test new ideas themselves. These competitions have created safe spaces for young people to innovate. This is the first time in the history of many educational and vocational institutions that the idea of changemaking is extended to young people.

Let me share with you the data of the changemaking competitions carried out by my organization during the last few years.

No. of Young People Engaged	Overall Investment in PKR	No. of People Served	Overall Profit in PKR	Percentage of Profit
16,010	7,123,712	620,617	6,667,740	93.5%

Table 14: Summarized Analysis of the YES Changemaking Competitions

Overall, the changemaking competitions provided PKR 7,123,712 to young people to initiate ideas or activities that produce social and economic benefits. A total of 16,010 young people participated in youth-led changemaking competitions. Being the lead users of many products and services, they did not have much trouble coming up with new ideas or solutions. They knew the strengths and weaknesses of products and services in the market. Young people were able to make a profit of PKR 6,667,740 on the invested amount in a short period of time. The percentage of profit on the investment was 93.5%. A large number of young people decided to take an incremental approach to create social and economic value. They did not try to create a new product or service that forces radical change or disruption in society. They preferred to improve the quality and accessibility of existing products and services. They focused on the fast delivery of their ideas. They used simple materials and tools to make an instant impact. A few of the young people came up with innovative ideas to deliver services to young people.

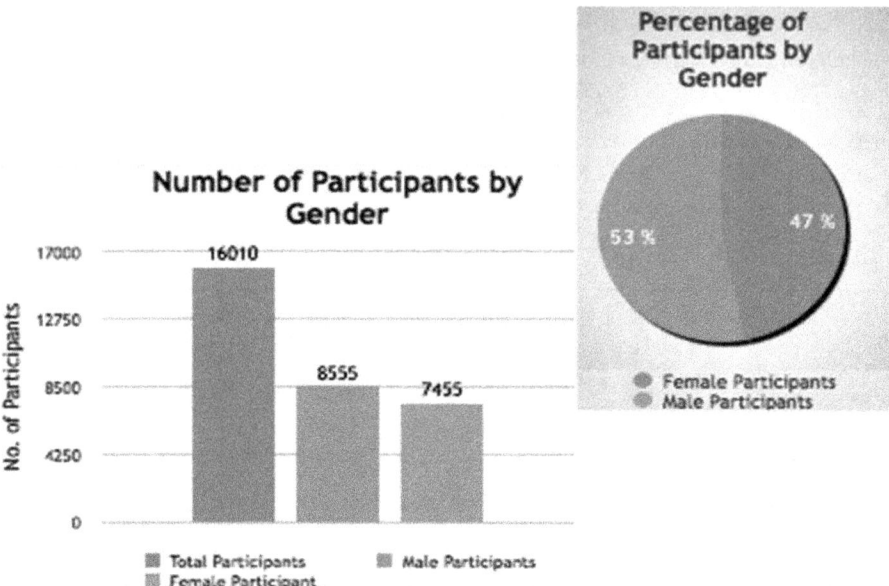

Figure 2: Gender Participation in the YES Competitions

Harnessing the latent changemaking potential of youth in Pakistan, the Changemaking Competitions engaged 16,010 individuals (47% females and 53% males) across the country, who in return, served 620,617 people in their communities. The multiplier effect created with these competitions has had a far reach, resulting in various teams continuing the project long-term. The Changemaking Competitions did not only allow the youth to be able to contribute to society in a positive manner, but also encouraged them to earn money for themselves and their families, even with small investments.

YES! Youth-Led Changemaking

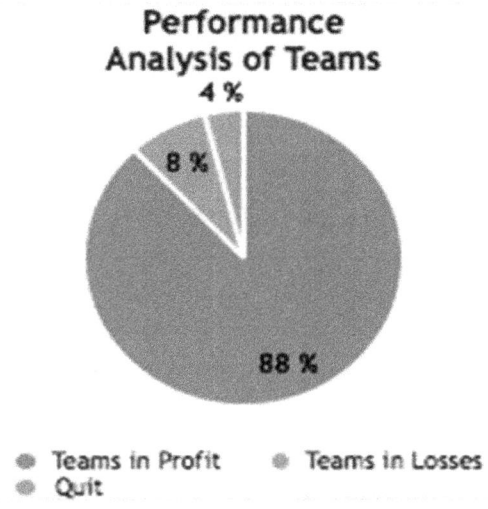

Figure 3: Performance Analysis of Teams in YES Competitions

A total of 3,717 teams participated in the competition (42% were female-only teams, 56% were male-only teams, and 2% teams were mixed-gender) out of which, 88% of the teams were able to reap profits, 8% experienced losses, and 4% of teams quit the competition before completion.

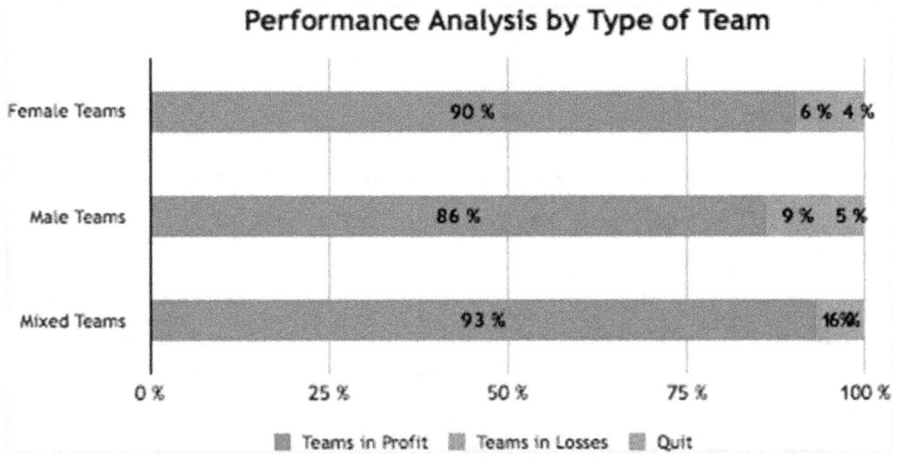

Figure 4: Performance Analysis by Types of Teams in YES Competitions

As the chart above shows, amongst the female groups, 90% of the teams were in profit, 6% faced losses, and 4% quit the competition. On the other hand, amongst the male groups, 86% of the teams experienced profits, 9% were in loss, and 5% quit. The mixed-gender teams experienced the highest percentage of teams in profit (93%), followed by 1% facing losses, and 6% of the teams quitting the competition.

The results show the remarkable rate of success for teams, and also highlights a small percentage of teams who faced challenges and/or quit the competition. A deeper analysis of the reasons for each will be carried out later in the report.

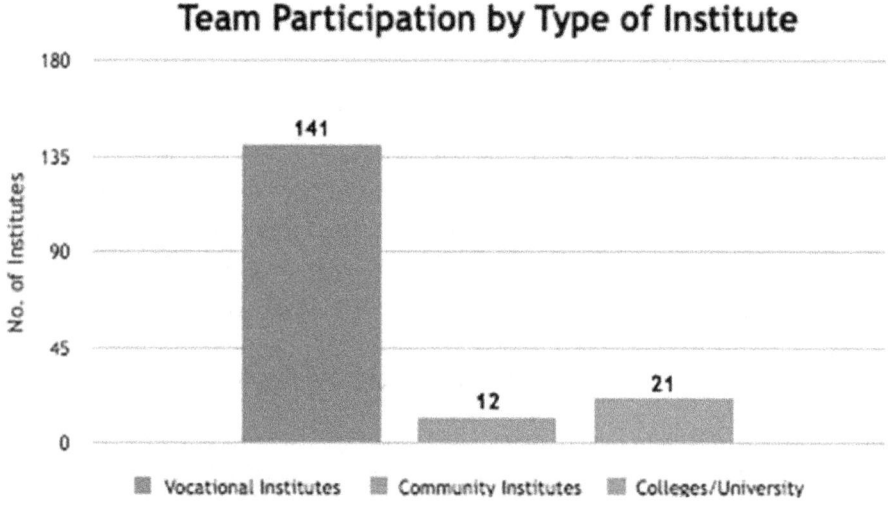

Figure 5: Team Participation by the Type of Institutes in YES Competitions

The data shows that a grand total of 174 institutes (141 vocational institutes, 12 community institutes, and 21 colleges/universities) engaged in the Changemaker Institute Award competition. However, the duration of the competition in each institute varied. 51 institutes carried out the competition for 5 weeks, 98 institutes carried it out for 4 weeks, 15 institutes conducted the competition for 1 week, 3 institutes spanned it over 5 days, and 7 institutes carried it out as a 2-day competition (see graph below).

YES! Youth-Led Changemaking

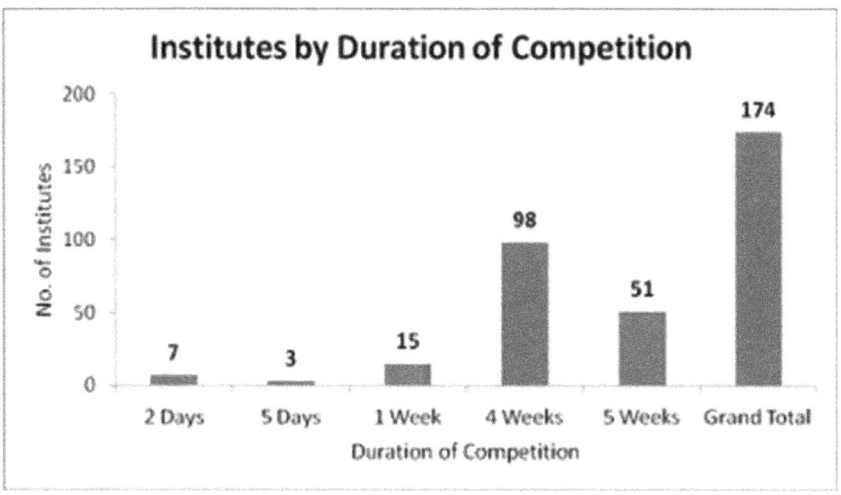

Figure 6: Participation of the Institutes by the Duration of YES Competitions

The diversity in the duration of the competition largely depended on the circumstances of each institute. Furthermore, the Changemaker Institute Award competition extended its outreach to different types of educational institutes. Out of the total of 174 institutes engaged in the competition, 141 were educational and vocational institutes, 21 were colleges/universities, and 12 were community schools. Amongst these different institutes, community schools emerged to be the dominant players, as they generated the highest percentage of overall profits (139%). Additionally, community schools also had the highest representation of females in the competition, (69%), followed by colleges/universities with 59% females, and educational and vocational institutes had 45% female participation in the competition.

A deeper performance analysis of each type of institute by gender reveals that 86% of the male teams of educational and vocational institutes made profits, 10% bore losses, and 4% quit the competition before completion. 87% of the male teams of colleges/universities were able to make profits, 1% suffered losses, and the remaining 12% quit the competition before completion. Similarly, 89% of all female educational and vocational institute team members generated profits, 6% suffered losses, and 5%

quit the competition. 94% of the female college/university teams made profit, 5% suffered losses, and 2% quit the competition before completion. Interestingly, all of the male and female community school teams had successful profitable enterprises.

The data above clearly highlights a huge population of youth in our country which, if given the opportunity and some guidance, can transform into unique assets contributing positively to our society by creating a chain of revenue-generating enterprises, thereby making our country more stable financially. If the energy and talent of these young individuals is tapped systematically, our country can have economic progress like no other. The data also draws attention towards a small percentage of teams which were unable to generate revenues and/or left the competition before completion.

The project engaged 3,717 teams by giving them an initial investment amount of PKR 100 to PKR 5,000 to showcase their skills and bring a social positive change to their communities through entrepreneurship. The projects ranged from providing door-to-door services, such as electronic repairs, stitching services, food supplies to offices during lunchtime by engaging home-based cooks, education fares, health awareness campaigns, entertainment in the form of fun-fairs, and many others. Each project touched upon a different element of our society and provided for a unique community-based solution. Some projects took a broader approach and focused on the promotion of peace and harmony in the community, such as the Peace Festival (arranged by one of the teams). Each project reaped phenomenal levels of profits. One project earned a profit of PKR 200,000 plus (on an initial investment of PKR 2,500). Three more projects had revenues crossing PKR 100,000 in a span of 5 weeks or less; and multiple others swept in profits of tens of thousands of rupees. Some praise-worthy welfare-oriented projects included the 4-week education program for street children, basic diagnostic testing services, such as blood and sugar tests at reduced prices, and the campaign "Keep Jutial Clean", which raised awareness amongst the community members on how to keep their town clean. These programs did not just improve the overall welfare of society, but also allowed these young individuals to earn decent profits. Students receiving funds as low as PKR 100 were also able to make huge profits percentage-wise. One female student who received the seed money of PKR 100 gave football coaching classes and earned PKR 4,500 in just a couple of hours. Another female student organized a fun-fair with her initial PKR 100 and turned it into a profit of PKR 7,600 in just two days. A significant majority earned profits more than 5 times the initial investment. This not only means that the competition was successful in providing a means of earning money for the young individuals in our society, but also encouraged these individuals to come up with unique cost-efficient solutions to the challenges of their community; thereby acting as multipliers to increase social and economic benefits for the community. Upon completion, the most common words used by participants to explain their feelings about the competition in one word were: **happy, amazing, hopeful, confident,** and **inspired.**

While focusing on the positive value creation of this project, it is equally important to draw attention towards the low-performing teams. These include the teams which could not generate profits or could not complete the competition. Out of a total of 3,717 teams, 284 teams (8%) finished as low-performing teams, and 165 teams (4%) quit before completing the competition.

Analyzing the loss-bearing teams further, the data shows that amongst these, 65% were male teams and 35% were female teams. A significant majority of the loss-bearing teams were from the educational and vocational institutes (63% males and 34% females). Only 2% of male and 1% of female college/university teams experienced losses. Amongst the loss-bearing teams, 58% (57% male and 43% females) teams experienced losses less than 50%, and 42% (76% male and 24% female) experienced losses more than 50%. The graph below illustrates a much more defined picture of the loss-making teams by decile.

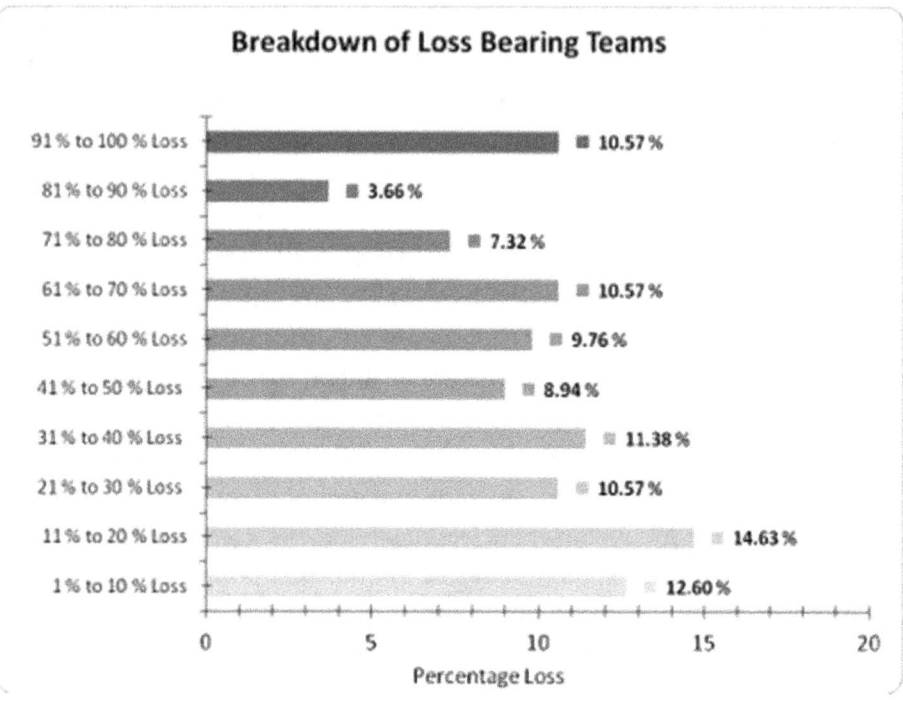

Figure 7: The Breakdown of the Loss-Bearing Teams

Looking at a much broader picture, if we analyze the percentage of teams which experienced a loss on their investment (i.e. experienced an 80-100% loss on their investment), out of the total teams which participated, the percentage is less than 1 (0.9%), thereby highlighting that investing in young people is one of the quickest and safest ways to achieve economic and social results.

The end-line survey carried out upon completion of the project revealed multiple reasons for the teams not being able to generate profits. Some major reasons included: a lack of support from teachers, poor product selection, a lack of community and parental support, intense academic pressure which made it difficult for the team members to focus on the competition, a lack of teamwork and coordination, difficulty with time management, and a lack of desire among students. These diverse reasons highlight the need for better coordination mechanisms at institutes to ensure that students participate in activities beyond academics. Capacity building of teaching staff to inculcate the spirit of entrepreneurship within students by making it a part of their coursework emerged as another significant recommendation.

Last, but not least, the results also show a small percentage of teams which quit the competition before it was even completed. Out of 3,717 teams that participated, 165 (4%) quit the competition. Follow-up surveys with these teams revealed that the major reasons for quitting the competition included: intense academic pressure, the fear factor, a lack of desire among students, poor team selection, a lack of parental support, and inadequate guidance from teachers.

The above-mentioned reasons for teams not being able to make a profit and/or quitting the competition clearly highlight the need for the rigorous training of teachers to provide the relevant support and guidance to students participating in the competition. It brings attention to the lack of communication and coordination among the teachers and the institute's administration staff to implement the project in its full capacity. At the same time, the results also show that the support of parents is also a major determinant in the student's success, as it is reflected in their confidence and their ability to perform.

Having mentioned the areas of concern as revealed by the data collected through these competitions, it is important to highlight the immense impact that these competitions have had on the lives of each and every participant and the beneficiaries. The project is an insight into the potential and ability of the youth that are ready to make a positive impact with minimal support and guidance. The Changemaking Competitions are an eye-opener for the politicians and policymakers of our country. They show the urgency and need to create institutional structures that aim at catalyzing youth-led changemaking in society. Changemaking Competitions provide a great opportunity to create new products, new services, and new ways of addressing local challenges. These competitions show that we can infuse the spirit of changemaking in thousands of young people so quickly. We have an unprecedented youth population in the world today. Youth-led changemaking presents the most exciting idea to realize the dream of a true demographic dividend. This demographic dividend can only be realized by developing and aligning structures that support youth-led changemaking.

I would like to share the names of a few young people that participated in and won changemaking competitions. It is important to mention here that almost all of these young people participated in a changemaking competition for the first time in their lives. A vast majority of these young people are from the vocational and technical institutions owned by the government, and are provided with a stipend to learn vocational skills.

A tiny majority of these young people are from universities. You will see in the table below how young people responded to the opportunity. They showed incredible talent and energy to create a social and economic impact in a short period of time.

Name of the Leader	Duration of the Competition	Investment	Profit	Percentage of Profit	Type of Business
Mr. Syed Haider Abbas	5 Weeks	2500	228150	9126.00	Blood-Screening Test
Ms. Sundas Dilawer	2 Days	100	7600	7600.00	Literature Festival
Mr. Azeem Sarwar	1 Week	1100	71500	6500.00	P. Test/ Diagnosis Disease
Ms. Hafiza Tanzila	5 Weeks	2500	155863	6234.52	Stitching and Designing Center
Ms. Taiba Batool	2 Days	100	4500	4500.00	Football Coaching Services
Mr. Fazeel	4 Weeks	2500	102600	4104.00	AC Repairing
Ms. Afshan Naz	4 Weeks	2500	102160	4086.40	Embroidery and Stitching

Ms. Shazia Malik	4 Weeks	1000	35000	3500.00	Creativity Competition
Ms. Zeest Mehmood	2 Days	500	7156	1431.20	Entertainment Services
Ms. Ghana Nasir	2 Days	300	3130	1043.33	Lemonade Water
Ms. Kanza Huma	2 Days	100	950	950.00	Cold Coffee
Ms. Ramla Moqatter	4 Weeks	2500	16260	650.40	Jewelry Making
Mr. Kashif Jalil	5 Weeks	5000	26000	520.00	Sugar Testing
Ms. Zohra Jabeen	4 Weeks	5000	20000	400.00	Shop for Ladies
Mr. Sajjad Karim	4 Weeks	5000	15230	304.60	Environment Protection
Mr. Shamoon Masih	4 Weeks	5000	15000	300.00	Hepatitis Awareness and Referral Services
Mr. Rizwan Shehzad	2 Days	800	2400	300.00	Essay Competition
Mr. Aun Ahmed	5 Weeks	5000	10790	215.80	Lunchbox Service
Mr. Amir Ali	4 Weeks	5000	5000	100.00	Art Competition
Mr. Mudasser Rehman	2 Weeks	1000	3050	305	Emergency Lights
Mr. Muneeb Abdullah	4 Weeks	5000	6290	125.8	Home-Based Cooks
Ms. Nasima Ali	2 Weeks	2500	11800	472	Basic Health Services
Mr. Saad Ahmed	4 Weeks	5000	5100	102	Sports Equipment

Mr. Taimoor Ahmed	4 Weeks	5000	32000	1280	Artistic Skills
Ms. Sadaf	4 Weeks	2500	18910	756	Beauty Service

Table 15: Summary of the Changemaking Competition's Winners

These are just a few names of the several thousand young people who trusted and engaged in changemaking competitions.

2.11.1 Twenty-Five Short Stories of the Changemakers

Below you will find the short stories of twenty-five Changemakers that emerged from the competitions:

1. Mr. Syed Haider Abbas: Haider, a 23-year-old student of Vocational Training Institute (VTI), Muzaffargarh launched a changemaking project to provide Hepatitis B and C screening services to the most deprived and marginalized people at a very low cost, right on their doorstep. A total number of 2281 people were provided with screening services for the first time. He earned PKR 228150 through his community service initiative. Due to his initiative, 200 people were found to be positive of both hepatitis B and C. Through this one-month activity, Haider stood out as an inspirational changemaker for other young community members.

2. Ms. Sundas Dilawer Ali: Sundas, a 21-year-old student of Lahore College for Women University (LCWU), organized a small-scale literature festival in a local private school aimed at "making learning fun for children". The project not only provided children with a break from their regular routine, but also indulged them in critical thinking activities in a

constructive manner. Within just one day, Sundas served more than 450 children and earned a profit of PKR 7600. Through this competition, Sundas set an example for her peers to become changemakers.

3. Mr. Azeem Sarwar: Azeem, a 30-year-old student of Vocational Training Institute (VTI), Kassowal, launched a project for artificial insemination testing. He sought the services of a professional doctor, offered diagnostic services, and started artificial insemination vaccination for animals. The project not only helped Azeem to make a profit of PKR 71500 but also provided awareness about `animal health among the community members. Through this one-month activity, Haider served 350 people of his community and stood out as an inspirational changemaker for other young community members.

4. Ms. Hafiza Tanzila: Hafiza, a 23-year-old student of Vocational Training Institute (VTI), launched a designing and stitching project after participating in a YES changemaking workshop. The workshop opened her mind to the idea that taking an initiative, no matter how small, is the first step towards prosperity and development. She formed a team and decided to start an enterprise. Her aim was to create an employment opportunity for home-based female workers by organizing them into a network. They designed, embroidered, and stitched clothes for small industries. She was able to generate a profit of Rs.155863 from only Rs.2500 investment in a period of weeks. She described her experience as a dream come true to have owned and run her own enterprise.

5. Ms. Taiba Batool: A very passionate girl, Taiba Batool, a student of physical sports science from the University of Sargodha (UoS) participated in the changemaking competition with an idea for football coaching. After physical fitness tests, she selected and trained 30 students from her university who faced problems during the sports gala. Within two days, she earned a profit

of PKR 4500. It was the first instance in the history of the university that a female led a sports initiative. She inspired many other girls in her university to become changemakers.

6. Mr. Fazeel: Fazeel, a 21-year-old student of the Vocational Training Institute (VTI), Rawalpindi launched a project to provide home services for electrical repairs. The project not only gave him hands-on experience, but also facilitated households who could not go out and get their electrical appliances repaired. Fazeel's innovative idea led him to make a remarkable profit of PKR 102,600 in just four weeks by serving 96 houses. Fazeel showed how a changemaking competition can help young people become changemakers.

7. Ms. Afshan Naz: 22-year-old Afshan Naz from the Vocational Training Institute (VTI), Nainsukh, launched a project selling multiple handmade items, including clothes, jewelry, and bags. Her project earned her a profit of PKR 102,160 in just one month. It aimed at providing high-quality homemade products made by females at prices lower than the market value. By empowering female home-based workers through this competition, Afshan showed other young members of her community how to be a changemaker.

8. Ms. Shazia Malik: Inspired by the changemaking competition, 30-year-old Shazia from Sardar Bahadur Khan Women's University (SBKWU) replicated the competition in a small school in her surrounding area, not only to learn more herself, but to extend the benefits of a changemaking competition to a larger audience. Within four weeks, Shazia earned a profit of PKR 10,300 and stimulated hundreds of other young students. Through this competition, Shazia came out as a true changemaking leader and an inspiration for other young people.

9. Ms. Zeest Mehmood: Inspired by the changemaker competition, Ms. Zeest of Government College University (GCU), along

with her team, launched a project to offer food items and entertainment services simultaneously with the aim of spreading sheer happiness and pleasure in the community. Ms. Zeest entertained 367 individuals and earned a profit of PKR 7,156 in just one day. Ms. Zeest stood out as an inspiration for other young community members to become changemakers.

10. Ms. Ghana Nasir: Ghana, a 21-year-old student of Fatima Jinnah University (FJU), launched a fresh homemade lemonade project to provide high-quality and low-priced organic drinks to peers. Her project not only solved poor-quality drink issues in the university, but also helped her earn a remarkable profit of Rs. 3130 in just two days. Ghana showed that the changemaking competition can help young people become changemakers.

11. Ms. Kanza Huma: At 20 years of age, Kanza from Lahore College for Women University (LCWU) was highly motivated to participate in the changemaking competition with the idea of providing cold coffee. She provided clean and healthy cold coffee to peers at a very low rate. Within two days, she served 10 people and made a profit of PKR 950.

12. Ms. Ramla Moattar: 18-year-old Ramla from the Vocational Training Institute (VTI), Governor House, launched a jewelry-making project through the changemaking competition. She provided homemade jewelry at a very low cost, and became a source of income for home-based female workers who did not have access to the market. She put up stalls inside and outside the VTI, and earned a profit of PKR 16260 in just four weeks.

13. Mr. Kashif Jalil: A 21-year-old student of the University of Engineering and Technology (UES), Taxila Kashif started a twin-project which included providing lunchboxes and conducting health tests, such as sugar and blood tests. The project aimed at offering homemade healthy and hygienic food to offices during lunch hours, and also carried out basic

health tests to create awareness amongst general community members. In just one month, Kashif reaped a profit of 26,000, and served more than 350 community members. Through this competition, Kashif served as an exemplary changemaker for other young community members.

14. Ms. Zohra Jabeen: Determined to be a changemaker, 23-year-old Zohra arranged for basic commodities of daily use to be available in the girls' hostel of her university. Her project not only aimed at making profits, but also to empower females with access to basic resources and facilities. In just four weeks, Zohra served 200 fellow students, earned a profit of PKR 20000, and became an inspiration for hundreds of other young females to become changemakers.

15. Mr. Sajjad Karim: Sajjad, a student of the National College of Commerce and Computer Sciences (NCCS), Gilgit, participated in the changemaking competition by pitching a very unique idea that no one else thought of. He offered garbage collection services to different residential areas, because there were piles of garbage outside each and every house in his society which were making the environment unhealthy. Through this project, he served more than 60 homes, and earned revenue of PKR 15230 in just four weeks. He is an exemplary changemaker for other young people of his community.

16. Mr. Shamoon Masih: Shamoon, a 26-year-old boy from the National University of Modern Languages (NUML), Quetta, was really committed to participate in the changemaking competition with an idea of health services-for-all. Shamoon took it as a personal challenge to create awareness about hepatitis in his community, because he saw many young people dying from hepatitis, and even his own sister of 32 years was a victim of this lethal disease. Within the time period of just four weeks, he not only reached out to 1500 people, but also made a profit

of PKR 30,000. He is a fine example of a changemaker in his community.

17. Mr. Rizwan Shehzad: Rizwan from GIFT University, Gujranwala, eagerly participated in the changemaking competition. He arranged a creative writing competition in his university to unleash the hidden talent of his university students. In just two days, he served 29 students and made a profit of PKR 2400.

18. Mr. Aun Ahmed: A 22-year-old student of the National University of Modern Languages (NUML), Aun started a project for distributing lunchboxes at reduced prices in his community. The project aimed at offering homemade quality food for lunch to individuals who cannot afford to buy expensive meals and are looking for home-cooked, delicious food. Aun earned a profit of PKR 10,790 in just two months. This competition made Aun stand out as an inspirational changemaker in society.

19. Mr. Amir Ali: Amir from the National College of Commerce and Computer Sciences (NCCS), Gilgit, participated in the changemaking competition by presenting the idea of an Art Competition. He organized a drawing competition in two of the largest schools of his city, and thus, provided a platform for the students to show off their suppressed talent. Within four weeks, he registered 100 students, collected revenue of PKR 5,000, and became a changemaker in his society.

20. Mr. Mudasser Rehman: A 20-year-old student of the Vocational Training Institute (VTI), Jhang, Mudasser set up a changemaking project to provide a cheap solution to his community members for growing load-shedding. He decided to create affordable and durable emergency lights. His invention earned him respect and admiration from his teachers and community members. He earned Rs.1000, and his hard work and diligence made him a handsome profit of Rs. 3050 in just two weeks. He earns from

his enterprise to finance his studies and support his family, which definitely makes him a role model for his community. "I want to expand this project and take it to a national level," says Mudasser.

21. **Mr. Muneeb Abdullah:** Muneeb, a 23-year-old student of the University of Haripur (UoH) started a lunch delivery system in order to provide high-quality homemade food to her peers. The project was not only aimed at making a profit, but also at providing a formal platform to the home-based cooks of his community. He earned a profit of PKR 6290. Through this competition, Muneeb emerged as an example for his peers to become young changemakers.

22. **Ms. Nasima Ali:** 25-year-old Nasima of Karakoram International University (KIU) launched a health program aimed at providing basic health services to her community members at their doorstep. Nasima realized that a large number of her community members, even her own parents, had to travel a lot to seek out basic medical services, such as measuring their sugar levels and blood pressure. She opened a health center to provide these services to the local people of her village. Her project not only yielded a profit of PKR 11,800 by reaching out to 500 people, but also saved her community members a lot of time and resources.

23. **Mr. Saad Ahmed Siddique:** Saad, a 20-year-old student of the Pakistan Institute of Emerging and Applied Sciences (PIEAS), launched a project to provide sports accessories, especially export-quality footballs, at the grassroots level. Saad started this project with the aim of unleashing raw talent at the grassroots level by providing community members with access to quality sports items at reduced rates. Within just one month, Saad generated a profit of PKR 51,000 and sold his product to 100 individuals.

24. Mr. Taimoor Ahmad: A student of St. Anthony's High School, Faisal Town Lahore, Taimoor started a project to sell paintings. Taimoor used his artistic skills to make paintings of various attractive landscapes of Pakistan and sold them to business elites. His aim was to spread awareness about the beautiful places in Pakistan. Taimoor earned a profit of PKR 32,000 by selling his paintings to only 7 clients. His successful and innovative enterprise highlighted his role as a young changemaker in his community – an example for others to follow.

25. Ms. Sadaf: Sadaf from the Vocational Training Institute (VTI), Bahawalpur, took part in the changemaking competition with her group fellows. Being students of the beautician class, the group provided door-to-door beauty services, because in their village, females don't have such facilities. They gathered a profit of PKR 18,910 by working for four weeks. Thus, the group set an example of how to create value in society.

My work has shown that young people present an infinite source of innovation in society. Changemaking competitions have helped young people to see things in a different perspective and to develop, implement, and evaluate new ideas and approaches. Young people were able to produce work that was missing. They developed and arranged better or improved products and services. They showed the ability to fill gaps and see possibilities that others have not observed.

The above data clearly shows that all young people have changemaking potential, and the problem is not the young people. The problem is the paradigm in which they are living and operating. When we change the paradigm of young people, we change the results.

Participation in changemaking opportunities triggers a new psychological and biological process that leads to a new self-belief and discovery. It develops a sense of belonging among young people. Students feel a strong sense of worth and acceptance that inspires them to go beyond their bubble.

Youth-led changemaking leads to results, product, work, output, or impact. This whole experience also tells us that a constructive environment facilitates young people to drive change by developing ideas and solutions, while a skeptical environment blocks the changemaking potential of young people.

Youth-led changemaking should be seen as a necessity, as it leads to new knowledge and invention.

There is a dire need to "set up new channels of youth-led changemaking" in the world. The digital world is providing a great opportunity to share and sell new ideas. I have no hesitation in saying that our schools are actually killing the inherent changemaking abilities of children and young people. I am saying this because, in schools, the major focus is on memorizing answers, thus restricting young people from creating and delivering something new.

Schools present the ideal time to engage children and young people in changemaking. Countries must find ways to "unlock youth's inherent potential for changemaking". Countries are finding it difficult to put this idea into practice. It requires both interest and investment to build a strong pipeline for youth-led changemaking.

Youth-led changemaking is about enabling young people to create social and economic value at the base of a pyramid.

It is interesting to note that many of the top-performing young people in all the competitions were not well-educated. They were living their lives in an environment of low-trust. I am not trying to devalue education. I am trying to identify the missing links in the education system. I believe my work in the field of youth-led changemaking will strengthen and add value to the current education system.

There is a dire need to provide better support to young people for changemaking at times of transition, whether from primary to secondary school, or from secondary school to further education. We must understand the vulnerabilities of youth during times of transition. Our major challenge today is not to improve our economy or increase the number of graduates. Our major challenge is to build trust with young people. Our future will not be secured by building new roads, factories, industries, or schools, but by extending and restoring trust with young people. If we want to speed forward towards peace and prosperity, we must restore trust with young people. No one is happy when they are not trusted. We cannot create a better world by mistrusting millions of young people.

When I was a child, my mother instilled a very strong belief system in me through her positive actions. It was my mother who inspired me to follow my dreams by focusing on what I have, and not by focusing on what I don't have. Now, I am trying to do the same thing in my work to help young people see more in themselves. I am trying to reach out to every young person in my country to present them with an opportunity to unlock their changemaking potential for personal and greater good.

I am uniquely placed, because I am asking young people to do what I have been doing myself for over 21 years. I have lived through this beautiful experience. Now, I want every young person to begin their journey. I feel so happy when I help young people find their worth in society.

The situation regarding youth engagement in changemaking has started changing incrementally. There is still a long way to go. With the publication of this book, I hope that we will add a new momentum to the field, both within and outside of the country.

Winners of Changemaking Competitions

Leader: Afia nazeer
Group: Female
Institute: Lahore College for Women's University, LHR.
Project: Nail Art,Mehndi,Jewellery
Amount Given: Rs. 5000
Profit Earnings: Rs. 13350
Location: Lahore

Leader: Afshan Naz
Group: Female
Institute: VTI, Nain Sukh, LHR
Project: Stiching
Amount Given: Rs. 2500
Profit Earnings: Rs. 102160
Location: Lahore

Leader: Aun Ahmed
Group: Mix
Institute: National University of Modern Languages (NUML), Islamabad
Project: Lunchbox Service
Amount Given: Rs5,000.
Profit Earnings: Rs. 10,790
Location: Islamabad

Leader: Azeem Sarwar
Group: Male
Institute: VTI, Kasowal.
Location: Kasowal
Project: P.T Test & Dignosis Disease
Amount Given: Rs1100
Profit Earnings: Rs. 71500

Leader: Ghana Nasir
Group: Female
Institute: Fatima Jinnah Women University, Rqawalpindi
Project: Serving Lemonade Water
Amount Given: Rs. 300
Profit Earnings: Rs. 3130
Location: Rqawalpindi

Leader: Kashif Jalil
Group: Male
Institute: University of Engineering and Technology, Taxila
Project: Sugar Testing + Lunch Box
Amount Given: Rs5,000.
Profit Earnings: Rs. 26,000
Location: Taxila

Winners of Changemaking Competitions

Code#16   Duration of the Competition: 2 Day

Leader: Muhammad Ali
Group: Male
Institute: Muhammad Nawaz Sharif University of Agriculture, Multan

Project: Food Services
Amount Given: Rs600
Profit Earnings: Rs. 1636
Location: Multan

Code#15   Duration of the Competition: 5 Weeks

Leader: Nadia Khan
Group: Female
Institute: VTI, Nain Sukh

Project: Stiching
Amount Given: Rs 2500
Profit Earnings: Rs. 155863
Location: Lahore

Code#17   Duration of the Competition: 2 Days

Leader: Nahid Akhtar
Group: Mix
Institute: Government College University, LHR.

Project: Entertainment Activities
Amount Given: Rs500.
Profit Earnings: Rs. 7,156
Location: Lahore

Code#14   Duration of the Competition: 2 Weeks

Leader: Naseema Begum
Group: Female
Institute: KIU, Gilgit-Baltistan

Project: BP Apparaturs
Amount Given: Rs1000
Profit Earnings: Rs. 11800
Location: Gilgit

Code#00   Duration of the Competition: 2 Weeks

Leader: Nazia Parveen
Group: Female
Institute: VTI

Project: Shop for ladies
Amount Given: Rs20000
Profit Earnings: Rs. 20000
Location: Sahansa, Kotli, AJK

Code#13   Duration of the Competition: 4 Weeks

Leader: Ramla Moatter
Group: Female
Institute: VTI, Governer House

Project: Jewelry
Amount Given: Rs. 2500
Profit Earnings: Rs. 16260
Location: Lahore

Winners of Changemaking Competitions

Leader: Sadaf
Group: Female
Institute: VTI, Bahawalpur

Project: Facial + Food
Amount Given: Rs. 2500
Profit Earnings: Rs. 18910
Location: Bahawalpur

Leader: Sajjad Ali
Group: Male
Institute: Karakoram International University Gilgit-Baltistan

Project: Tuition Center
Amount Given: Rs 5000
Profit Earnings: Rs. 20000
Location: Gilgit-Baltistan

Leader: Shamoon Masih
Group: Mix
Institute: NUML, Queeta

Project: Diagnosed of Hepatitis
Amount Given: Rs5000
Profit Earnings: Rs. 30000
Location: Balochistan

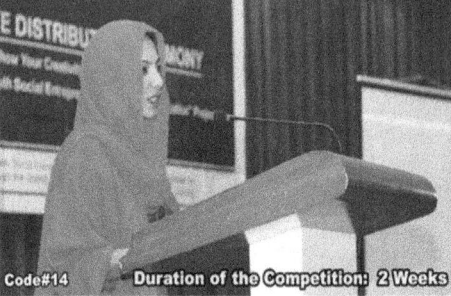

Leader: Shazia Malik
Group: Female
Institute: Sardar Bahadur Khan Women's University Quetta

Project: Peace Festval
Amount Given: Rs 1000
Profit Earnings: Rs. 35000
Location: Quetta

Leader: Sundus Dilawer
Group: Female
Institute: Lahore College for Women's University, LHR.

Project: Fun Fair
Amount Given: Rs. 100
Profit Earnings: Rs. 7600
Location: Lahore

Leader: Taiba Batool
Group: Female
Institute: UOS, Sargodha

Project: Training Football
Amount Given: Rs. 100
Profit Earnings: Rs. 4500
Location: Sargodha

Winners of Changemaking Competitions

Leader : Syed Haider Abbas
Group: Male
Institute: VTI, Muzaffargarh

Project: Blood Screening Test
Amount Given: Rs. 2500
Profit Earnings: Rs. 228150
Location: Muzaffargarh

A Glimpse of Changemaking Competitions

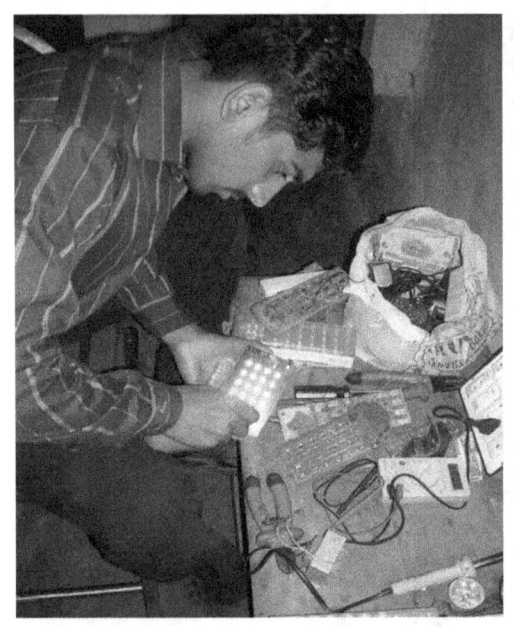

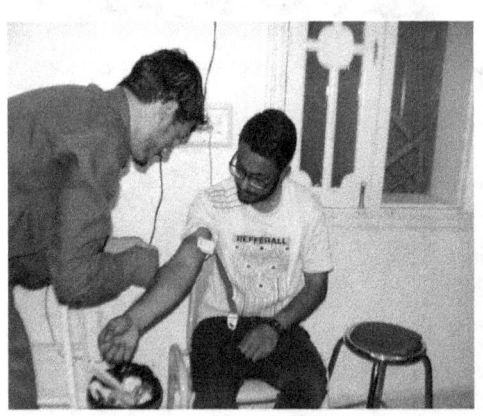
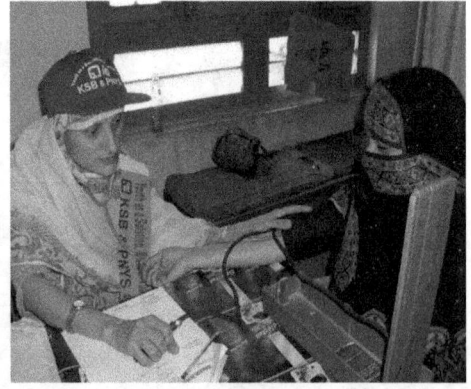

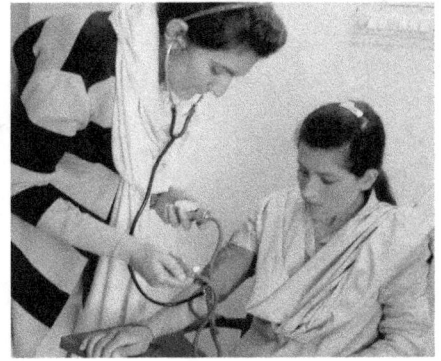

Part 3

Chapter 7

BECOME A CHANGEMAKER, CREATE VALUE, GIVE ABUNDANTLY, DISCOVER THE GIANT WITHIN, AND MAKE A LIVING ON THE WAY

Introduction

What if anyone can learn how to be a changemaker? What if we got it all wrong and it doesn't require a fancy diploma, a wealthy family, or roman numerals at the end of your name to lead a great life; to create, contribute, and explore your potential?

Well, as we already laid out in Chapter One, it is highly likely that if tens of thousands of the most neglected, destitute, marginalized, and half-educated youth studying in the state-owned, charity-based technical institutions in the Punjab province can not only start businesses, but can do so within only a couple of weeks (sometimes days), with minimal funds, and the vast majority of them are able to create a profit, then it is highly likely that you can do it, too.

And not only that: We are convinced that anyone with inner will and basic integrity can do it. That is good news. It means you can do it. And it means that you can create. And if you can create, and even earn while you create, you can make the world as perfect a place as you wish it to be.

The transformation begins within. It is a shift from a victim mentality, and a mentality where we expect to be served, to a mentality where we ask ourselves how we can be of value to others, how we can contribute, how we can provide services, sell products, create merchandise, and come up with new ideas that add value.

You already have the basic tools that you need to be a changemaker. This chapter will give you some ideas and inspiration for how you can use your toolkit, what has worked for others, and which mental models might help you launch your new venture.

We will look at ways to create value, how to deliver value, how to earn money, how to start a business even if you have no initial capital, the mindset most changemakers we know bring to the table, and how this mindset translates into Changemaking Behavior.

However, as you already know, and as one of my mentors likes to put it, theory does not cover the price of admission for actually being a changemaker. In order to be a changemaker, you have to put your ideas into practice. So, read this chapter only as a companion guide. A theory that is not tested is of no value. So, go out and apply yourself in the real world.

Ready? Let's get started.

The Changemaking Kit

Let's begin with the basic tools that every changemaker needs and which, gladly, everyone already has. We call these tools the "Changemaking Kit".

Your Changemaking Kit is made up of your:

1. Physical Body
2. Mind
3. Heart
4. Spirit

As you can see, you and everyone around you already has this basic toolkit. The good thing about this toolkit is that no one can ever steal it from you during your lifetime.

Your house burns down? Okay, you still have your changemaking toolkit. Someone steals your phone? No problem. You still have your changemaking toolkit. Someone is rude and calls you names? No problem. They can do what they want, but they can't take away your changemaking toolkit. Your real value resides inside of you. You are it. Your changemaking toolkit is a part of who you are in this world, and you have the power to decide how to put your toolkit to use in a way that creates value for others and for yourself.

Let's take a quick look into the components of your toolkit, and define how you can put them to use.

The Physical Body

The physical body is a superb tool to get you from Point A to Point B, and to help you act on your intention and decision to create value.

The body usually takes care of itself and is fully autonomous. You can't imagine what would happen if every single thing that is working in your body would need a conscious decision from your mind.

Breathing, pumping blood, creating new cells, keeping the heart beating; all of this is going on without you ever having to think about it. It is said that there are over five trillion cells in your body which are alive in and of themselves, and they are all working in perfect harmony; each one being part of a complex, intelligent system and interacting with the whole. However, your mind, when making a conscious decision, can direct your body to do certain things in time and space. So, if the body and mind work together, they can create value for others.

The Mind

Although the mind is a superb tool that can be used *by* you, it is important to note that the mind is, more often than not, actually *using* you. Where are thoughts coming from? Who is creating them? Most of us have a lot of "talk" going on in our heads; often, repetitious thoughts that serve no purpose at all, just aimless thinking that requires energy and distracts us from being in the present moment. If the underlying consciousness is predominantly negative, then the mind can turn from an inner tool, into an inner enemy. If your mind is telling you that you are not good enough, it is important to realize that thoughts are just thoughts. They have no independent reality of their own. Most of our thoughts are just borrowed thoughts, abstractions, and ideas that we have inherited from someone else; from our peers, parents, schools, society, television, or strangers. Most of the thoughts we are habitually thinking are ones that we have never stopped to question the truth of. We just accepted ideas and concepts into our consciousness. But are they really true? Or are they just thoughts?

When you realize that your thoughts are limiting you, and telling you that you can't do things, that you are not good enough, old enough, or smart enough, that you don't have the right family background, or if they attempt to keep you in a place of low energy, depression or fear, realize that you have made an idea with no independent reality of its own your master, and you have made yourself its slave.

You are not your thoughts. You can use your mind to solve problems, yes. But be careful to observe the thoughts you are thinking, and if they are negative, or loaded with fear, guilt, anger, or worry; realize that this is just a habit of thinking, and choose a new way to look at things. Thoughts that are not serving you or making you into a braver, more loving, more compassionate, more inspired, and more authentic, free, and creative human being can be discarded. What is the use of holding on to them? As soon as you realize that there is a thought, you can choose whether you want to believe it or not.

If it is not serving you, simply choose to discard it.

If you want to be a changemaker, it is of importance that you use your mind as a tool that helps you create value. Practice thinking empowering and engaging thoughts. Remember, truth is what is true for you. Choose your own truth carefully, because your thoughts shape your experience. What you think, you are likely to attract. If you think the universe is essentially good and friendly, this is likely what you will see in the world. If you think of the world as a scary place, this is what the world will reflect back to you. *The world "out there" is a reflection; a mirror image of your beliefs and thoughts about the world.*

Imagine how nice it would be if the voice in your head told you all the time that you were born great, that everything is designed to work out well, that God loves you, and that you can be anything in the world, as long as it speaks to your heart.

You would be the powerful creator that you were born to be.

The legend of the grandfather and the grandson illustrates this well.

The grandfather tells his grandson that, inside each of us, there are two wolves, and they are fighting with each other.

One wolf is greedy, angry, violent, arrogant, and envious, full of false pride, ego, sorrow, and resentment.

The other wolf is nice, friendly, compassionate, generous, kind, humble, truthful, serene, and loving.

The grandson asks his grandfather which of the wolves will win the fight. The grandfather smiles and replies to his grandson, "The one that you feed."

Thinking positive thoughts, acting from inspiration and compassion, and treating humans and all living beings with respect and love is the equivalent of feeding the loving wolf. *Investing energy* into angry and resentful thoughts is the equivalent of feeding the ugly wolf. In each moment, we can make a new decision about which wolf we are going to feed by deciding which thoughts we are going to invest energy into.

Here are a few thoughts that are true for us. Whether you choose them as your own truth is up to you. But if you do, make sure that you look at them regularly, and write it down in a journal every time you see proof in the world that these thoughts are true. This is how you build an empowering, strong inner foundation.

- I was born great.
- I am a Changemaker and I have the power to create value for myself and others.
- I have everything I need to be successful in the world.
- I can learn and achieve anything, as long as I apply myself and believe that I can.
- Every problem that I encounter is, in truth, a beautiful challenge that was created so that I may have an opportunity to grow and become a kinder and better person.
- If something inspires me and I take action towards my goal, I can trust that it will happen, even if I don't know exactly how. I can act and move towards my goal with a calm and relaxed sense of certainty, and trust the river of life.
- If I keep asking the right questions, life will give me the answers and allow me to find my purpose and serve from love and compassion at the highest level.
- If my heart and mind are aligned and I act with pure motive, then I can trust the flow of the river and can be certain that life is helping me achieve my goals.
- The journey gives birth to the leader.

If you keep thinking empowering thoughts and "installing them on your inner hard-drive" so that you have constant access to them, then your thoughts will empower you and help you on your journey. Because when you change the way you look at things, your interaction with them changes, and thus, your perception of these things changes as well.

This way, you have turned your mind into a tool that supports your vision, instead of a barrier to your success.

But what if you realize that you are persistently thinking negative thoughts about yourself, your life, or others? Here is a tool that is called "The Work", and it was developed by Byron Katie. It is a beautiful and simple tool that teaches you to question any thought or belief that is pulling you down, limiting you, or making you unhappy. It is a form of written meditation, so it requires becoming still and allowing the answer to find you. But it works beautifully, and I use it myself as part of my regular practice.

Here is how it works:

The work consists of four simple questions and a turnaround. It does not require you to follow a specific belief system, religion, or to have any prior knowledge of anything, really. No one is telling you what to think or how to act. All you do is ask yourself questions. It is self-inquiry. It is meditation. If you become still, the answers will come from within you.

If you are thinking thoughts that cause you stress or unease, you simply isolate and question each particular thought.

Here are the four questions you must answer:

1. Is it true?
2. Can you absolutely know that this thought is true?
3. How do you react, and what happens, when you believe this thought?
4. Who would you be without this thought?

The final step is to turn the thought around, into a positive thought, and look for examples that make the positive thought truer than the original, negative thought.

Here is what this could look like, in practice:

Let's assume that, I, Thomas, think that I am not smart enough to be an entrepreneur, and let's assume that I didn't already have a business. My answer to these questions could be as follows:

1) Q: Is it true?

A: Well, I can't really know whether this is true or not. All I know is that I don't have a business yet. But I don't know for sure that I am not smart enough to start a business. For all I know, I just haven't started a business *yet*. And for all I know, there seem to be a few people in the world that are not "very smart" and still have businesses and are entrepreneurs. So, the answer to this question would be NO.

2) Q: Can I absolutely know that this thought is true?

A: So, if in question one I had said on impulse, "Yes, this thought is true", then this question would give me another shot at questioning the thought. Maybe I missed something. So, if my answer in the first question was a YES, then I would have the opportunity to become even more still, and see what answer comes from within me. So, my answer here would again be that NO; I can't say with a hundred percent certainty that this thought is true.

3) Q: How do I react, and what happens, when I believe this thought?

A: Well, if I think I am not smart enough, then I might feel afraid, because I may think I will fail. I might also feel discouraged. I might also feel sad or regretful or depressed. Or I might feel self-critical, negative, and tense. I will surely be discouraged from starting a business. I wouldn't even try. I would be upset with myself. I might blame myself. I might be envious of other people who I believe to be "smart enough". I might hide when the opportunity to start a changemaking project arises. I might tell myself and others that becoming a changemaker is very hard, even though I have never tried it. I will put others up on a pedestal and put myself down in my mind. I might be depressed at the thought of my opportunities in life if I think I am not smart enough.

4) Q: Who would I be without this thought?

A: Well, I guess, without that thought, I would simply be me. I would feel free to act, and would not be afraid. I'd be courageous and authentic.

I wouldn't feel that I need to prove anything to anybody, and I would feel trust in in my abilities, especially my ability to learn. I might be curious to learn and seek out more information, and contact people who have already walked the path before me, so I can learn from them. And I might envision enthusiastically how I would help people once my business is up and running.

Now, you might already see that question 4 and my answer to it would really start to free my inner potential if I managed to let the negative thought go. So, let's have a look at the turnaround part.

What could the turnaround of this thought look like?

Possible turnarounds:

- I am smart.
- I am smart enough to become an entrepreneur.
- I can learn anything if I really want to.
- My thinking is smart enough to become an entrepreneur. (Here, I replaced "I am" with "My thinking", which can be quite a powerful realization.)

So, now that I have a few possible turnarounds, I will look for proof that these positive turnaround thoughts are truer than the original, negative thought, and I will try to find at least three examples that each turnaround is true.

Here is what these examples could look like:

- I can read and write, and I have heard that some entrepreneurs can't even read and write, and they managed to be successful anyway. So, this is a strong indicator that I am smart enough.
- I never thought that I would be smart enough to understand English, and yet, I learned a few words. So, this means that I have the ability to learn and improve. Therefore, I think I can also learn how to become an entrepreneur.

- I read about the 6,000 students from the Vocational Training Institutes that successfully started changemaking projects. At least some of these 6,000 kids are surely not smarter than I am. So, if they can do it, then I am sure that I also have the basic ability to achieve what they have achieved.
- And yes, if my thinking says, "I am not smart enough to become an entrepreneur", then this "thinking" is not smart enough. Smarter thinking would allow me to be an entrepreneur. So, it is not about *me*; it is about the way I *think* about me. Thinking "I am not smart enough" is blocking my success, because it is fallacious thinking.

So, this is how I might write it down. Generally, after such an exercise, if we found turnarounds that are true for us and answers to the questions that are true for us, we can already feel the burden lift off our shoulders, and we come to see that our mind created a thought, and it was really nothing more than that: a thought. It was not true. And since it was limiting us, we are free to choose a turnaround thought that is more empowering and feels much better.

You can do this with any thought that feels negative to you, whether it is a thought that makes you angry, sad, or fearful. This is about facing the truth, and it is about dissolving the inner stories that are limiting you and making you fearful.

"The Work" by Byron Katie is one of the best tools to transform belief systems and create change in your life. Other tools are prayer, visualization, and a strong spiritual intent to create, which is a powerful catalyst if it comes from an aligned heart and mind.

If you are interested in practicing "The Work" in your own life (which I suggest you do, if you have any negative beliefs or emotions), you can access a few of Katie's worksheets and learn more about Katie's work if you go directly to her website: http://thework.com, or learn about the process in more detail here: http://thework.com/en/do-work. This written meditation can also be used to reduce anger, improve your relationships, give you more energy, and bring more peace into your life.

When you remove the inner blocks, success as a state of being will come naturally, because you are aligning yourself with a higher power and with life.

To sum up this part:

Learn to understand the mind and how it works, and be aware of your thoughts. When you learn to program yourself with empowering thoughts that help you take action, a positive outlook on life, and beliefs that enable you to live a life filled with gratitude, joy, and peace, then you are already becoming successful.

What you think, you will become; and what you become, you tend to attract in your life.

Think positive, empowering thoughts, and turn the negative ones into thoughts that enable you, and you will start to see that your perception of the world will begin to shift. This might not happen immediately, but if you persist, and turn around all negative thoughts, the results will manifest in your life.

The Heart

The next tool in your toolkit is the heart. The heart is the first organ to form in a fetus. When the heart starts to beat, it creates an electromagnetic field that encompasses the entire body. The brain also has an electromagnetic field, but its strength is only a fraction of that of the heart. Also, your heart seems to send signals to every cell in your body, and even seems to have an impact on which DNA gets activated and which remains deactivated, via communication with the membrane of the cells in the body.

The heart is a powerful ally in your changemaking journey. Scientists have discovered that the heart is not only receiving signals from the brain, but is also sending signals to the brain, and influencing and altering the brain's chemistry.

But not only that, you also have approximately 40,000 neurons in your heart area, which act together as the heart's brain. In this sense, there is quite literally a heart intelligence.

So, why is the heart important for your changemaking journey, apart from its physiological function of pumping blood through your body?

The following fable that one of my mentors shared with me made it clear for me:

The story goes that, in a village, there was a blind man and a cripple. The two hated each other. One day, the village caught fire. All the villagers fled. Only the cripple and the blind man were left.

The blind man could walk, but couldn't see the safe path out of the deadly firestorm. The cripple, on the other hand, could see the path, but couldn't walk, and thus, couldn't escape to safety alone.

So, in order to save their lives, they started working together. The cripple climbed on the shoulders of the blind man. From the shoulders of the blind man, he told the blind man where to walk, and the blind man carried them both to safety.

Your mind is the blind man. Your heart is the cripple.

Your heart can see in which direction to walk. But you need your mind to act and think in order to get to your goal.

Your heart is in touch with the spiritual side and has an intuition about right and wrong. It knows the goal and can "see" intuitively. Your mind can't do that.

Your mind is good at linear thinking and problem-solving. But only your heart can ensure that you are working on the right problems.

Let your higher heart, the heart that is in touch with love and compassion and inspiration, guide you and tell you the way.

Then use your mind to carry it.

If your heart and mind are working together, you tap into a power that few people ever realize they have. In order to hear the voice of your heart, sometimes it is required to be still and calm your mind.

The mind is always busy with thinking. The voice of the heart is subtler and much quieter. Make sure that you take time to just be still, and sit, and look inside, and observe the space between your thoughts. While this might seem impossible initially, after a while, you will become quieter, and in the space between thoughts, you can get in touch with your heart intelligence.

If you create from the desire to contribute, the desire to share and love in action, and the motive of helping others and creating value, then your heart will signal to you that you are on the right track, and your mind can walk towards your goal.

The Spirit

People understand different things when we speak of the human spirit. What I am referring to here is the spiritual side of our human experience. All the wisdom and traditions tell us that there is more to life and creation than the physical and visible side of things. Some of us have come to realize this as true, not because they read about it in a book or have a purely mental concept of it, but through subjective experience of it. It is part of a complete journey to inquire into our spiritual nature, the impersonal, the universal, and the higher part of human nature that connects us to everything beyond the visible and linear reality that is so easy to get trapped in.

The power that sustains life and enables you to do what you do. To align oneself with a higher power, which is also present in us, as we are expressions of it, is what ultimately enables you to be a changemaker.

To know that, to be connected to this knowing, and to step beyond the ego is what will allow you to grow without pain, as your growing will be based on humility.

The Changemaking Journey

There is an African saying that I cherish: *"The journey gives birth to the leader."*

So, what are the stages of the journey you embark upon when you decide to become a changemaker?

Well, to begin with, there is the decision you make that you ARE a changemaker. Something that I learned from a coach of mine is that it is not the businesses I have that made me a changemaker and entrepreneur. It is who I choose to be every single day. If my businesses went bust tomorrow and I would have to close them down, would that make me less of a changemaker and entrepreneur in my mind? Probably not. I'd most likely start again.

So, maybe a good question to start with before we have a look at the changemaking journey is: What are the character traits of a changemaker?

Some character traits that come to my mind are:

- They are people that do not just talk, but walk the talk.
- They are people that take positive action.
- They are people with courage (and this simply means being willing to step outside of your comfort zone).
- They are people that believe in possibility.
- They are people that have hope.
- They are people that are willing to learn and improve upon their abilities.
- They are people that are inspired by a cause and are daring enough to take the first step towards their vision, even if they cannot see the entire way to their goal from where they stand.

- They are people that are proactive.
- They are people that ask and act upon the simple question: How can I add value to this group of people or this person?

Those, to me, are some character traits of changemakers.

So, in order to be a changemaker, just look at your character traits and develop your changemaking traits as much as you can.

So, what is a possible journey for changemakers?

We could come to think of the journey as composed of three stages.

Stage 1: The Beginning Stage

This is where everyone gets started. First, we must accept the fact that we were born with natural changemaking abilities.

On an inner level, we must accept the fact that we, too, can create change, and that the sky is the limit. We must accept that we were meant to create value for others, and that our mind and our habitual thoughts determine where we go. Positive habitual thoughts will create positive results in the long run. Negative habitual thoughts will result in negative outcomes in the long run.

This is also the stage where we first get encouraged. Maybe there is a spark of inspiration and we actually start believing that we are great, by the grace of God. That our journey lies in realizing our gifts and using them for the benefit of humankind and the planet.

This is also the stage where we might have the first ideas about how to create change. Maybe the idea is not perfect yet, but that is okay. We must start practicing our changemaking abilities with the first idea and try to create value for others.

The success will most likely come mainly from gathering physical evidence that we can actually do something. We start moving from being passive recipients to being active contributors of value in society.

Maybe we are met with resistance or skepticism. Our friends, parents, teachers, or surroundings might not necessarily understand why we start behaving differently, why we start believing that we can change our circumstances, or why we want to do something with our talents beyond what is "normal" in our community. That is okay. How could they understand if all we've ever been trained to do is accept the status quo, follow what others say, and be passive?

If we were raised in poverty-whether mental, emotional, spiritual, or materialistic-we might think that poverty is normal. However, if we start to see that it is not, and that we can create abundance from the way we think and act; not just for ourselves, but for our communities, it is possible that we will be moving against the current for some time. In general, however, we can expect that people will, over time, become used to us being different. In this stage, it is of the utmost importance to fill your mind with inspiration and positive food for thought. Surround yourself with people that are supportive of your inner spiritual, emotional, and intellectual growth.

On the outer level, it is likely that you will create your first product or service, or sell someone else's product or service. You will likely have your first customers, and the excitement of seeing the results of your courage will give you more confidence. Moving from trust and belief in your abilities to the physical evidence of your abilities, and the resulting surge in confidence, might also make you envision more opportunities. You might become an inspiration for others in your environment and share what you have learned with them, and thereby increase the value that you create even more.

This is also the stage of much experimentation. You find out what works and what doesn't. Not by reading about it in a book, but by actually testing your ideas in the real world. This is not theory, but one hundred percent practice. Some things will work, and others won't. If you discover the joy in trying things, you will be ever more innovative in finding ways to deliver value to your customers and the community. Maybe you will even drop one project and idea that you have already started working on and switch to a project that looks more promising. Maybe you will discover that there is a bigger demand in a different field. Or you may learn that the margin (the difference between the selling price of your product or service and the cost to create and deliver that product or service) is too small with one type of product or service, and much better with another one.

All of this is absolutely typical, and part of the adventure of starting an enterprise and being a changemaker. Experimentation and what look like setbacks are absolutely normal in this stage. Don't be discouraged. You will only fail if you quit before you have truly discovered the potential you have as a changemaker.

And then there is also another aspect: Even though you might start with a simple product or service and sell it in the marketplace, you might soon have even more innovative ideas, and even an alternative vision for how your community could look.

If you are inspired by a vision that is bigger, and that could help people live more amply, with more hope and courage, and with a greater vision, you might not just meet the needs that are already visible in the market. As a matter of fact, the people that you are trying to serve might not even be aware of their unmet needs. It could require you to educate them and raise awareness first.

A common example that is given is a quote by Henry Ford, the founder of the Ford Motor company, and one of the great car manufacturers, entrepreneurs, and visionaries of the 20th century. He was quoted as having said: "If I had asked people what they wanted, they would have said faster horses."

And this is exactly why changemakers will start envisioning beyond what already exists. We will start operating from imagination, and not from memory or what we already know. This is the work of true visionaries, and if we allow ourselves, we might find that part within ourselves, whether it be for small or big projects.

Leading from an envisioned future, and not from our memory of the past or our limiting belief systems, is what is required in order to provide services that might not have been available before.

However, this is also a challenge, as you might face resistance. But if you believe in your idea and you see evidence of it working here and there, and you stick to it, and it inspires you and speaks to your heart, then you should go for it and make a difference.

A last word on this stage: Even if you are starting with a product or service that is not an innovation, that is still okay. In this stage, it is all about getting started and discovering your innate abilities. Simply by taking entrepreneurial action, you are already transforming your own life and making yourself more powerful. Additionally, you will inspire others, and thus, also transform your environment. This is all that is required for this stage.

Stage 2: The Driving Stage

This is the stage where you have already demonstrated the impact of what you are doing for society if you have a social project or you have shown that you can actually find customers and create value.

This is the stage for quick wins. Demonstrate that what you are doing works, and ideally, demonstrate it quickly.

Think about how you can scale up what you are doing to reach more people, spread the message, and deliver your product, service, or offering to more people.

As you do this, it is likely that you will find repeat buyers who will want or need your service again and again, and who are recommending you to others. Depending on what you do and how you do it, you might also create a small community of people that are inspired by your mission, and that want to help you carry it out.

These might be fellow students, co-workers, business partners, or beneficiaries of what you are doing. It might also be parents or friends or NGO's that do related work or speak to the same audience as you.

See who understands your mission, and if their vision resonates with you, bring them on board. The earlier you start getting more energy from people and getting partners on board with your project, the sooner you can expand your outreach and impact.

Stage 3: The Institutionalized Stage

If things are going well, it is likely that there will come a time that you, as the founder and chief changemaker in your project, will require serious support and help. As a project grows, you simply can't do all of it by yourself. Neither will you be able to be everywhere at once.

And if you don't want to become the bottleneck in the growth of your project or business, you might want to think about how to cement the change, the creation of value, and what you are doing so that it can work independent of you.

At this point, it is important that the values which you and your project have are documented, and that the spirit of what you have started is sustained in your project, even if you are not around.

This has been a crucial stage in my projects, as I always wanted to ensure that the people we serve are still getting their products and services delivered, even when I am not around.

Value Creation

In the preceding chapters, we have been talking a lot about adding creating value. But what exactly do we mean by this?

Value creation is the backbone of changemaking. Value creation is the major objective behind every action of changemakers.

Basically, when you create value as a changemaker, it means to create products, services, or other types of offerings or activities which:

- Fulfill a need;
- Solve a problem; and/or
- Cater to a dream, wish, or desire for someone or a group of people.

You can do this by applying energy and ingenuity to the implementation of an idea. All it needs is the intention and decision to do something and sustained energy towards the implementation of your project idea so that it can materialize. All it needs is for you to use your inborn abilities as a creator.

Once the need or opportunity is identified, a mechanism is developed by the changemaker to create, deliver, and capture value.

As I pointed out before, creating value is something that comes naturally to us. As children, this is something we don't have to think much about. We create something from nothing. We imagine. We implement. We build. Only when we are told that we have to sit still and listen to the wisdom of someone else do we start to lose this natural tendency for creative, innovative, fun, and productive self-expression.

So, what are the components of value? Which needs, problems, or wants can it address?

In general, we are thinking of value in the following components:

- Economic component of value
- Ecological component of value
- Social component of value
- Spiritual component of value

Of course, this is just one possible categorization, and you can come up with your own, but in general, this might help you look at creating value from different angles.

It is very difficult to give equal importance to all components of value. The question is, how do you decide which type of component to pursue? Each component of value is useful. It depends on what you want to achieve. Are you aiming for a single bottom-line, a double bottom-line, a triple bottom-line, or a quadruple bottom-line? It is important to define your reason, and know your WHY.

YES instructs young people to begin their changemaking journey by creating social and economic value. The idea behind it is to help young people and society simultaneously. In the beginning, a vast majority of young people rely on taking an incremental approach to create value instead of advancing entrepreneurial solutions to problems or opportunities.

Young people often create or improve upon a product or service to meet the needs of others. Many factors play a role in the selection of changemaking projects. It includes young people's personal experience, talent, skill, or success that inspired them to start a changemaking project.

Young people are often the lead users of a new product or service; sometimes, they prefer to play a catalyst role when introducing a new idea or innovation to peers and the general public. A few of the youth-led changemaking projects also encompass radical innovation. Young people initiate a new product, service, or method to create and deliver value by using simple tools, processes, and materials. They implement their changemaking projects in difficult conditions, discover problems, make revisions within hours, and try again.

Youth-led changemaking can have profound effects when income generation strategies are well-integrated into their ventures. Income generation through programs provide changemakers with an opportunity to create a sustainable social impact and build a powerful organization capable of scaling-up and providing blueprints for replication. If changemakers are unable to integrate income generation strategies into their programs, they must rely on donations, fundraising, grants, and leadership qualities to create social value and achieve sustainability. It would be very difficult for young people to continue their changemaking journey if they are not expected to generate income through their changemaking initiatives.

Common Characteristics of Youth-Led Changemaking Projects

The common characteristics of the youth-led changemaking projects are as follows:

- Focus on dual value creation (social and economic impact);
- Work in a team (3 to 5 people);
- Address a gap or need;
- Multi-sector approach (health, education, sports, entertainment, etc.);
- Reach out to people at the base of the pyramid (low-income communities);
- Have an enterprise orientation (sell a product or service); and
- Distribute profit equally.

Youth-led changemaking has become a new marketplace where value is created, not only for social impact, but for economic impact.

Changemaking has a great scope in developing countries to activate in-school and jobless young people to address gaps that the government has failed to fill.

For instance, suppose young people don't have access to clean water. Instead of waiting for the government to do something to clean the water, some young people can decide to provide clean water to the local community at a low cost.

Another example is from *one of my own companies.*

EcoToiletten is selling and renting mobile ecological toilets to outdoor events in Germany, and stationary composting toilets to municipalities. Part of the money we make is used to build toilets in villages in South Asia via a non-profit. The components in this venture are (a) Economic value, because we are adding a component to the festivals and events that helps them sell tickets, and we are also creating an economic value for ourselves, because we charge for the rental; (b) Ecological value, because our mobile toilets work without water, and the feces can be composted after use and turned into fertilizer, thus, the use of this toilet, compared to the competitors' toilets, is saving water and energy, and creating an ecological benefit; (c) Social value, because we create jobs, but we also use some of the project resources to build toilets in villages and schools where there is a lack of proper sanitation infrastructure; and (d) Spiritual value, because we inspire ourselves and others with the passion and enthusiasm with which we implement strategies for wholeness within our team.

Value can be created in many ways. You can inspire people and uplift them spiritually. You can offer services in any sector, from health to education or sports and recreation. You can build on existing products and services. And you can take someone else's products and help distribute them in areas where they are not yet easily available.

We will never run out of ways to create value for others. Ideas are plentiful. There is no lack of ideas or opportunities. It is all about the implementation of these ideas, and the vision and courage to become a changemaker.

Share Your Gifts

When I talk about becoming a changemaker, I always encourage people to build on their strengths. Not everyone can create value in the same way, and that is okay. You are unique in the way that you express your changemaking abilities.

Many people are so focused on the areas in which they are lacking that they forget to be grateful for the areas in which God endowed them with a special gift. Build on your strength. Acknowledge what is great about you. Everyone has areas in which they naturally shine, and these areas can be developed.

Yes, your weaker areas can also be developed, and the saying goes that *hard work beats talent that doesn't work hard* most of the time. And yes, if you truly want something, then applying yourself and persisting will eventually get you there.

But if you build on what comes naturally to you, and you learn how to share your gifts with the world while at the same time creating economic value and developing your strengths, you will likely have a much easier time, because you are connected to your authentic self. So, don't compare yourself to others. Learn from others, but find your own way.

Share Your Story

Can you build a story around what you are creating and WHY you create it? If you have a big vision, then it is probably worth sharing your story. What is inspiring you to do what you do? Why do you want to help your community? Why do you want to serve your customers? Why do you go out and do what you do?

Stories, if told well, touch the hearts of people. Can you name a person who has had a powerful story to share? Often, it is the identification with these stories that propel us to action. This is also the case for customers. If you have an inspiring story to tell, this will be of great use.

An example I love to share is the story of the founder of Tom's shoes, Blake Mycoskie. He started his company in 2006, after having visited Argentina on vacation, where he met an American volunteer that provided shoes to children in need. Seeing the infections and injuries that the children had due to having to walk barefoot, he decided to start a for-profit company to tackle the problem. He set up a company that sold stylish shoes. For every pair of shoes sold, he donated one pair of shoes to children in need. The promise to his customers was that every time they bought a pair of shoes, they actually helped a young child. This story, and the social value he created with his company, greatly appealed to his audience, and the story spread widely. In 2013, the company had already donated over 10,000,000 pairs of shoes to people in need all over the world.

Crafting a good story around your efforts, and even sharing your own story and passion, is a great way to attract a loyal audience, fans, and supporters to your business and changemaking efforts.

The Changemaking Paradigm

We are probably living in the most exciting time in human history. There is an unprecedented change happening around us. The main driving force behind that rapid change is not technology. It is the growing ability of an average person to unlock their own changemaking potential, which doesn't have to be, but is often aided by, technology, making it ever cheaper and easier to create change. The key question is: How can we create a society where the changemaking potential of every person can be harnessed and explored? Should we let this happen by chance or by design? I believe we have a remarkable opportunity to lay the foundation of a changemaking paradigm where everyone is able to discover their true worth and changemaking potential. This new changemaking paradigm has to be designed and embedded consciously. We have seen that old paradigms have failed to produce the desired results. The new changemaking paradigm will be entirely different from the old paradigms.

Changemaking-The Conscious Changemaker

Times are changing, and so is what is required of an entrepreneur and changemaker. So, if you are thinking about starting a project or business and creating value, it may help you to get acquainted with a new paradigm for changemaking. The table below is incomplete, but may give you hints and ideas as to what mindset to operate from.

Areas	Old Paradigm	New Paradigm
Good Social and Economic Returns	Achieved by efficiency in repetition	Achieved by constant change

Good Leadership	One leader at a time	Everyone leads and contributes
Sound Success	Success depends on expertise and authority	Success depends on the ability to break down walls
Sound Communication	Achieved through authoritative voice	Achieved through storytelling
Good Information Management	Limited distribution of information	Open and transparent communication

Table 16: Difference Between the Old and New Changemaking Paradigms

Repetition vs. Change

In the old paradigm, we were taught that efficiency is achieved by repetition and economies of scale. What we can observe today is that, in many industries and markets, the established companies are being outperformed by more innovative and flexible young companies that do not necessarily win through economies of scale, but by learning faster, handling the constant change in market conditions, using and developing technology, and reacting faster to new information. Being able to handle, and even benefit, from constant change is what ensures that you will survive and thrive in a world that changes faster and faster.

Leadership

In the old paradigm, there was one leader at the top, and everyone had to follow. This is changing, and we can see this in many successful organizations. Leaders are the ones that make decisions. If we empower everyone to make decisions in their field of expertise, and be transparent and share the information that is necessary to make good decisions, then we can really benefit from the potential everyone has to be a leader, innovator, and changemaker. In my own companies, my role as a leader is to create more leaders, and not more followers. I ask and challenge team members to think for themselves, make decisions, and think as entrepreneurs within the company. This not only leads to more proactivity from the team members, and allows them to feel more like they are a part of a family, but it also has the side effect of everyone giving their best, because everyone is rallying for the same cause. Also, employees will learn much faster, and we all benefit from their ideas, input, commitment, and changemaking skills that we would not benefit from had we not asked them to step up as leaders, take responsibility, and make decisions within the framework of a few golden rules, our values, and our mission and vision statement.

Success

In the old paradigm, success was seen as being driven by being an expert in one area, and by amassing massive authority. In the new paradigm, success may depend much more on tearing down walls, forming coalitions and partnerships, being innovative, and having broad expertise over several fields. The integration of information from different backgrounds as a generalist, rather than as an expert in just one area, may allow you to see opportunities that an expert in just one narrow field might have missed completely.

Communication

The communication style is changing as well. Whereas, in the old paradigm, it was about an authoritative voice, one strong leader, and following orders, the new paradigm is more focused on storytelling and inspiring through a mission that aligns a team, and might help in awakening unknown potential and energy within teams. A team acting from inspiration, which can be achieved through storytelling, is more likely to outperform a team that is merely motivated by a paycheck and is just receiving orders. But storytelling is also important to elicit support and the goodwill of customers. Tell your story. Inspire. Give people a reason to rally behind you and your mission.

Information Transparency

In the old paradigm, the distribution of information was limited within companies and within teams, but also in general. In the new world, information is widely accessible online, often for free. Information and data that would have cost a fortune just a few years ago can now be accessed for free by high school kids and anyone with an internet connection. But there also seems to be a change in information distribution within organizations. New software tools make it easy for teams to speak with each other, even if they are spread out all over the globe. And last but not least, many companies decide to give their employees and team members access to information that would have been closely guarded under the old paradigm.

To give you a few examples: One of my companies, Strandschicht, has a team of full-time employees and freelancers, working for several client companies. Of the staff of forty-seven people, I have only met two people in person. The rest I have only spoken to online via email or Skype. We share all our information through mostly free software tools, like Google Drive or Dropbox. We don't require an office, which saves us a lot of money, and the information we need to exchange as a team is exclusively exchanged online.

An interesting example when it comes to the sharing of information not just within the team, but also with the public, comes from a software company called ConvertKit. They create software that allows you to send emails to your customers. I am one of their clients. The founder of the company shares his revenue numbers, clients that signed up, and a bunch of other data on his blog. He makes all this transparent, because transparency is one of the values of the company. These figures would normally be closely guarded secrets, but he trusts that his openness and transparency will bring good to the company, and not hurt the results. Although this might seem counterintuitive and even lunatic under the old paradigm, I think he is probably right, and his company is just one example of several companies making a move towards sharing more of their core with the general public.

Decide to Act

People think that it takes a long time to change the direction of their life. Such is not the case. Actually, changing your life doesn't take time at all. You change your life the moment you make a conscious definite decision. Making a definite decision doesn't take time. It does, however, require energy. From that decision, everything unfolds. Your life is changed. You may not see it right away. People around you might not see it right away. What you see before your mind's eye might not yet have materialized, but the most powerful act of creation has happened; the moment you changed or made up your mind, and thus, changed your world. Again, the results might not be visible instantaneously, but within, you can be certain that a profound shift has taken place.

Make a decision and trust that everything will change if you stick with it. The manifested material universe might not reflect your inner decision right away, but if you stick to it and choose a new path, everything and everyone around you will adapt sooner or later.

So, the secret to changing your life within one minute is to make a definite decision.

In order to make the decision definite, it greatly helps to connect the decision to a positive emotion that is so memorable, your body can never forget it. An emotion that you can connect to again and again. In this way, you can be more certain that your heart and mind are aligned, and you can always find the motivation to extend energy towards your vision.

If you are not inspired, or filled with joy or excitement at your decision, maybe it would help to connect your decision with different images. As human beings, our subconscious mind and our emotions control a great deal of our behavior.

So, if you don't want to rely entirely on willpower when making your decision and working towards your goal, connect it to a strong emotional response, so that your subconscious mind and your body are cooperating in the journey to integrate the decision into your life.

Nurture Your Intention

If you have made a definite decision to become a changemaker, to take control of your life, to become an active citizen, to create value, and to explore your potential, it is helpful to nurture this decision and intention.

Your ambitions and dreams have to be nurtured, just like a seed. By making the conscious decision and connecting it with a strong, empowering emotion, you have planted a seed in your mind.

Now it is time to water the seed so that it can grow and take roots.

Great ways to nurture your intention and decision are to:

- *Journal*-Write down each day what you have done in accordance with your decision. You can also write down evidence that your decision is benefiting you (i.e. because you learned something, got positive feedback, or just feel great about your new abilities).

- *Reconnect to the empowering emotion*-Remember WHY you made the decision, and relive the emotion you felt when you made the decision. You can also visualize the outcome that you are aiming at with your work, and play a mental movie of the results you wish to obtain. This is a technique employed by many professional athletes and successful entrepreneurs. It is a great tool, and absolutely free of charge. And even if you cannot see a clear picture of your ideal outcome, it doesn't matter, as long as you have an emotional response to your inner mental movie. It is about *feeling* your vision. Again, this is a technique to get your subconscious mind working for you, instead of against you. The most important thing, in my experience, is to know that it is possible. There are endless possibilities, so what you want to create is also possible, and by setting your intention and accepting the result in advance, you can choose what to create and bring it about.

Commit

If you made a decision from inspiration, then commit to it. Give it a real chance. One of my mentors always says: Tentative has no power. If you commit, you will have the energy and focus to get results. If you doubt and are hesitant, then you are already defeated before you even get started.

Decide where you want to go and why you want it, make sure that your heart and your mind are aligned, and then trust that it is going to happen. It might not happen in the most linear way that your mind craves, but if you are persistent, then it is going to happen.

Thomas Edison was quoted as saying, "Many of life's failures are people who did not realize how close they were to success when they gave up."

There is much truth to this quote.

Yes, sometimes it requires a change of plans, and maybe even an entirely different approach to a challenge, but you should never doubt that you were born with great gifts, that God gave you the ability to be a changemaker, and that you were born great.

Trust in this and act accordingly.

Time and Resources

So, you want to be a changemaker and creator? Great. Congratulations! But what is expected of you in order to succeed? Just as in any endeavor, you need to commit time in order to make the project successful.

A new enterprise is similar to a rocket. It takes a lot of energy to get it off the ground, but once it has taken off and it is in space, the pull of gravity becomes less and less, and you might not have to invest as much time and effort as you did in the beginning.

With that said, in the beginning, you will have to make a real time commitment. Later, you might be able to hire people to help you expand your business, and you might not have to do all the work alone. But in the beginning, it is likely all about you, and your creativity and resourcefulness. It doesn't mean that you have to do all the work alone, but it will require energy and faith to get momentum. Most projects that have gone through the YES Network Experience have dedicated at least 30 hours per week to their businesses, while many projects worked overtime to make them a success.

Remember, though, that this time you are not working for someone else. You are not working for your teachers. Nor are you working for your parents or the government or anyone else. You are working solely to create value for your customers and for yourself. And you are working on yourself and developing yourself. And if you love what you do, and find joy and excitement in your new business, then more often than not, the time you commit will not feel like "work", but more like a fun adventure and a calling.

Changemaking Mindset and Changemaking Behavior

This part is all about the mindset of a changemaker and changemaking behavior. We want to share a few of the most common belief systems and patterns that help changemakers create and make a real difference. Again, you don't have to use the same belief systems, and you can choose your own model of the world, but these mental models have worked for many successful entrepreneurs and changemakers, and it would be unkind to leave you in the dark about the operating system that many of these highly successful people use.

Ground Zero-An Exercise

Before we start, it makes sense to do a quick evaluation of where you currently are, and take inventory of your current belief systems. This will (a) help you to recognize what might be blocking you from success on your journey, and (b) help you track your inner progress as you develop new models and trust more and more in your changemaking abilities, so you can look back again and again at where you started from.

So, here are a few questions that might be helpful when mapping out the status quo:

- What is my current mental model and success model?
- What is my current way of thinking doing to me?
- What kind of person am I becoming through my current education?
- Am I becoming more active or more passive?
- Am I acting more from love or from fear?
- Am I acting more from a need for certainty and security, or a need for growth and contribution?
- What would I do if I could not fail and it was 100% certain that I would succeed?
- What is stopping me from doing it now?

Please take the time to answer these questions for yourself before reading on.

Achievement

When I talk about business and the benefits of learning how to use your entrepreneurial skills, I am often faced with an audience that has very different concepts of success.

Many people believe that the people who are successful are the ones who have a lot of money, or have accumulated a lot of wealth.

This outer component of what many believe to be success is easily visible, and seems attractive to many people because they cling to the flawed belief that, somehow, having a lot of money makes a person better or more successful.

By this definition, if someone with a lot of money suddenly lost their money, they'd also become unsuccessful again.

But success can also be viewed from a different perspective, and that is the perspective of character achievement. The questions then become:

- Am I becoming a better person with the choices I am making?
- Am I choosing love above fear?
- Am I choosing growth in character over the need for certainty?
- Am I choosing to contribute, serve, and share instead of holding back?
- Am I doing the right thing instead of the thing that seems to be the easiest?

This is a perspective that has very little to do with your bank account balance and your wealth. From this perspective, you don't pursue recognition, worldly success, and wealth, but rather you pursue a life lived from ethics, personal character growth, and contribution. And the result of this might very well be wide recognition, wealth, and outer success.

However, you will always know that achievement cannot be taken from you, because achievement and success then become an inside job. Your fulfillment in life will not be dependent on the transient world "out there".

This perspective, which I greatly favor in comparison to the belief in achievement measured by the amount of money in your bank account, gives you the control.

There is no need for someone else to tell you that you are successful. As a matter of fact, many people have told some of the greatest entrepreneurs and most successful changemakers that they were out of their mind, that they tried something that was impossible, and that they could never achieve their goals.

As a changemaker, you can't be dependent-at least not for long-on the definition by which success and achievement is usually measured.

However, you can measure it for yourself anytime by asking yourself whether you are doing the best you can do at this moment to grow your character and contribute value through your business from an energy of love, kindness, compassion, joy, inspiration, excitement, and enthusiasm, and never from a need for security, certainty, or the thought that "I am not enough if I don't own XYZ". You can evaluate for yourself whether you are acting and being (in thoughts, emotions, choices, and actions) the person that you'd like your future self to be. This is not about the *material possessions* of your future self, but about the *state of being* of your future self. If you visualize and emotionally connect to your future self, and start making decisions as that future version of you would, then you are successful already, as you are making the choices that future self would make, and you are moving towards your vision, taking actions, and making choices that are probably vastly different from the choices you made and the actions you took up until now.

This may sound a bit like head-in-the-clouds thinking, but it has become a valuable compass for me that I regularly consult for decision-making and checking whether I am meeting my own standards for achievement. In this way, success and achievement is also not something that I arrive at, but a continuous journey that I am enjoying more and more.

Perception

As children, we are born innocent.

As we grow up, we are being programmed with beliefs, dogmas, patterns of thought, and values. We might come to believe that our personality is really who we are, but if we look closer, we will likely observe that the ideas, thoughts, and beliefs that we cling to are mostly borrowed. Society's programming that we believe without ever questioning its innate truth and reliability.

As such, we are stuck with "programming" from our environment, and now we are running these "software programs, thinking that is who we are, without ever coming to the conclusion that we have a choice in the matter.

Once we recognize that we are all programmed, but that the programs that we are running are not fundamentally who we are, we can start to check whether the programs we are currently running are quality software that help us live lives of peace, joy, contribution, growth, connection, and happiness, or whether the programs we are running are blocking us and slowing us down, or worse: breaking down our systems because they came with a virus.

The fact is that we are seeing reality through several filters, and if we want to change what we see in the world, it is best to start with changing the perception and the angle from which we look at things.

For example, if we say, "this is a flower", we might think that we know what a flower is, but we don't really know. Most of us rarely take the time to observe a flower; to see its shapes and colors, or smell its scent.

Even if we did, seeing the colors is our subjective experience of different wavelengths of light, which is colorless. Also, the scent is not a reality in and of itself, but our sensual interpretation of the molecules coming from the "flower".

*The fact is, we cannot know the flower. We can only know **about** the flower. Having a word for "flower" does not change that.*

We will only know about the flower from our subjective experience, interpretation, and perception, and thus, the flower as it exists for me, exists in this exact way, only for me. I am creating this world from my perception of it. What I am seeing, and how I experience it, is tied to my perception of it. If I were to change the way that I look at what I am perceiving, then the thing that I am perceiving would change.

And on the level of words: If we don't take the time to look at the flower, then we are not relating to this particular flower, but to the memorized concept of the flower in our mind.

The reason I am going into this is that we do not only rarely take the time to look at flowers, but we also rarely take the time to look at our thoughts, beliefs, and how we look at the world.

If you look at the world:

- Do you see a threatening world, or a world full of wonderful opportunities to make a difference?
- Do you mainly focus on seeing people being kind and helpful to each other and being helpful to them, or do you focus mostly on the news and the media that portrays a world that is dangerous; a world in which people cheat, lie, and steal from each other?
- Do you focus on thinking about problems, or thinking about solutions?
- Do you focus on blaming others for taking the "wrong" actions, or do you get busy taking the "right" actions?
- Are you spending your time and energy demanding that the government should solve problems, or do you get busy creating solutions that can solve the problems yourself?
- Are you busy explaining why you can't, or are you busy finding a way that you can?
- Are you busy following change, or are you busy driving change?
- Are you demanding that others should be better and kinder to you, or are you challenging yourself every day to be better and kinder to others?

You see, perception creates the world as you see it. Your desires and fears create the world as you see it. And what you focus on creates more of the world as you see it. Your reality, right now, is a result of your habitual thinking, your habits, and your beliefs.

Consciously change what you focus on and what you believe, and you will inherit a vastly different world.

If you don't know that the software that you were programmed with is responsible for how you experience life, then you are a victim of circumstances.

If you realize that you can, with conscious effort and intention, discard some of the software that doesn't serve you, practice a different angle of perception, and install "software" that *is* serving you and society more, and at a higher level, then you are taking responsibility, and you gain the power to create and contribute as a changemaker.

Whenever you limit who you think you can become, what you can achieve, and how you think you can serve others and contribute value, realize that this is only a perception. It is part of your social programming, and it might be blocking you from discovering more of your potential. You are neither serving God, nor yourself, if you keep yourself small, and deny your abilities and power to contribute to yourself and humankind.

Look back at history and see if someone has ever done what you want to do in the spirit of love and contribution, and if you can find someone that has done it, and you realize in your heart that it is your calling, then you can do it also. Yes-time, sustained commitment, high energy, and a heartfelt desire are necessary. However, the limits to how much we can serve were never put on us by our creator. They exist only in our minds, and are part of the limits that we, as the human race, have put on ourselves with our limited thinking. If you truly desire it, you can transcend these limits, and create a positive change the way you feel called to do.

Power of Peer Groups and Environment

The human mind works as a powerful adaptation machine.

Your environment is influencing you every minute of every day. Most of the time, you will not even be aware of this. Most of the information that comes into your mind is only registered by your unconscious mind. Only things that are being selected as noteworthy are ever reaching your "conscious" mind.

This is because your conscious mind has a limited capacity for processing input, and so, it needs a filter that only lets through the bits and pieces that are seemingly "relevant" to your conscious decision-making process. A lot of stimuli, however, will not be noticed by your conscious mind. However, they still influence you. Your mind is always tuning in to the energy of your surroundings and adapting, whether you are aware of it or not.

So, what is the practical implication for you as a changemaker?

Build your surroundings in a way that supports your mission and vision. If you are around people that inspire you, believe in you, and support you in becoming a changemaker, your chances of succeeding are much higher than if you choose to be around people that always look down on you or tell you that you can't succeed.

Creating a peer group of people that are on the same path as you is one of the best ways to ensure that you learn and become successful. Your peer group can be real people, friends, fellow students, or mentors that have already done what you want to do, or are at least encouraging you to follow your dreams. However, I also found a great peer group in inspiring books about entrepreneurs and changemakers. From every book that I read about someone who changed the world, created successful businesses, or was an inspiring leader, I learned something that I can now integrate into my own life.

The question is: What kind of thoughts are you feeding your mind? What kind of energy are you absorbing? And what kind of person do you want to become?

Spend time in the kitchen with a great cook and you will likely learn how to cook. Spend time with people that gossip, and you will likely become like them, unless you decide to leave. Spend time with changemakers, and you will likely become one of them.

Our environment, and the people we spend our time with, are massive influences on us. Our environment has a great impact on our habits, thoughts, and actions. And our actions determine where we go in life.

So, if you want to change yourself, and if you want to explore your potential and become a changemaker, then surround yourself with people and books that tell you that you can. Create an environment that enables and supports you.

Your body and your mind are adaptation machines, and if you spend time in an environment that inspires and uplifts you, you are soon going to feel the impact in your own life. Choosing or creating an environment that supports your dreams and ambitions is one of the best ways to success that I know. The people and thoughts you surround yourself with are one of the strongest indicators of where you are heading.

When I wanted to start my own business, I started reading books about how to start a business that were written by people who had actually started a business, or several businesses, themselves. I also started spending a lot of time with a friend that had started a business and was much more of a changemaker than I was. I learned so much from him in such a short time that my three years of studies at the university seemed like a joke in comparison. Today, we are business partners, and we still help each other expand our awareness and create an inspiring environment that helps us grow and prosper.

If you don't have changemakers in your direct environment, you can still seek them out. Creating an empowering environment and having a peer group of fellow changemakers is one of the best shortcuts to your personal development.

Embrace Being Overwhelmed

This guide may be a lot of new information for you. And the challenge of starting a business, becoming your own boss, developing your changemaking abilities, and stepping outside of what is normal and comfortable for you, might lead to the feeling of being overwhelmed.

There are so many things to take into consideration. There is so much new information, so many challenges, and also probably a lot of emotions, such as the excitement and joy of trying something new, or maybe feeling worried about whether you will succeed and if you can really do it.

Let me tell you: Being overwhelmed is normal.

When you try something new, it is absolutely normal if you don't start out already knowing how to do everything. *Not knowing how to do something is no reason not to do it.* And feeling overwhelmed is no reason not to take action.

The real question is, what do we do when we are overwhelmed? Do we let being overwhelmed lead to confusion, and confusion lead to inaction? Or do we embrace being overwhelmed, accept the confusion, and pick out a single task that we can start acting on, regardless of whether we already know every single step to take or not?

Changemakers choose not to let being overwhelmed or confused trap them into inaction. Instead, Changemakers choose to take positive action towards their goal, no matter what.

Imagine that you want to walk to a distant mountain and climb to its top. You are still several miles away, but you can see the mountaintop. On the way, you still have to cross vast stretches of forest and jungle. There is fog. There are lakes with alligators in between you and the mountain. And of course, there is also the rocky trail leading up to the mountaintop.

From where you stand, you can't possibly know every single step you must take to get to your goal. And the straightest route to take is also not the fastest. It would be very impractical to take a straight line to the mountaintop, which would force you to swim through the lake with the alligators and cut down the trees that get in your way. No-the fastest way to get to your goal is to walk around the lake and the trees, and enjoy the scenery while you find a path.

So, all you have to do as you walk towards your goal is figure out the single next step to take, use the flashlight you carry with you to figure out a path through the fog, and keep your self-esteem, your positivity, and your inspiration high.

And if you encounter an obstacle, you accept it and find a way to walk around it.

This is how changemakers choose not to let being overwhelmed and not knowing every single step of the way just yet stop them from going where their heart tells them to go.

Yes, some planning might be required from time to time, and can be helpful. But never let planning and theory stop you from trying and learning as you go.

Many changemakers and entrepreneurs could not even have imagined the kind of support that they would get once they started taking inspired positive action towards their dreams and visions. You don't know what will come up along your journey. There might be shortcuts that you can only discover once you've already moved down the road a bit.

So, take action. Don't let being overwhelmed put you into *paralysis by analysis,* as best-selling author, Tim Ferriss, puts it. Get out there, trust life, and you will find a way to succeed.

Ask for Forgiveness, Not for Permission

In the world we grow up in, other people make the rules and we learn to follow and obey. Our traditions, our parents, our political system, our teachers, and our peers introduce us to rules, and we adopt them without ever questioning why.

That is not a bad thing in and of itself.

Many rules, customs, traditions, and standards were put into place to make our lives easier and help us live together.

Other rules, however, are there for no apparent reason. Maybe they made sense a long time ago, but they might have become outdated, or they might simply not be helpful for you and what you want to do in life.

And again, other rules were put into place by the people in power to help them control others and gain even more power.

There are two kinds of rules: Written rules, such as laws or religious rules, and rules that don't exist in writing, but that are prevailing belief systems.

The prevailing belief systems and habits of collective thinking are often as powerful, or even more powerful, than written rules. Again, some of them might be helpful for the community and support its development and prosperity, but other rules might be harmful for the expression of human potential and the ability to make a real contribution.

The challenge is: If we blindly follow rules, we become docile and passive, and we might never be able to explore the potential we have as changemakers. Rules are mere mental constructs. They don't exist in the real world, only in our heads. However, they do manifest around us through our individual and collective actions.

But then the question becomes: How do we deal with rules that are not serving us? And do we really have to follow all the rules? What about rules that are immoral? Or rules that are not serving you and aren't there for any reason whatsoever? How do you deal with the rules that aren't contributing to your life, and are not serving you or anyone else in becoming who you are meant to become?

I don't advocate breaking the law or being ignorant of your culture and traditions-not at all. But I do challenge you to see if you can learn to ask for forgiveness instead of permission, if that is what is needed in order for you to be yourself and find your own way as a changemaker.

Sometimes, we seek permission to do something or become someone, but in many cases, the only person that can really give you permission is yourself. If you really want to create something, explore your potential, or follow your dreams, but no one will give you the permission to do it, then maybe it is time to stop seeking permission and instead, act on your ideas and dreams, and ask for forgiveness later.

My experience is that if I am not afraid to make a bold move and follow my dreams, the world will adjust to my persistent, positive, and inspired action. Sometimes, this requires letting go of the need to get approval or permission from everyone around me. And I have found that if I have accidentally really upset someone, then asking for forgiveness works in most cases. People are willing to forgive if they receive a sincere apology more often than you think, if you have truly upset someone.

This way of moving ahead works better for me than always seeking approval and permission, and possibly never getting it. If I want to take control of my life, and serve God and other human beings as a changemaker on the highest level that I can, then sometimes, it requires taking the risk that not everyone will approve of my actions. In almost all cases, it is never too late to apologize afterward. In many cases, people adjust and get used to the new circumstances.

If we are addicted to seeking approval, permission, and the good opinions of other people, then we will likely block our own road to success and development.

In Thomas' family, for example, everyone has always worked for someone else. There were no entrepreneurs, and all Thomas learned while growing up is that starting a business is very risky, that almost everyone fails, and that entrepreneurs and business is basically bad. So, this is the unwritten rule and belief system that his Mom instilled in him.

It was only after he became exposed to other information when he learned that changemaking could also be fun, exciting, and a way to express his love for God and fellow human beings by helping them and providing services and products that they needed and that enriched their lives.

When he wanted to start his first business, his Mom cautioned, asked, and begged him to delay the decision. But he knew that if he delayed it, he might never again find the courage to do it. Now is the only moment there ever is. So, he decided to act and start a business. He figured that, if he asked his Mom for permission, she would likely never give it to him. But if he asked for forgiveness for his bold move after he had already done it, he would likely be forgiven.

Today, his Mom is proud that her son is starting and creating businesses that contribute to life, and is even interested in learning from him how to start her own enterprise.

If you start asking for forgiveness instead of permission, it might be wise to start with small things. Slowly but surely, your friends and surroundings will get used to the change in you. Show them empathy if they are worried. Be humble. Don't argue. Assure them that you respect their opinions and beliefs. And don't be shy to apologize if someone is really hurt. But also, don't let the need for the good opinion of other people determine how you live your life until the rest of your days. The mantra is: *In general, ask for forgiveness, instead of permission.*

Become an Active Observer and Identify the Missing Value

Changemakers become good at identifying the needs of other people and then finding ways to close the gap and provide what is missing.

One of the easiest ways to find what is missing is to become an active observer and student of life. Look around you: Everything you see that is manmade is likely to be a product or service that someone is creating, selling, or distributing.

When you walk around, it might be a good exercise to think about:

- How can this be created?
- How could I create something like this or find someone to create it for me?

- How would I bring this product or service to the market?
- How could I do it better than the person who is selling this product or delivering this service?
- Could I be friendlier to the customers?
- Could I provide a better service?
- Could I be cleaner, faster, more fun, or could I provide the service or product closer to people's homes?

It can also be a fun exercise to just observe someone and their business and learn about it, or even ask questions, such as:

- How much do their products or services cost?
- Where are they buying their products from?
- Are they creating these products themselves, or are they bought from someone else and then resold?
- Can the products be sold on a commission basis?
- What is the process behind this?
- Who are the customers that are currently buying this product, or similar products, and why are they buying it?

There are dozens of questions you can clear up by observing businesses. You don't have to attend a business course in order to learn about business. Observing other entrepreneurs, business owners, and changemakers is likely to be the fastest way to learn. Asking questions and learning from them will even accelerate your learning process.

Observing existing businesses is a great way of learning from practitioners, not from theory. Make life your university, and you are sure to get a top-notch education.

All it requires is being aware and a keen observer, having a vision and a goal, and showing an interest in learning.

Go out and learn. Observe other businesses, but also observe where people have unmet needs. If people are unsatisfied with a situation, you have a good indicator that there might be a business opportunity waiting for you. Do you hear people complaining about something that they are missing in their lives? Maybe there is an idea waiting for you. Ask people directly: What is your biggest frustration at the moment? Ask someone that is already running a business, and they might tell you several things that are frustrating them which they might need help with.

As a changemaker, it is your job to make other people's lives more beautiful, stress-free, and safe, or help them in any other way by creating a product, service, or offer that enriches their life.

Get good at finding the missing value, and you can start a business from scratch at any time.

Money Mindset-Part I: Money as a Measure of Creating Value

Let's discuss the topic of money. Money is a mystery to many people, and most people think that there is never enough of it. Some people say money is the root of all evil. Others claim that rich people are bad, or that you have to cheat and exploit others to make a lot of money.

As a changemaker and entrepreneur, it is important to recognize that all the stories about what money is are merely belief systems and mental constructs.

Nowhere in the universe does money mean anything other than in the mind of a human being. No tree and no animal cares about money. Neither do the stars, the sea, or the planets.

Only humans have managed to give pieces of paper so much meaning.

It is important to recognize that you are the one that gives money its meaning. Only the fact that you believe in money allows it to have any value to you.

So, if money is just a story that we believe in collectively, then it might be helpful to think of it in a way that serves us, rather than hinders us.

So, instead of seeing money as the root of all evil, or something that is scarce, it might be more helpful to see money as a tool and a means of exchanging value, and recognize that money is there in abundance. They print more money every day.

So, if money is simply a tool for exchanging value, then the amount of money that flows to you is primarily determined by the amount of value you create and deliver to others.

In other words: How many people do you serve? And how much do they value the service you provide to them? The amount of money that you attract to your business will have a strong correlation with the number of people your business is serving, and the degree to which you serve and contribute to their lives.

If you create a product or service that enriches people's lives, and that you charge enough for to make one dollar of profit per sale, then you will be a millionaire if you enrich a million people's lives. And yes, you can use the money you make to create even more value for people, which reinvests it in your purpose.

So, if you see money as a means of exchange for value, and recognize that money flows abundantly to those that help solve problems and needs through business, then you will not think of money as something that is in short supply, but you will start asking better questions and think of how you can have a positive impact on more people's lives.

Does that mean that all people get money in a fair way that benefits everyone? No, that is not what is being said. But you can attract money in a way that benefits everyone. The people you serve, your community, the environment, yourself, and your family.

The only limit to how much money you can attract is how big you allow yourself to think, in terms of how much value you can create for others through your business and the products and services you deliver.

I encourage you to start asking yourself how you can serve more people in a way that is good for everyone involved, and start seeing money as a tool that can be used for good.

This way, money will not be an issue for you. Those that know and learn how to create value for others can attract money at any time by providing an equal or better exchange for the money that they get in the form of value.

Money Mindset-Part II: You Don't Need More Money, You Need a Better Strategy

You don't need more money, you need a better strategy is the credo of one of my mentors in business. And I couldn't agree more.

One of the limiting beliefs that kept me from starting a business when I was in college was that I thought that starting a business takes money. It was only when I learned from the examples of friends and coaches that you can start a business with no money at all, that I recognized the thought *"I need more money"* was simply another limiting belief, and that I could choose a better belief that would serve me more. I started choosing the belief that I don't need money to start a business.

Here are just a few reasons why you don't need money to start a business:

- You could sell someone else's products or services with their permission, and for a share of the profit. This way, you wouldn't have to invest any money.

- You could sell a service that doesn't require an initial investment. The money you earn could be reinvested into hiring staff or buying the tools that would make your job easier.

- If you need tools, space, or other resources to offer your service, you could find someone to partner with that already has those tools or resources, and ask them whether you can use them in exchange for part of the profit you make.

All of the companies that I have started were launched with very little or no initial capital. Only later, when the companies grew, did I sometimes rely on money from a bank or someone else to expand my business. But not having access to a lot of capital has not stopped me from starting businesses and projects again and again.

If you think you need money for what you want to do, always remember that it is probably not more money that you need, but a better strategy.

Choose Your Script

We have now spoken quite a bit about the mindsets and behaviors of Changemakers. I have found that one of the essential qualities of Changemakers is that they don't believe that life is only happening *to* them; that they are playing the victim role in someone else's movie and they have to follow the script given to them.

Changemakers will always take part of the responsibility and realize on some level that they can edit, rewrite, or tear up the script that was given to them, and come up with a script for the role that they choose.

If we think of the experience of this lifetime and in this body as a movie, continuously unfolding before our eyes-or rather, before our perception-then wouldn't it be great if you could influence which scenes are coming up next? If you could write the script in a way that inspires the audience, and is not the most boring movie ever?

Well, in a way, you can. You might not be able to influence every single frame in the movie right away, but you are able to influence the general direction that the plot of the movie called *Your Life* is taking.

How do you do it?

First, decide that you are the writer, director, and star of your own movie.

Then decide what kind of movie you would like to watch. Is it a movie in which the hero learns, develops, inspires, and goes beyond what they thought was possible, or one where the hero sits at home and complains all day?

Once you have decided on the version of the movie, you can start editing the script accordingly.

What would the goals of your alter-ego be? What kind of courageous decisions would your movie character make? How would the star in your own movie contribute to humankind? How would they express their feelings? And how would they become more spiritually aware and connected to God? What would your hero be like at the end of their life? Would they say that they have lived life well? That they have loved? And that they have given everything to be an inspiration and to realize the potentials and gifts that they were given?

Once you have determined what your hero would be like, and how they would look at life, realize that this is actually your movie script, and you are the director and the hero in your own movie.

You are now free to get inspired from what you have just written. If you have done it in a moment of inner peace and an energy of possibility, then you have likely created a script for yourself that has the potential to inspire you.

You can be the person that you have just written about. You can choose who you want to be and which direction your life should take. Knowing that you create the script of your life, you can start out on an incredible journey.

You are now really in power. The power to create your life, and the power to create change for others as well.

Trust the River

If we want to grow and stretch beyond who we currently are to see who we can become, it is not only necessary to show great discipline, but we also need to be able to trust.

If we don't trust that it is possible, then we will not act accordingly. Either we will not go outside of our comfort zone at all, or we will do so halfheartedly. And you will learn in another chapter that *tentative has no power*, as one of my mentors always proclaims.

But how can you trust? How can you KNOW that life is taking care of you, and that you can follow your path without fear or doubt?

This is a spiritual question, and everyone has to find the answer to this within. However, I would like to share my experience of how I have been able to move past my doubts and dedicate myself fully to a purpose I have chosen. From my experience, two things were essential for me:

- Firstly, I now operate from a belief system that if I act on a purpose that inspires me and gets my enthusiasm, then I know that I am not only intellectually in tune with what I am setting out to do, but that my heart is in it as well, and I can trust that this is my path to follow. From a purely logical standpoint, this makes sense, because if I am inspired by something, it is much more likely that it will be easy for me to dedicate time and positive energy to this project than it would be if I was not emotionally moved by the project.

- Secondly, I believe in a higher power; a power that guides me if I am willing to listen and put aside my fears and habitual negative thoughts. I believe that I have been guided many times, and that often, it has only been clear to me after the fact. From my perspective, the things I am doing are done not *by me* but *through me* if I act from inspiration and love, and with a purpose that is bigger than myself, which speaks to my heart. I have observed several times that in situations where I didn't know the next step, a way presented itself suddenly and unexpectedly, and allowed me to move forward and towards what inspired me. To onlookers, it might have seemed that I had done something amazing, but I know that the universe, or life, has always been cooperating with me. Knowing this from experience allows me to be a lot calmer and more confident, and I know that I can trust the river of life if I follow my heart.

Knowing where I want to go and why, nurturing the emotional connection to this goal, and then trusting that it is possible and will eventually happen, is likely to have shortened the time it takes to attain my goals tremendously.

Failure as A Delay, Not A Defeat

A failure is not really a failure. You cannot really fail. As long as you get back up when you have fallen down, and progress and learn from the experience, there is no real failure. Only *failing forward*.

In the years that I have worked and been active as a changemaker, I have made quite a few decisions that I would make differently today. I take that as the price to be paid for learning.

There is a quote by Thomas Edison that I cherish: *"Many of life's failures are people who did not realize how close they were to success when they gave up."*

This is why, from a certain perspective, you can only fail when you give up. As long as you learn, try again, improve, and build on top of your experiences, your failure means you are actually making progress. Your breakthrough with your Changemaking project might come slowly over time, or as a sudden success. Your past failures are the learnings that have laid the foundation for any visible success to come.

The truth is: All success is gradual, even though it might seem like it happened overnight. All the failures, all the preparation, all the successions of trial and error, and all the experimentation and tweaking are necessary to get the end result, which again, is only another step on the journey.

So, don't discredit your failures. Rather, celebrate them as opportunities to learn, just as you can take any "problem" and call it a "challenge" instead, and welcome it as an opportunity to grow.

This way, you will never have to deal with a problem again, and you will never fail, but will only be confronted with opportunities.

Remember: Your perspective on things creates your reality.

Courage Attracts Support; Purpose Fosters Relationships

An interesting observation I have made over the years, in personal endeavors and in reading the stories of great men and women, is that something magical tends to happen when we go from an energy of pride or fear, where we are constantly trying to protect our "ego" and constantly afraid to fail, to an energy of courage.

Courage is vibrating at a higher energy than fear or pride. When you switch from worries and fear, or from making yourself too important and being stuck in your own pride, to an energy of courage, all of a sudden, the universe seems to cooperate more with your plans.

Courage not only enables us to do things that we were previously stuck on due to old, limiting patterns of thought, but it also seems to attract support.

I also find this to be true because I, myself, feel inspired by the courage that people exhibit.

For example, a young man once contacted me and told me that he had quit school, although his parents were quite critical of his decision. He thought that he did not learn much of value in school, and that the environment he was in at the time was not conducive to his personal growth. Quite the contrary; a lot of young people in his surroundings were getting into trouble, and he wanted to choose a different path. So, instead of continuing in school, he wanted to start a business or help build a business, as he thought he would learn faster if he learned in a more practical manner.

He asked me if he could come work for me, as he knew that I had several businesses and might need some help. I was impressed with his direct approach of looking for guidance and an opportunity to learn. So, this young man and I worked together for a few months, after which, he moved on to other projects, but because of his courage, we stayed in contact.

About one year after I had initially met him, he sent me a message saying that a company had hired him full-time. He had moved to a different country, and they had paid for his relocation and his apartment. He loved the new job, and raved about the new challenge. But what was most impressive to me was that he had gotten the job even though more experienced and much older applicants had also applied for the position. The difference, he told me, was that he had applied a skill that he had learned while working with me. That skill was that he had learned to look for how to add value, whether as an entrepreneur or as an employee, and to communicate the value he could bring to the table.

So, instead of telling them how great he was, he first studied the company, and in the job interview, he told the company how he would help them and how they would earn more, serve their clients better, and have a bigger impact, and he gave them very specific examples of how he could help them achieve this. But not only that, he also asked very specific questions, looking and digging deeper into how to help them improve, and he told them how he thought they could do it and the specific steps that they could take.

His relentless focus on adding value got him a well-paying job at a time when most of his former classmates were still going to school. Also, he found a way to finish his school degree on the side, while already earning money and making a real change.

Hearing these kinds of stories, or being a part of them, always delights me. And it shows me how much support can come from courage. But courage has to come first. The outer world seems to be like a mirror with a delay on it in this regard. If you start acting courageous, the world will start helping you, possibly with a delay of a few weeks, but it will eventually happen. So, the key is to keep up the courage.

Another way to enlist the support of the world is to have a clear purpose. A clear purpose that inspires and is meaningful in that it does not solely serve your ego but contributes to the lives of other human beings, nature, or animals, can be a powerful catalyst to bring people together and align them with your mission.

I have witnessed this many times. When I see changemakers talk about their projects designed to help others, and I see the light of enthusiasm and inspiration in their eyes, I can't help but be inspired as well. Immediately, my mind is searching for ways to help and support them, be it with advice, encouragement, funding, or contacts.

If you have a mission that goes beyond the economic value, in that you also add social, ecological, or spiritual value, it might be well worth it to focus on telling an inspiring story that shares the purpose of your organization or project with others. You might be surprised by the amount of support you can enlist.

Tentative Has No Power

If you decide to become a changemaker, make it a clear decision. If you give it your best and commit an act with full engagement, then the results will happen.

However, if you doubt and don't take care of your attitude, and if you think negative thoughts and get yourself down due to fear and doubt, then your success is being compromised. Whenever you catch yourself thinking these thoughts, become aware of them, decide to get inspired again, and connect yourself to thoughts about why it is possible that you will succeed.

Commit to becoming a changemaker. Act decisively. Don't take your eyes off the goal. Decisiveness, conviction, and boldness carry power, whereas *tentative has no power*.

Take care of your frequency, and make sure that your heart and mind are in alignment and that you act from courage, inspiration, love, and enthusiasm.

This way, you can be certain that the doors will open for you. Keep at it. Dissolve doubts. The worst thing that can happen is that you learn a whole lot about yourself and the world.

Becoming a changemaker gives you the shortcut to a free business education that many students at expensive business schools in the world would envy you for. If you are committed and willing to step forward without hesitancy, the world can be yours.

Nurture the Vision

When we work on our projects, it can happen quite easily that we get lost in the many tasks and things that seem urgent to work on. While you may have started out with a clear idea and a strong and inspiring vision, many entrepreneurs and changemakers that I know find it difficult to maintain a helicopter perspective on their project.

When you are busy with all the small details, the main reason-the WHY-and the purpose of the project can get lost in the urgent demands of the moment.

And my experience is, that if we lose our connection to the WHY, and the vision of the project we are working on, it is easy to also lose the inspiration that was driving our initial desire to create something from scratch.

The best way I know to deal with this challenge is to take time off regularly and just reconnect with the purpose of WHY I am working on the project, and to also reconnect with how I hope my work will benefit others.

While writing parts of this book, for example, I took time to visualize and imagine again and again how this text, and my work with the YES Network team, might inspire and touch young people's lives. I imagined that, by being exposed to this material, some people might be able to change their perspectives and realize the potential they have within to create value for society, for themselves, and for their families. Getting back from my visualization to the work on these pages, I felt inspired and deeply grateful to be given the opportunity to contribute in this way.

Nurture your vision and connect to the purpose regularly. If you are creating from vision and from inspiration, you will vibrate at a different energy than you would have if you lost sight of the bigger goal and the WHY.

Establish the What and the Why, and Let the How Present Itself

This is one of my favorite learnings on my journey thus far. If you decide "**What** it is you want" and "**Why** you want it", the "**How** to bring it into your life" will eventually present itself.

Before I set out in business, I had a clear idea of **What** I wanted and **Why** I wanted it. But I had no real idea of **How** to go about creating such a business for myself. My **"What"** was an online business that would be fun, that I could learn from, and that would give me a somewhat reliable income, no matter where I was in the world. My **"Why"** was that I wanted to learn, but also have the freedom to travel and visit other countries instead of working in an office, or for someone else, for the rest of my life. And I wanted the time to work on solving social and ecological problems. This was a really strong motivator for me, and inspired me enough to be courageous. But I didn't know **"How"** to go about setting up my own business. I just knew that I had to take the first step, and that any kind of step towards my goal would be okay. That I would learn on the way and figure things out as I went.

So, I simply went out to register a company. Meanwhile, I kept reading and reading about how to start a business on a budget. I also read stories of successful entrepreneurs and changemakers. A few days later, a friend approached me and asked me whether I would like to help him with an idea that he had been working on. He already had the first customers, and needed help growing the business. So, I said yes, and the way towards my goal was clear. About 8 months later, I had my stable income from this company, we had 27 employees, and I had sufficient time and funds to travel and pursue new projects. I could not have planned for something like this to happen this quickly.

Was it pure luck? Maybe. But similar things have continued happening to me whenever I was deeply inspired and had a strong desire to create something, learn, and grow.

On a different occasion, I decided that I wanted to ride a bicycle from Germany to India, through Europe, Turkey, Iran, and Pakistan. I wanted to use this event to raise donations for a social project of building toilets in villages where people were without sanitary infrastructure, and I wanted to make a film about the tour. This was back in 2011, and I had absolutely no idea about toilets, raising funds, or making a movie.

Within a very short amount of time, I found a friend that wanted to cycle with me, and that also had a camera and filmmaking experience. Additionally, I recruited another NGO from Germany that were experts in the field of sanitation, and they gave me a contact in India that helped me realize the project there. And, last but not least, I found a sponsor for the bicycles and a lot of support with the fundraising efforts.

So, within only four or five months after the initial idea, we were ready to start the project, from which we have now sprung even more projects in the field of sanitation and environmental protection.

Again, I could not have planned for these things and these people to show up in this sequence, or that they would all be ready to contribute. But it happened, and I was so inspired by this project, that for me, there was no turning away from it. I was inspired, excited, and ready to give it my all. I knew **What** I wanted, I knew **Why** I wanted it, and the **How** revealed itself along the way.

Trust the river. You only need to know the next step, not every single step, to reach your goal. Take the next step, and then the next, and then the next, and then you will see that doors will open and opportunities that were simply not visible before will present themselves.

If you are inspired, and you are not acting from ego, but from a desire to create, grow, and contribute, people and the world around you will likely be there to help you. You have to take the first step and trust that there is always a way.

The Power of Partnerships

Most of us were trained and brought up to believe that we should know how to do things ourselves, and that hard work is something positive and something to be proud of.

Hard work is a strong value for many people.

While I do agree that "work" can be very enjoyable, I also realized over my years as an entrepreneur and a Changemaker that I neither need to know everything myself, nor do I necessarily have to work hard to achieve results, and that trying to do everything myself can actually be a hindrance to getting results fast.

Yes, initially, when starting a project, often there is a lot of work to do, and because I might not have much or any experience in the field, I might have to make an extra effort. However, through observation, it also became clear to me that I achieved the most in the shortest amount of time when I wasn't simply working hard, but also smart, with a great focus on how to leverage my own resources.

And this brings me to the topic of partnerships and deal-making.

There are some fundamental beliefs that I carry, and that many of the successful changemakers I have met also hold:

1. If I don't know how to do something, there is probably someone out there that knows how to do it and would be glad to do it for me.

2. I can (ethically) use other people's time, money, investments, know-how, and resources to create the value that I want to deliver.

3. If I become good at combining resources, connecting people and offers, and creating deals whereby everyone wins, I will have access to almost unlimited opportunities at virtually no risk or expense.

Now, whether these statements are true or not, you will have to figure out for yourself. I am certain, though, that you can make them true for yourself.

Here are three examples from my own experience, where I used partnerships and/or deal-making to make things possible without spending my own money.

Example #1: Starting A Shared Office Space/Co-Working Space with No Money Down

A few years ago, I wanted to work in a huge and beautiful house with my friends, where we could invite friends, hold workshops and seminars, and develop our businesses. I found a beautiful and big loft in the center of the city, but at that time, I didn't have the money to rent it for myself.

Become a Changemaker, Create Value, Give Abundantly, Discover the Giant Within, and Make a Living on the Way

So, we came up with a plan.

First, we asked the landlady whether she would: (1) Be willing to give us one week to decide whether we'd rent the place or not, and reserve the place for us, and (2) Agree to accept 50% of the rent for the first month, as there was still work to be finished on the space. She agreed to both points.

Then, we recorded a quick video of the space in which we spoke about the inspiring vision that we had for the place, that we wanted it to be a place where Changemakers could work together and create projects that would have a positive impact. Then we shared this video via YouTube and Facebook with all of our friends and their friends. Within a week, we had interviewed 12 applicants that wanted to join the co-working space in exchange for a monthly fee. We also negotiated a down payment with them that they would receive in return at the end of their contract with us.

So, within a week, we knew that we would have sufficient revenue every month to cover the cost for the co-working space, and that we could confirm the place with the landlady. We had mobilized several thousand euros in a few hours, and had a base from which to move forward.

Creating a deal with the landlady and our new co-workers in a way that we would not need any cash of our own was necessary for us to be able to create this space. While we have since moved on to other projects, the three years in which we ran the space were very exciting, and I made some crucial business contacts and connections there that have helped me greatly since.

Example #2: Cycling from Germany to India, Building Toilets in Villages, and Starting an Ecological Toilet Company with No Money Down

When we first had the idea to cycle from Germany to India and build toilets in a village there, we didn't have the slightest idea about how to do it. All we knew was that it was going to happen somehow.

So, true to our mantra that you don't have to do everything yourself, and that there is probably already someone out there that knows the **"How"** to do it, I started researching.

The first thing that I did was contact someone that had already cycled for more than 1000 kilometers, and I interviewed him about all the essentials. This was really helpful and gave me the confidence that it was, indeed, possible.

The second thing that was crucial were the bicycles. I had recruited another two people to cycle with me to India, but we didn't have proper bicycles. So, I asked an assistant working with me at the time to write a short letter to all the manufacturers of bicycles in Germany, Austria, and Switzerland. In the letter, we offered to create pictures of their bicycles, write articles online, make Facebook posts, and create videos about their bicycles on our tour from Germany to India. We also said that it was likely that we would be featured in many press articles and on TV. Of the 100+ companies, the assistant sent the letters to, two responded that they would like to sponsor us. One was a big e-bike manufacturer, and the other one a small, local manufacturer. We decided for the small manufacturer, because it seemed that there was less bureaucracy involved, and also, we didn't want e-bikes. Where was the fun if we didn't have to peddle hard to reach our goal?

The third challenge was that we didn't know much about toilets at the time, and we also didn't have any contacts in India, or any idea what we were doing in general. So, again, I did some research and contacted an NGO in Germany by the name of the German Toilet Organization. I asked them if they would be willing to partner with us on this project, and told them that this would give them great publicity, more possible donors, and that it was for a "good cause". So, they said yes and came on board. They also had a contact in India; an NGO that knew more about these types of toilets than we did. So, by bringing them on board as well, the tasks were well-distributed. The Indian NGO would build the toilets in the village, the German Toilet Organization would take care of the administrative part of the project and collect the donations, the manufacturer would sponsor the bicycles, and one of my friends was going to film and create the documentary. So, my part basically came down to cycling and keeping everyone motivated. The tour and the project became a huge success, and, in the end, everyone was happy. Had I tried to do everything myself, I would not have known how to do it. By contacting people with expertise in different fields, by bringing them together, and by sharing an inspiring vision, I basically got dozens of years of experience, and tens of thousands of euros' worth of hours and equipment for the project, without having to pay a single cent myself.

After having built the first toilets in India, we wanted to start an ecological toilet rental company in Germany. The idea was to use profits from that business to continue supporting humanitarian work in the area of water and sanitation. But again, we didn't have a lot of know-how or money to start such a project in our hometown. So, we did some research for potential partners. One company that we found was already renting out toilets in the South of Germany. They were a very small business with around 30 toilets for rental. We contacted them and asked them whether they would give us a few of their used toilets that they didn't have a big need for anymore and that were to be replaced soon anyhow, and they agreed. Since we weren't willing to invest from our own money, we arranged a deal with them that basically stated that they would give us the toilets with no money down, and that we would pay for them little by little every time we had a client and money was coming in. Also, we included in the agreement that we could give back the toilets at any time, since we wanted to remove the risk for ourselves, and first wanted to test this business idea and see whether it was promising. We also included in the agreement that we would rent-to-buy, meaning that, after we had paid them a certain amount, the toilets would be ours. This approach made it relatively risk-free, or at least immensely lowered our risk. Also, this company taught us their entire system, told us the prices that they were able to charge, and even sent us our first clients when the request came from our geographical area and they couldn't fulfill the job themselves. So, this was a big win for us, and made it much easier to start this business from scratch, but it was also a win for the other business, since they could get rid of their older toilets and still get a good price for them. Also, we sent them clients later on that were interested in renting toilets in their geographical area, and our two companies have been exchanging know-how together ever since. This was a win-win, and enabled us to start our company as cheaply as possible and without access to funds.

Example #3: Selling Information, Online and Offline

In 2015, one of my projects was aimed at selling videos on how to start a business over the internet. I had done something similar before with a different company, but I had left because we really had a different vision, and I didn't want to compromise on following my heart.

I already knew how to record and edit video material and such, but a challenge I faced is that I didn't have much of an audience. My website was relatively new, and had very few visitors.

Nevertheless, I didn't want to postpone the launch of this business.

So, I asked myself who had a huge audience, and how I could help those people and create a win-win situation.

I made a list of a few names that I knew, and a few of which I had already been in contact with. I sent them an email and offered them a free online lecture/webinar for their followers, and on top of that, I would also gift their audience with a six-hour long, free video course, that I would normally sell. I told them that they could offer this to their followers. Additionally, I told my contacts that if any of the people that signed up for my free online presentation and the gifted course then decided to also purchase my other product, I would pay them a commission, as a token of appreciation for introducing me to their followers.

I was able to negotiate this deal with four influencers within two weeks. The result was that they sent me over a thousand sign-ups, and quite a few of these signups turned into customers for my paid program. So, through these partnerships, I went from not having much of an audience myself to having my first customers and a five-figure revenue within weeks, and I also helped the partners make a good impression in front of their audience and earn a nice side income.

Those are only a few examples. Yes, not all the partnerships that I wanted to set up worked out. But, in general, if you find a way to create a win-win, or even better, a win-win-win situation in which the other party, your clients, *their* clients, *and* you, benefit from banding together, then I am sure that you can make partnerships happen in wonderful ways. I am sure that if you start thinking in creative ways, you can figure out how others can help you with your efforts, and in ways that are beneficial for you, as well as for them.

Always think of ways that you can:

- Help someone else make more money;
- Help someone else save time;
- Help someone else save money, or not lose money;
- Help someone get into an area or a new market that they couldn't access before;
- Help someone use vacant resources that they are not using for a profit;
- Help someone get their products or services into more hands; and/or
- Help someone else that doesn't have a product, but has a wide influence and reach, create a product or sell a different product.

Those are just some ideas. They might not be meaningful to you right now. But once you have started your project, looking at this material might be an eye-opener to think about your project from yet another perspective.

Always remember: You don't need to know everything yourself. You can always find people that are already doing a good job, and tie up their knowledge and resources with your own if you make a good win-win deal with them.

The Outer Follows the Inner

The world, as you see it in "normal" consciousness, is largely a projection of your thoughts and beliefs.

If your being is love, then this is all you will see in the now, and you will radiate it and change your surroundings accordingly, because they are a direct result of who you are.

If your being is optimistic and courageous, the world will show you plenty of opportunities and possibilities. So, what you believe inside is true for your outside, and is carried forward into the future.

The same is true for "negative" thoughts and belief systems. If you believe the world is basically evil and dangerous, then your mind will gather all the evidence to support this belief. Our minds are always busy gathering proof to create a coherent story.

You decide which story you want to believe. Believe the story that YOU CAN and act on faith, and you will see the proof showing up all around you. Believe the story that you WERE BORN GREAT, and that all you have to do is awaken your latent potential, and you will start acting on this belief with faith, and the results in the outer world will follow.

There might be a time delay of a few days, or a few weeks, or a few months. But the results (meaning the proof) will always show up according to your thinking and your beliefs.

So, if you want to change the world, start inside yourself:

- The world is evil? *I am evil.* Are you thinking evil thoughts sometimes? If you find this to be true, then practice being kind, forgiving, and loving, and the world around you will appear more kind, forgiving, and loving. It can't do this otherwise, as it is a projection of your mind.

- You cannot trust people? *I can't trust myself* or *People can't trust me.* Could this be truer? If so, when? When should other people not have trusted you? When have you been untrustworthy? Again, if you start practicing being more honest and more trustworthy, the world around you will start to shift, because it is a projection of your own mind and your own beliefs.

Changing the outside world is a struggle if you don't change yourself first. However, you can make a shift within seconds, if you start changing yourself first. Yes, the outside will follow. Everything is set in motion by your own belief system, and the thoughts you think about yourself and "the world out there".

Start gathering evidence that this is so. Journal your experiences and look for the proof that the outer follows the inner, and you will have found the key to changing your experience of life in a way that is likely to lead to more peace, happiness, and success.

Labels and Identities

Our mind loves to identify with things, and so we put labels on each other and on ourselves that give us an identity of sorts, which again tells us the story of how we should act and how we should think and feel.

The labels you use for yourself are not who you really are, and the labels you use for others are not who they really are.

Using labels, is normal, but just because it is normal to do it, does not mean that it is sane, especially when the labels, or your thinking about those labels, can cause you shame, guilt, fear, anger, apathy, or make you believe that you are a victim of circumstance and can't change anything in your world.

If a label inspires you, then by all means, use it and be inspired. If a label that you use makes you happy and peaceful, or is likely to make you see your latent potential and take action, then great, on you go.

But it is the labels that frighten us and cause us pain, worry, fear, anger, and hate, which imprison us in a limiting, unfriendly world that exists only in our heads.

Those are the labels that can be questioned, and if you can go beyond them, you are free to live from a different energy and manifest the things your heart desires.

"Changemaker" is a label that is likely to empower you.

Choose labels that allow you to live life fully and bring out the best in you. Create an identity that you like, and change your identity if you don't feel that it inspires you and helps you to grow, contribute, and love.

Patience

When you start out on your Changemaking journey, it is essential to believe that you can learn anything. Neuroscience has proven that the brain can change itself. Your brain is actually changing its shape, and the neuronal connections are constantly adapting to the demands you put on them.

So, when you start learning a new skill or practice new ways of thinking and being, your brain adapts itself.

This being said, be patient with yourself, and don't get frustrated if things don't seem to work out right away. Learning to become a Changemaker is a journey. It is not a destination. It is a continuous practice, and if you keep practicing, and connecting to inspiration, purpose, and the material in this book again and again, without giving up or quitting, it is almost guaranteed that you will make quantum leaps towards a new you.

If you do get frustrated, and you think that the results are not showing up fast enough, recognize that many of us go to school for 10 or 12 years; even longer if we go to university. All this time, we are supposedly practicing and working towards being "ready" to get a job. So, if society allows us to practice for 10 to 12 years, or even longer, for a "normal" job, then you can surely allow yourself 2 or 3 years of practice to become a Changemaker; something that can be decidedly more challenging than a "normal" job.

Everything you practice for long enough, you will get good at. If the baby practices walking, after some time, it will be able to stand up on its own two feet. And if a young child starts learning about IT and programming, they can become experts in their field or successful software business people by the time they are young adults.

Anything can be learned with enough time, sustained commitment, and persistence. Of course, it will be much easier to persist and make the time if you practice something that genuinely interests you. That is the reason why, if you look for your changemaking project, it is wise to choose something that speaks to your heart.

But other than a sustained commitment and sufficient time applied to practicing, as well as the desire to master what you have set out to do, nothing is required. Your body, your brain, and your being will naturally adapt in order to allow you to grow in the direction you have set course on. All you need is the knowledge that this is so, and the patience to gather the evidence for yourself.

Keep practicing and you will get good at it. Keep working towards your vision and it will show up. Trust the river, and be patient in the knowledge that you can achieve anything you truly want if you keep a clear focus on it.

Belief

Believing in yourself, and in possibility, is a great help on your way to creating and exploring your potential.

But how do we actually start to believe? How do we discard doubt and recognize that we are capable, that we were born great, and that we can achieve anything if we trust our path and our innate greatness?

In the beginning, we might not be able to fully believe this. If I tell you that you were born great, that you can become anything you want, and that you can do anything your heart truly desires, you might think that this is not the case. But even if you don't believe it, you can at least acknowledge that there is a possibility that it is true.

And if you see the possibility, this might give you enough hope. Hope is already more powerful than negation and disbelief. If you have hope, you can start taking action. As you take more and more action, you will see how things around you start to change. You will notice that things are coming into your life that you might not have thought were possible before. Take notes in your *Success and Evidence Journal,* and proactively collect indicators that you are, indeed, a changemaker.

Then, slowly but surely, your mind will become convinced, and you will move from hope, which was necessary to get you started, to a place where you can say: *I don't have to hope that I can become what I dream of. Now I know it. I have the intention to become my dream, and I know that, if I take consistent action towards it and act from the alignment of my heart and mind, I am living my truth.*

Science tells you, "Show me and I will believe you", and faith says, "Believe me and I will show you". All visionaries had to live out of their imagination and believe that something that had not yet come to fruition was possible. And so, they created reality. As a changemaker, you have to trust the creative potential and the non-physical power of imagination. Everything is first created in the non-physical realm of thought, creative imagination, and intuition. Only then is it transferred into the physical realm through creative expression. The act of creation begins in the realm of the non-physical.

Trust your inspiration. Trust your heart. Trust that you can create, and hold the image of what you want to create and what inspires you in your mind, and you will move towards it, and see it manifest in the physical world. There is a time delay, but if you stick with it, don't get distracted or discouraged, and nurture your belief, then you will be moving towards it with clear certainty.

This is what belief can do for you. Act on your hope and nurture your belief in your positive and inspired vision, and you won't waste so much energy with doubts and fears. Things will come to you with greater ease.

If you believe that you are a changemaker and you create experiences for evidence of this belief, meaning you start acting on your belief, you start believing it so clearly, so perfectly, and so thoroughly that, when other people encounter you, they can't help but believe it themselves.

Thinking in Models: Blueprints, Frameworks, and Examples from Past Competitions

In this part, we want to give you a few models that we hope will give you a good orientation when you think about business and explore your opportunities for creating value. Also, we want to give you a few selected examples of businesses that were started by other students. However, please do not let the theoretical distinctions or examples overwhelm you and stop you from taking action and learning on your own. The presentation of these models and examples are merely to inspire you, and provide you with a broader perspective.

B2C vs. B2B

If you create value, your first impulse might be to think about serving people that are in similar circumstances as you are, or who belong to the same group of people. For example, if you are a girl, your first impulse might be to create products for other girls your age. And if you are a student, you might first come to think about how to serve other students and how to create value to solve their challenges. Thinking about yourself and wanting to create services or products for the same group that you belong to is natural, because those are the kinds of people we know best. In business terms, selling products or services to other private individuals is called "Business-to-Consumer" transactions, or in short, "B2C".

However, it might be helpful to at least consider that we do not have to only create value for other consumers. We might also think about creating value for another business. This would then be called a "Business-to-Business" transaction, because your business would provide a service or product to someone else's business. I find this distinction very useful because it widens my focus and lets me see opportunities that were previously hidden to me.

Here are some examples for business-to-business transactions:

- I might provide a professional cleaning service to another business. If I get enough good contracts, I might hire people and expand my company.

- I might offer security and guard services to another business. I could look for and train security staff that will work for me and provide security to my business clients.

- If I create clothing, I might distribute my clothing to a store that sells my clothing to the end customer.

- If I live in a village and produce products there, but I would like to sell them at a higher price to wealthy families in the city, I could look for a store in the city that has access to this target group and distribute my products to that store.

Those are just a few examples to show you that private individuals don't have to be the only target market to think about. In many cases, businesses can be good buyers for your products or services. They might be able to spend more money than private individuals, and they might also buy a higher quantity from you.

Business Model Blueprints

If you are at the stage in your journey where you are looking for an idea of what you can bring to market and how you can create value for others, sometimes, a bit of inspiration can be helpful. One tool that I find helpful is to think about different models for changemaking and creating businesses.

These models I call "Business Model Blueprints". Here are some models that you can take inspiration from to create and come up with new ideas. Again, it is important to only take this as a starting point for creativity. In the end, it is important that you feel emotionally connected to your idea and project. If it excites you and creates value, then you have a great starting point.

Here are some of the Business Model Blueprints that I keep in mind when searching for new ideas. They are not complete, however, and you could come up with more ideas.

My Business Model Blueprints are as follows:

- Create a product for a specific audience.
- Sell a product that someone else created to a specific audience.
- Rent a product that someone else created to a specific audience.
- Create a service for a specific audience.
- Sell a service that someone else is offering to a specific audience at a commission.
- Create an experience for a specific audience; for example, an event or a conference.
- Create content; for example, a book, brochure, or CD for a specific audience.

Further Blueprints for creating value are as follows:

- Make an expensive product cheaper.
- Bring a service that is physically far away from customers closer to them.
- Make a service easier for customers to access.
- Educate a target group about a service or product that is yet unknown to them but might be of value to them.
- Create a service around a product (e.g. don't sell the hammer and nails; sell the construction service).
- Make a service that people will buy repeatedly, such as a subscription service.

You could take these business model blueprints, add them to a matrix, and ask specific questions for each blueprint regarding a certain specific audience that might help you come up with new ideas.

And for each box, you can ask yourself:

1. What problem, challenge, or desire does this specific audience have?
2. How could I help solve one of their challenges, or supply something they want, through that specific Blueprint?
3. What could be my specific offer and how much will I charge to provide this value?

Here is how such a matrix could look:

Specific Audience / Blueprints	1st semester students at university	Shop owners	Farmers	Elderly people	Construction workers
Create a service					
Create a product					
Sell someone else's product					
Create content					

Table 17: Business Model Blueprints Case Studies of Projects from Past Competitions

Another great way to come up with new ideas, and to learn and find "models", is to model the behavior or successful ideas of others, and then find ways to improve upon them.

In order to give you some inspiration, we wanted to share examples of business projects that other young people started in past competitions. Again, we are sure that you will be able to come up with your own ideas, but sometimes a little bit of inspiration can be helpful to start setting our minds in motion and on the path of creativity. Here a few case studies of past ventures.

Case studies from past ventures are as follows:

- Sami Ullah Khan started his changemaking journey at the age of 17. He came across the founder of YES Network Pakistan, Mr. Ali Raza Khan, in a community session. Sami expressed his strong desire and commitment to providing education and skill development opportunities to the children of his displaced community members who migrated from Bangladesh and were living in deplorable conditions in Green Town, Lahore. Mr. Ali was very impressed by his missionary spirit and decided to work with him to establish an education center for the displaced children and young people of his community. They decided to engage half-educated young people, mostly girls of displaced families, to serve as teachers and administrators due to the absence of government support, infrastructure, and financial means. Ms. Anjum Rasheed, who discontinued her education after the 8th grade, Ms. Saeeda Rasool, who quit her education in 10th grade, and Ms. Yasmin Khan, who discontinued her education after 9th grade, joined as the first batch of teachers and counselors for children. This youth engagement strategy worked out very well, as not only did it engage left-out young people in the delivery of education to underserved children, but also helped them resume their studies from the nominal stipend received from the education center. The journey started by setting up camps in empty plots. Sami made the best use of the limited resources available, and without the support from the government, the education center managed to benefit over 3,000 children and young people. 250 people completed their graduation and 125 were provided with job opportunities.

- Muddasir Rehman is a compassionate young man. He started his changemaking journey when he was a teenager. He was lucky enough to get an opportunity to participate in a session on "Youth-Led Changemaking" in his vocational training institution in Jhang City. The session changed his life and mindset. The session helped him to look at his life in a different way and realize that opportunities are far greater than problems. He was inspired by the idea of driving a change in his community. He was genuinely concerned about the excessive energy crisis in his area, and decided to take seed money from YES to produce low-cost emergency lights. With the seed money, Muddasir began his changemaking journey. He put in a lot of hard work, and soon, created a successful prototype. His invention earned him the respect and admiration of his teachers and community members. He got excited and decided to expand his project. Today, he is the owner of a solar company which is providing services across the country. He is also teaching students in the institution where he got the education. *"I give all the credit of my success to YES Network Pakistan for helping me break personal and psychological barriers in order to become a hero from zero. I am also thankful to my teachers for arranging the opportunity for me to participate in the changemaking project of YES. My life altogether has been changed. I never realized before in my life that I am so gifted and talented,"* says Muddasir.

- Shah Mehmood is a young man from the Federally Administered Tribal Area (FATA), who is proud of his heritage and wants his area to be seen in a positive light in the world. Shah Mehmood realized that the best way to build a positive image of his area in the world is to showcase the local sports talent. He strongly felt that due to a lack of avenues for recreational and outdoor activities, the youth is badly affected. Instead of engaging themselves in productive and constructive tasks, young people are getting involved in violent and criminal activities. The young residents of Mehmood's area have no sports facility, whereas the youngsters are quite talented in the region, particularly in cricket and other sports. He was lucky to participate in a "Changemaking Session" organized by YES in his area, and a world of possibilities opened up for him. He came up with an idea to set up a "Cricket Academy" in his area. He arranged the required items for starting a coaching academy, including bats, balls, nets, and a physical trainer. The players who were playing in the streets got the opportunity to play in an environment where they could actually practice their best cricket techniques. Mehmood knew that the youngsters were full of talent, but due to an unavailability of coaches and guidance, these players could not make their place in national cricket yet. Mehmood's academy focused on teaching batting, balling, and fielding techniques. In a short period of time, his cricket academy has produced and unleashed outstanding local players who have been selected by the National Cricket Academy of Pakistan for further training and coaching from international coaches. He has established strong links with the supreme cricket governing body of Pakistan. He has met the chairman of the Pakistan Cricket Board at several locations and is often invited for meetings and consultations. Not only did Mehmood manage to provide a platform to the several hundred vulnerable youth of his area, but he is also earning by providing coaching services to them. *"I am committed to train young players of my region to help them grow in their favourite sports, such as cricket,"* says Mehmood. Mehmood aims to start coaching academies in other Tehsils as well.

Further Case Examples: Starting Up a Health Service Enterprise

- Enrolled in the Masters for Business Administration program, Zabi Ullah took part in "Show Your Creativity" with the intention of getting practical experience of the theories he was studying in his coursework. He involved four other classmates who were interested in setting up a small-scale social enterprise. The team met quite a few times before deciding on their final product idea. They opened up a small-scale laboratory in their local area which provided services such as blood tests, sugar tests, and cholesterol tests. With the initial investment, the group members bought the required instruments. They pitched in some personal money, as the cost of instruments was more than the initial investment. *"I knew this was a brilliant concept which not only helped the community create health awareness, but which we would also be able to make a profit from. Therefore, being the team leader, I encouraged all the group members to invest some money of their own,"* says Zabi. After buying all the required instruments, the team hired some medical experts to run the tests, as they themselves, were business students and did not have the relevant expertise. Zabi was successful in getting voluntary services from some of the medics in the area, as he explained the concept of healthy community to them. The experts committed to giving some time from their jobs to the social cause – these voluntary services helped them save a lot of money. Furthermore, the team kept the tests at a low cost so that more and more people could afford it. Together, the team served more than 200 individuals, and earned total revenue of PKR 10,500. Zabi explained that the exercise was extremely helpful for the entire team, as they understood the nitty gritty of conducting a business.

- At the young age of 18, Asia has already designed a strategy to address the rapid increase of Hepatitis B and C cases among the poor families in Pakistan. A student of the Vocational Training Institute, Asia got involved in the Social Enterprise competition initiated by the British Council and YES Network Pakistan. Her entry focused on ways to reduce the threat of Hepatitis B and C among impoverished communities in Lahore. Backed by her training and the seed money, Asia developed a system of services that addresses prevention, treatment, and rehabilitation. She started by going door-to-door in selected communities to carry out tests to efficiently identify people at risk. Then she recommended interventions to manage their health issues before they get worse. Finally, she gave reference support to people who are suffering from Hepatitis. Breaking down social and cultural barriers to create awareness and establishing her own credibility among the community proved challenging. Dedicated to her cause, Asia has provided services to more than

5,000 poor people so far. *"Participation in the social entrepreneurship project was a life-changing experience for me. I used to only see problems and never bothered to look for solutions."* says Asia. *"Now, all I think about is finding solutions to problems."* Asia also prepares girls of her community to participate in such projects. Determined to take her idea to the national level, Asia wants to establish collection centers in Lahore and its adjacent areas and to construct a hospital for patients of Hepatitis.

- Childhood is an age of playfulness, dreams, and freedom from the cares of the world. For Yousaf, a young man from Multan, childhood memories included the haunting images of many men, women, and children from around his community dying from the much-feared Dengue fever. Now, many years later, the threat of the fatal fever was still present. Yousaf knew that using mosquito repellent was not enough to keep the threat of Dengue at bay. He wanted to come up with a solution that would help keep away all types of mosquitoes, and other insects, too. When Yousaf found out about the Social Enterprise Challenge Competition, he rushed at the opportunity to participate. His idea of creating an effective and economical insect repelling device was appreciated, and Yousaf was granted the seed money that he needed to start his project. After receiving the required technical training and finances, Yousaf set about creating the insect repelling device. He faced initial hurdles and delays when importing most of the components of the device, but he kept on working on his dream of a Dengue-free environment. His perseverance paid off and he was able to complete his project. He spread awareness amongst the people about his device by going door-to-door and convincing people about its affordability and usage. At present, over 250 households in Multan use his device. Yousaf has managed to make over Rs. 45,000 because of his hard work, and he feels proud that he made such a positive contribution to his community.

Further Case Examples: Starting Up a Project Caring for the Environment

- Belonging to the district of Sibbi, Nargis had big dreams when she was enrolled in the Bachelors program in a university in Quetta. At the age of only 19, she was not only studying Environmental Science, but was an active member of the university and taking part in various extracurricular activities. She had passion for growth and learning new concepts. Hearing about the "Show Your Creativity" competition in her institute, she immediately made a team of four members, including herself, and got registered. Nargis and her team brainstormed for a couple of hours before deciding on using waste material to make attractive decoration arrangements. *"I was studying environmental science; therefore, I knew the importance of keeping the environment clean and healthy. In this competition, I wanted to highlight how every individual could use certain material from their daily waste and put it to some good use,"* shared Nargis. Nargis and her team collected various materials for the decoration arrangements to ensure that they would be attractive so that their products would be bought by the people. With the initial investment money, the team bought raw material, such as baskets, colorful ribbons, shining spray, and multicolor markers. The team used other waste material, such as empty tissue boxes, to come up with a list of decoration items which could be put up in homes. They made fancy dustbins, baskets for oral arrangements, photo frames, wall hangings, tissue boxes, and pencil boxes for children. Nargis mentioned that while the team was working, customers had already started booking their products. She mentioned that some of her products were sold even before the team set up the display at the stall. The team earned total revenue of PKR 4,000. *"One should always put in hard work and dedication. This is the way to go, because if you put in these two elements anywhere, you will get great results,"* said Nargis, while sharing how her team was completely supportive of each other. She mentioned that they not only learned new things, but also enjoyed taking part in the competition.

- A young man hailing from Toba Tek Singh, Usman is a firm believer in the power of the human spirit. He believes that there are no boundaries and limitations to what people can achieve, and that if they work hard enough, they can get whatever they want. Fate provided him the opportunity to follow his beliefs when he participated in the Social Entrepreneurship workshop held by the YES Network Pakistan and the British Council. His city suffered from a major energy crisis with 20-hour long load shedding on a daily basis that crippled its entire infrastructure. Businesses came to a grinding halt; daily household chores became an impossible task, and life, in general, became miserable. Usman decided to help his community by manufacturing solar energy panels for homes. Armed with the technical training and finances required for his project, Usman started installing solar panels in people's homes. His community welcomed his brilliant effort, as they no longer had to worry about prolonged power outages. Attending the workshop proved to be a major turning point for Usman; it gave him the training to use his idea to benefit his society and make a positive difference in the quality of life within his community.

- Like his peers, Nazim believed that people in his community did not possess any social conscience or desire for prosperity and development, as they had become accustomed to poor living conditions and a substandard lifestyle. His instructor at the Vocational Training Institute, where he studied, attended the social entrepreneurship workshop organized by the British Council and YES Network Pakistan, and then encouraged his students to participate as well. The information and encouragement he received from the workshop revived his faith in the human spirit, and he started to believe that if a change was needed, then all one had to do was take the initiative. He formed a team to pitch an idea to help the environment by starting a community-based solid waste management system, in which they would collect, manage, reduce, and transform waste material to manure and biogas. They faced a lot of discouragement and skepticism from their families and community members about the nature of their job. The Local Municipal Corporation and sanitary workers also refused to cooperate with this unpleasant project. However, the team did not give up, and decided to collect and lift the garbage themselves. They helped 342 households by collecting their waste material and improving their sanitation system.

Further Mixed Case Examples

- Being a humble resident of Rawlakot, Azad Jammu and Kashmir, Bilal Akhtar did not have the faintest idea of the turn his life was going to take a few months down the road. He was a natural-born entrepreneur, but his dreams of making a difference lacked direction. When the YES Network Pakistan visited his hometown, he was more than just keen to attend the workshop on youth-led changemaking and learn from it. Guided by the training provided by the workshop, Bilal put forth his idea of setting up a beekeeping farm to produce honey on a large scale. After conducting an initial market survey on honey farming in his area, Bilal began setting up his own farming facility with the help of the money granted by the YES Network Pakistan. He hired six young people from his locality and was soon producing honey for his community. He says that even though running a beekeeping business was not an easy profession to choose, he took it very seriously and was soon reaping profits from his hard work. In the first year of production, he and his team earned a profit of Rs. 150,000. At present, Bilal runs a private technical institution in Rawlakot where he encourages innovation, creativity and self-employment among his students. According to him, 'Participation in the changemaking competition was the most rewarding experience of my life. It altered my thinking and philosophy of life. I learnt that one has to take personal responsibility for living a better and happier life.'

- 29-year-old Nazia Parveen is a student of the Vocational Training Center in Sahansa, Kotli. During her time at the Vocational Training Center, Nazia developed a desire to utilize her skills to help young girls and women around her. After consulting with her teacher, Madam Farzana, Nazia set about her dream by conducting stitching classes of her own for young girls. She is a firm believer in the independence and self-reliance of women, and by teaching them how to stitch, Nazia says she can help them achieve that goal. Through unparalleled devotion to her work and a sheer passion for pursuing her dream, Nazia manages to earn up to Rs. 20,000 per month. Forever thankful to her teacher for her guidance and opening a completely new world of possibilities for her, Nazia is looking to expand her business and explore new avenues of providing entrepreneurship opportunities for the women of her area. At present, Nazia teaches around 20 to 25 girls how to stitch, and urges more women to come forth and play an active role in society and participate in new projects and initiatives.

- *"Working as a female social entrepreneur in a strictly male-dominated society is a challenging job,"* says Shaiza, a young resident of Kotli, Azad Kashmir. The women of Kotli had great difficulty purchasing certain items of necessity, like undergarments, from shops run by men, because their community is strictly conservative. With the seed money received as part of the Social Enterprise Challenge, Shazia, along with a group of girls, decided to open a shop exclusively for women, which was also run by women. Shazia is a strong advocate of female empowerment, and this shop is a bold step in her effort to bring the world of social enterprise to the women of her community. *"Becoming an entrepreneur at this very young age feels great. Women come to me and appreciate my effort, and get inspired to do something of their own,"* she says. Shazia is now considered a successful entrepreneur in her community; she has employed 2 women who support their families through this job.

Okay, we hope that you got a lot of inspiration and encouragement from the examples mentioned above. In the end, the most important thing to remember is that you have all the tools and everything you need to move forward. All it requires is courage. Courage is the key to take the first step into the unknown. Everything unfolds from there. Trust yourself, and trust that you are greater than your doubts or fears. You were born great, and if you have a dream and an idea that inspires you, then you can trust that it will set you on the way to personal growth and becoming a changemaker.

The real measure of success is not how much money you have or how many people applaud you. The real measure of success is within: Did you dare to dream, take action on your ideas, and have the courage to trust? Did you dare to explore your potential and follow your heart? Did you dare to take a leap of faith? Or did you always hide in the safety zone where you were robbing yourself and the world of the potential you did not choose to activate and explore?

We encourage you to live more fully; to create, to contribute, and to trust the magnificence that resides within you to create and make a positive change.

Chapter 8

STARTING YOUR OWN CHANGEMAKING JOURNEY

Introduction

This chapter is written to facilitate young people in doing things which are beyond their home and school. Young people are encouraged to act and lead to improve the quality of life around them.

We are living in a society which is facing unprecedented challenges to address, and which provides plenty of opportunity for sincere and selfless actions to take, inspiring stories to write, new laws to be made, real problems to be solved, greater justice to be sought, and unconditional efforts to be made to preserve landscapes and heritage.

Unfortunately, our society has failed to produce changemakers at all levels of society. Our institutions are developing a *one-track mind* in young people. Our families, communities, and educational systems are following a very passive and exhausted track to empower young people.

They have failed to unlock the changemaking potential of young people. It is a sad reality that millions of young people are out of touch with society, and too busy with their hectic routines and repetitive procedures. They are pre-occupied in gaining only knowledge and skills from society. It is high time to shift the focus of young people from reading heavy textbooks and memorizing what other people have done, to unfolding their own myth. There is so much left for young people to do.

Young people can't afford to miss this remarkable opportunity to make a difference in the lives of others. This book is written to enable young people to begin their changemaking journey and to take control of their lives at an early age. Equipping young people with a new vision to become changemakers will not only help them escape poverty, but it will also help them address serious issues that are slowing down the progress of our society. It will help young people look at their lives in a different way and realize that the opportunities are far greater than the problems.

Instead of repeating knowledge and skills, young people will be involved in discovering their inherent changemaking potential for paving new paths by leaving behind their doubts and the idea that ending up with a well-paid job is the only way forward in life. There is a serious shortage of material available on the market that prepares youth to become changemakers.

This chapter provides basic information about starting and running a changemaking project. Hopefully, it will inspire young people to consider self-employment, Changemaking, and conscious entrepreneurship as viable career options.

This chapter guides young people through the various steps of turning an idea into reality. At each step, young people will learn how their natural changemaking abilities can be used to address a community need, create a social and economic impact, solve a social problem, or create an enterprise that empowers people and spreads the wealth equally.

I want to ask a few simple questions to young people. Are you waiting for a good job? Are you tired of broken promises? Are you sick and tired of endless persecution? Are you tired of seeing people in hopeless and helpless conditions? Do you have any desire to serve others? Or are you just waiting for things to happen?

Starting Your Own Changemaking Journey

We spend most of our lives waiting. Waiting for the right opportunities, waiting for jobs, waiting for promises to be fulfilled, waiting for references, waiting for money to start a new business, waiting for someone to trust in you.

While we wait for all these things to happen, we miss out on the things happening right now.

This book is written to break this old paradigm, and to assist young people with becoming changemakers during their studies, turning their dreams into reality, and helping young people to think big. Young people studying in schools, colleges, universities, and technical institutions are growing up with the hope that, as soon as they finish their education and training, they will find exciting jobs. They are unable to see that there are already little-to-no jobs on the market. Their desire to become self-reliant and independent will remain a fantasy for many of them. It is important for young people to find and use their naturally gifted changemaking abilities.

This book is meant to provide an inspiration to young people to build a new societal structure by doing what they feel needs to be done.

It is not enough to just think about government jobs. Your goal in life should not be to secure a government or long-term job.

You are blessed with natural changemaking abilities to start and run your own business with social objectives. These natural powers include your abilities to express yourself, inspire others, drive change, and show love and respect to others. Your passion and ideas are needed. You can produce a product or a service that you can sell. And you can make a difference.

There are several benefits of becoming a changemaker. These benefits include:

- You can drive a change;
- You can choose your own path;

- You can change lives;
- You are responsible for your own income;
- You are responsible for your own progress;
- You are free to experiment and test new ideas;
- You can show creativity and innovation;
- You decide your own working hours;
- You can't get fired from your job;
- You are not required to report to someone;
- You can choose who you work with;
- You can choose to work cooperatively; and
- Depending on the set-up of your business, you can also decide where you work from and how often you work.

Breaking the Myths About Changemaking

A large amount of money is required to begin a changemaking project: It is a myth that a large amount of money is required to start and run a changemaking project. We have already proved this wrong in our work. We have engaged over 16,000 young people recently in changemaking by providing them with a very small amount of money. We have mentioned above that students receiving funds as low as PKR 100 (US$1) were still able to make a serious social impact and a huge percentage of profits in a short period of time. The most important thing young people need today is trust. Young people thrive on trust. When young people are trusted, they immediately bring into play their inherent changemaking abilities. Trust breeds desire in young people. We have found through our work that strong desires produce strong results, and weak desires produce weak results.

Changemaking requires a lot of degrees and diplomas: Young people believe that changemaking is only possible if you have a large number of degrees and certificates. Degrees and certificates certainly help you in many ways, but they are not the only decider of your success or failure. There are many examples of leading changemakers who, without even having basic degrees, accomplished unparalleled success. We should remember that Thomas Edison had only 3 months of formal schooling, after which his mother homeschooled him. Henry Ford had less than 6th-grade schooling, but he managed to do pretty well financially. Albert Einstein was a high school dropout before completing his schooling and becoming the most well-known physicist. He went on to publish more than 300 scientific papers. Abraham Lincoln was not well-educated. William Shakespeare was a middle school dropout. He is a man credited with the invention of 1,700 new words. Lastly, we should not forget the example of Bill Gates, who dropped out of Harvard University to pursue his dream. In short, changemaking is possible without a formal degree. Any person who can inspire people with knowledge, skills, resources, and the achievement of a plan is just well-educated as anyone else.

Changemaking is not possible at a young age: We are indoctrinated to believe many untrue things. One of the myths we are following is that changemaking is not possible at a young age. In my work, I have thousands of examples of children and young people who embark upon a changemaking journey at a very young age. Many great changemakers of the world started their journey when they were in their teens. It is an open secret that changemaking is possible at any age. There is no pre-condition or specific age to become a changemaker.

Changemaking requires skills: I believe changemaking requires the application of inherent changemaking abilities. I met so many young people in my work who are highly skilled, but seriously struggling to find a place in society. Their skills are not helping them move forward in life. I believe that you don't need to go somewhere to learn changemaking. It is already a part of you. You don't pray for something you already have. You don't go and buy something you already possess. You need to simply capitalize on it, or connect to it. God has equipped everyone with a changemaking kit. The most important part of the kit is the human heart. I reckon that all successes and failures depend on the condition of your heart. I firmly believe that every success starts from the heart. We are often worried about equipment and tools, but they are not necessary. Only from the heart can you feel, heal, and touch the sky.

Changemaking is the domain of the privileged few: Many of us believe that changemaking is the domain of the privileged few. I find this to be completely wrong. It is not the domain of the privileged few. It is in the domain of everyone. Human beings are designed to create value and add value to society. It is amazing to see how many young people have given up so early in their lives, while they have forgotten that a goldmine lies within each of them. Everyone has the ability to deliver good and discard bad. I believe my work with young people, especially disadvantaged youth, has busted the lone hero myth. Out of 16,000 young people, 88% of them were able to create a real social and economic impact.

Changemaking is a risk: Risk is involved in everything we do. Risk is involved in excessive eating. Risk is involved in driving. Risk is involved in walking on the road. The most important thing is how you do it. Risk can be minimized by careful and creative thinking. All risks are not equal. A risk which is taken to create a value in society is far superior to a risk taken to seek short-lived pleasure. One might fail while doing something valuable for others temporarily, but one should not be worried about it; rather, one should wear that failure as a badge of honor. Like beauty, risk is in the eyes of the beholder. What looks risky to someone from the outside does not look risky to someone who is passionate about something. All great successes are built on risk-taking. I remember when I decided to engage the first batch of 6,000 young people from poor families in changemaking by providing a small seed funding, everyone thought I made a big mistake and took a huge risk. I knew inside that, if I am able to extend and restore trust with these young people, they will be successful. The results showed that my conviction proved true.

Key Steps to Begin a Changemaking Project

I firmly believe that human beings were originally created for changemaking. My mother gave me a very useful piece of advice very early in my life: that the purpose of your life should be to become useful for others. I firmly believe that changemaking is the real purpose of life. Learning about changemaking begins at home. If there is a weak foundation, or no foundation, offered to children for changemaking, it will weaken their changemaking spirit. The changemaking spirit dies when we live in an environment where changemaking abilities are not practiced. Good actions strengthen our changemaking spirit and bad actions weaken our changemaking spirit.

Changemaking begins with your ability to see the difference between right and wrong, and good and bad. The drive for changemaking often stems from our moral training and moral responsibility. Changemaking abilities are nurtured in an environment filled with love, care, respect, and responsibility. The degeneration of the changemaking spirit is done at an early age. It is very sad to see that a large number of young people have abandoned and gotten out of touch with their changemaking abilities and inherent potential.

How can we begin the process of regenerating the youth-led changemaking spirit?

The best way to begin this process is to engage young people in changemaking in an organized and structured manner. The superior ability to contribute of one individual in comparison to another does not come from the possession of a greater amount of education and skills, but from the more developed ability to use their inherent changemaking abilities.

We are all born with a Changemaking kit. I reckon the most important tool of this changemaking kit is the human heart. If the heart works well, everything works well. The heart is able to direct the ears, eyes, and the brain. If the heart gets filled with greed, all other human faculties ceased to support changemaking. A corrupt heart is not fit for changemaking. A conquered heart is a heart where changemaking is the central motivation.

Often, a changemaking journey starts when someone shows trust in your abilities, when you feel the need to bring change in the lives of others, and when you decide to change the status quo.

Build a Youth-Led Changemaking Team

The best way to begin your changemaking journey is to form a youth-led changemaking team. The size of the team should not be very small, nor too big to handle. In our work, we recommend that young people form a youth-led changemaking team of 3 to 5 members who share a common interest and are committed to bring change to their personal lives and their community.

It is important that all the members of the youth-led changemaking team are willing to give a few hours of their time on a daily basis. For a changemaking project to be successful, you need the right team members. It is very important that all team members share the same passion, goals, values, and vision.

A person should not be selected into the team simply because they want to be on the team. The goals of the team should be considered as the yardstick for the selection of team members. Before selecting any team member, ask yourself: Does this person have something to contribute to the team? Can they be trusted with working towards the common vision?

Also, the necessary size of the team is based on the requirements to accomplish the task at hand.

Take a cricket team, for example. The selector and coach invest a lot of time in making sure they choose the right players for the team. The players don't have the power to put themselves on the team. It is the job of the selector and coach. It would be imprudent for them to select someone who does not deserve to be on the team. The best team members know and understand each other, they support and respect each other, and they share credit with each other. If one incompetent person is selected on the team, the whole team's dynamics can be destroyed.

Here are some ways to make a youth-led changemaking team successful and effective:

- Aims and activities are set by the members of the team.
- There is open communication and discussion within the team.
- Everyone participates in discussions and exercises.
- Team members attend meetings regularly.
- There is a method for coping with new members and for what happens when people leave the team.
- Evaluation and feedback is encouraged in the team.
- Acceptance of all the team members is encouraged.
- There is a high level of trust in the team.
- Conflict or disagreement is open and constructive.

Developing a Changemaking Plan

The following are the basic steps for developing a changemaking project:

Identify the Problem (Opportunity)

The next step in starting your changemaking journey is to identify a specific problem or opportunity. Remember that you can't solve all the problems simultaneously. A problem is a gap between what you would like to see in the world, or what you would like to be, and what it actually is. The best way to select a problem is by using different techniques, such as the observation technique, the personal experience technique, the survey technique, and the data analysis technique.

Talk to the people to find out how they feel about the problem. You can get the best information directly from those who are affected by the problem, or from other sources, such as newspapers, local stakeholders, and local organizations. Verify the information gathered by making observational visits to the target communities.

One good way of identifying and understanding the problem further is to gather as many people as you can from a variety of interests for a **problem tree session**.

Discuss with them what the main problem is and what the causes are, and try to get to the very bottom of every cause. Stick some cards on a wall or use sticky note paper to "drill down" and get to the root of every cause. Then, look at the effects of the problem in the same way. This exercise will help everyone understand the problem fully and enable the institution or community to see what can be solved through a changemaking project, and who you need to work with to attack other causes of the problem.

The other way is to look around at your institution or community. What are the major problems? Are there any areas which are totally neglected? Are there any places which are being destroyed? Are there any people who are seriously struggling due to poverty, homelessness, drug abuse, or hunger? Are there any people who are facing inequalities? The challenge won't be finding a problem. The challenge will be creating a solution.

Developing a Vision

What change in the environment would you ultimately want to see? Imagine what the change would be if the problem was solved. The vision would give you a sense of power and a reason for your changemaking project. If the vision is speaking to your heart and inspires you, you know that you are on a good track. The vision is also something that you can turn to, again and again, to gather the strength to continue on your changemaking journey.

Establish Goals and Benchmarks

Creating specific goals and benchmarks based on your vision and priorities is very important. It helps you break down the tasks that are needed so that you can organize your plan, explain it to others, and get everything done in the right order. It also allows you to focus on specific priorities, rather than becoming overwhelmed by the entire task. BE REALISTIC with your goals! Things take time.

Your short-term goals should be fairly specific, as you will start to work on them right away. For now, your mid and long-term goals can be more general. You need to expect them to change somewhat as the initiative, project, or program begins to take shape. As you complete the first set of goals, be sure to go back and revise and expand upon the next set.

Theory of Change

Every changemaking project has a theory of change. The theory of change can be described as a pathway, blueprint, or theory of action. It could be described as a hypothesis about which actions and conditions will lead to which results, or in mathematical terms: is something like if "conditions = X then change = Y".

Without a clear theory of change, a youth-led changemaking team cannot accomplish anything. A theory of change is a way of thinking about how the outcomes of your activities will ultimately lead to your desired social impact. For example: If low-income, disadvantaged girls have first-hand experience for running a business, they will be more successful in their lives. This is a hypothesis or theory until it is tested practically and validated through observation.

Solutions

Solutions can be defined as your response to the problem in the shape of the creation of a product or a service. Solutions describe the key activities needed to achieve your vision and mission.

The solution is developed in light of the existing services or products that are provided to your target group. In the solution stage, you investigate the lifestyle of your target group. For example, what is their socioeconomic background? Where do they live? What does their typical day look like?

Then you can get busy creating a solution aimed at solving the problem. Always keep customer feedback and your personal observations in mind. Think up as many ideas as possible. After you have made a long list of potential solutions, analyze each one carefully.

There might be many ways to accomplish a goal. If you wanted to help young people, for example, you could have many approaches that might benefit young people, such as:

- We will help children learn to read by serving as tutors.
- We will help children and girls learn computer skills by serving as trainers.
- We will help reduce crime in our community by organizing a public dialogue between police authorities and community members.
- We will install a water filtration plant in a village to provide clean drinking water.
- We will establish a hepatitis diagnostic center in a village to provide low-cost testing and referral services to poor people.

Social Impact

It is the effect of changemaking projects on individuals, families, and society. The purpose of launching a changemaking project is to bring a social change. The assessment of social impact helps to measure the performance against the established goals and objectives. It helps youth-led changemaking teams with planning better, implementing carefully, and scaling-up successfully. Remember that, in most cases, the only ones who can truly measure the successful impact of the changemaking project are those who are directly affected by the problem and the ones you are trying to help, so get them involved in this discussion from the very beginning.

Financial Plan

A financial plan is the most important component of the changemaking project. The first step to develop a financial plan is to identify costs associated with implement a changemaking project. The financial plan must also include an income generation plan.

Good changemaking projects pursue both earned and unearned income strategies to meet their goals. The major difference between a changemaking project and volunteer work is the creation of social AND economic value simultaneously. A charity-based organization always looks for donations and funds to meet its expenses, while a changemaking project relies on both approaches for sustaining and expanding its services. Changemaking projects should look to exploit additional avenues of finance and resources that a normal business cannot access. The institution or community being helped may be prepared to support the changemaking project through their own fundraising, using their own resources (e.g. allowing the use of a building for free or other such non-monetary resources).

Today, many philanthropists prefer to look at social investments, rather than donations to charities. You can also raise social investments from many small investors working together (also known as crowdfunding or crowd investing). When solving a social problem, also think about how your changemaking project is contributing to the global picture.

Your financial strategy should also include raising money from that contribution by joining international partnerships or working with others who are carrying out similar interventions. You may also use these avenues to set up a model that you can franchise to other communities or countries.

Setting Up a Changemaking Organization

A youth-led changemaking idea can be incorporated as a separate entity in the three most prevalent types. These are:

1. **Non-profit organization:** Ideas that focus sharply on social impact tend to convert into non-profit organizations.

2. **Profit organization:** Ideas that focus on economic value creation prefer to convert into profit-oriented organizations.
3. **Social enterprise:** Ideas that focus on both social and economic impact tend to go for social enterprises.

While selecting the nature of the institutional structure, several factors should be taken into consideration:

- *Legal Environment:* The legal environment varies from country to country. The legal framework for setting up non-profit and profitable organizations is available in both developing and developed countries, while the legal framework for setting up social enterprises is non-existent in many countries, with the exception of the developed countries such as the United Kingdom, the United States, and Germany. When selecting the type of institutional structure, the purpose of existence, impact measurement, source of income, use of income, and ownership-related issues should be considered carefully.

- *Funding and Income Generation:* Organizations secure their financing through a variety of different instruments, such as donor funding, loans, and selling a product or service. When selecting the legal status, the income generation and business plan of the organization should be examined carefully. For-profit organizations generate income by providing products or services. Non-profit organizations generate their income mainly through donations and donor funding. Social enterprises use entrepreneurship approaches to create social and economic value.

- *Ownership Structures:* There are three main types of ownership structures that currently exist: public, private, and collective. Public ownership means "property of the public". It indicates that the governing body has the major responsibility to ensure transparency and accountability. The income generated should be reinvested, or can be paid out through dividends to the shareholders. Non-profit organizations have public ownership.

The founder of the public (non-profit) organization has no power to sell the organization or liquidate the assets for personal profit. Private ownership means "ownership by a single individual, a family (family business), or by several people that are not family members, or even different entities (for example, in the case of a joint venture)". The owner or owners of the private enterprise have the power to sell the organization, take all the profit, and expand or reduce business operations. The individual or family, or their entity, is liable to pay taxes. Collective ownership means that "a group of individuals, non-profits, or for-profits come together to achieve intended objectives (social or economic or both)". This collective ownership can be registered as a non-profit, for-profit, or social enterprise.

Young people often find it difficult to choose either a non-profit or profit-oriented structure to set up a separate entity. There are advantages and disadvantages of setting-up profit-oriented or non-profit organizations.

Profit-oriented organizations	Non-profit organizations
Can reinvest the profits or pay them out to the owners.	Has to reinvest all the income back into the programs.
Workers are mostly employees only. In some scenarios, there can also be incentive programs, such as an employee shareholder program.	Can develop a highly motivated team of workers who may share ownership of the programs and are committed to the social purpose.
Has no real connection with the community built into its DNA by default. If a connection to the community is to be established, it requires willing leadership in the company.	Is likely to have full support of the community who will be willing to help the programs in many ways.

Long-term customer loyalty might be more difficult to be achieved by a "normal" business than by a non-profit, or a business with a double or triple bottom-line.	Have loyal customers who buy the added value of the social benefit being created.
Mostly more difficult access to donor funding. There might be grants or prizes available for social enterprises with a double or triple bottom-line, or especially innovative businesses.	Creating benefits can also attract additional funding from donors who are also concerned about the problems being solved.
Mostly rely on commercial loans only.	The social purpose of the programs can attract social investors who are happy to give loans at very favorable rates.
For-profit enterprises have to make an extra effort to mobilize the support of volunteers. Some social businesses or businesses that have raving fans can win people and organizations to join in their mission.	The social purpose can attract volunteers to either help with the delivery of a service, provide free advice and support, or be volunteer board members.
For-profit enterprises have to make an extra effort to gather the support of networks and civil society organizations.	Are supported by networks of civil society organizations who will gladly help each other.

Table 17: Differences Between Profit and Non-Profit Organizations

How to Establish a Non-Profit Organization

The following are the steps to establish a non-profit organization:

Forming a Board of Directors

When setting up a changemaking organization, the founder(s) must recruit the board of directors carefully. It is important to understand that the first board of the changemaking organization plays a very important role in determining the future of the organization. Various factors should be kept in mind while recruiting the first board of directors, such as relevant experience, technical skills, credibility, availability, legal and financial knowledge, integrity, and commitment, as well as current profession. Common mistakes made when recruiting the first board of directors include: selecting relatives, selecting political leaders, selecting friends that are not otherwise qualified or interested, selecting highly influential personalities that use the position only for marketing purposes without adding any other value, and/or selecting someone who is not available.

Choosing a Name for the Changemaking Organization

Choosing a name for the changemaking organization is a very important task. The name of the changemaking organization should be chosen after critical thinking and reflection. It is important to check with intellectual property organizations and copyright organizations about the availability of the chosen name. It is better to avoid any jargon, flashy words, or languages while choosing the name of the changemaking organization. It is better to choose a name which is easy to pronounce and remember. The same thinking should also be applied to the logo that the changemaking organization is going to have.

Drafting Bylaws of the Changemaking Organization

Bylaws of the changemaking organization will specify how it will function. They explain the purpose of the organization, the board size, the responsibilities of the board members, the criteria for selecting the board of directors, the length of memberships, the structure, the distribution of power, the financial accountability, and the decision-making process. Bylaws are the ruling documents of an organization. It is better to keep the bylaws as brief as possible. Bylaws should set forth the basic structure and abilities of the board. Everything else – such as policy recommendations – should be kept elsewhere. It is good practice to set up a rulebook and make sure that it is present at all meetings. These rules can cover a wide variety of things, like personal conduct or office procedure, and can be changed at any time through agreement. It is useful for new people to read when they join, but the rules should be looked at from time to time to see what sort of values are being expressed. Ensure that you also add those values to the values statement.

Registration of the Changemaking Organization

There are several categories of registration available. Changemaking organization can be registered as a non-profit, a social enterprise, a hybrid, or a private enterprise. More information and application forms for registration can be sought on the internet.

When setting up a changemaking organization, you should answer these questions before deciding on the legal route to pursue:

- Who will be the owner(s)?
- Who will govern and who will manage?
- Who will be accountable for it?
- Who will be the main beneficiaries?

Setting Up a Financial System for the Social Enterprise Business Organization

Every organization needs a sound, transparent, and efficient financial system. A financial system records where funds come from and how they are used. It also ensures checks and balances, as well as internal control. It is important to decide whether the bookkeeping should be cash or accrual. In cash-based accounting, the revenue is recorded when added to a bank account, and expenses are recorded when money is withdrawn from the bank. This is a very simple system. It tells how much funds are available in the bank account and nothing more. It does not reveal how much money might be owed to the organization.

In accrual-based accounting, you record revenue when it is earned (even before or after it is received) and expenses when incurred (even before or after payment). Accrual-based accounting is efficient because it provides a broader picture. It allows an organization to see not just its immediate payments and deposits, but also what kind of money they owe or may be receiving in the future. This allows an organization to be more aware of its financial situation. It is very important to seek the services of an accountant who can help with financial management. Board members can be very helpful in finding or referring someone for financial management. Often, start-up organizations start with a volunteer accountant or a part-time accountant. The characteristics of an ineffective financial system include: the founder/CEO managing finance in isolation and with inadequate board oversight, no system of reporting financial information, no connection to outside financial expertise or resources, and/or no system for managing accounts payable and receivable.

Developing an Income Generation Plan

Developing a sound income generation plan is crucial to the success of the organization. It is important for the founder and board of directors to develop a fundraising plan that is realistic and reasonable for the organization's situation. It is important that the board members are willing and able to help raise funds for the organization, and that they understand that funding often comes from both earned and unearned income strategies. It is important for the organization to move away from relying solely on donor funding. There are several possible revenue sources for non-profit organizations, such as government schemes and donations from corporations, foreign funding agencies, charitable trusts, individuals, and fundraising drives.

Developing a Sound Communication Plan

The next step to establish an organization is to develop a sound communication plan for the organization. A sound communication plan helps to achieve organizational goals, showcase the success of the organization, engage diverse stakeholders, and ensure that people understand what we do and why we do it. The sound communication plan develops specific strategies for reaching out to relevant stakeholders. An effective communication plan includes the following elements:

- **Specific Audience:** Communication should be audience-specific-communication efforts that are appropriate to the different audiences the organization wants to reach or engage.

- **Reason/Objective:** The objective of the communication should be clear. Why do you want to communicate? What do you want to accomplish?

- **Channel(s) of Communication:** What methods of communication should be adopted? Today, we have many channels of communication available, both offline and online, such as websites, social networking, mobile, and blogs. When selecting a channel of communication, the target audience's access to the channel should be kept in mind.

- **Message with Benefit:** It is important to remember that, for effective communication, the benefit(s) to the audience being addressed have to be clearly communicated.

- **Frequency:** Communication must be ongoing and consistent.

Setting Up a Human Resource Management System

A human resource management system is another important step towards the establishment of an organization. An effective human resource management system includes recruitment, performance management, reward and recognition, and training and development. The features of a sound human resource management system are as follows:

- Personnel policies and procedures are in compliance with state and federal laws, are reviewed regularly, and continue to meet the needs of the organization.

- Employee information and records are kept confidential.

- Programs have accurate and clearly written job descriptions that are tied to program outcomes.

- A recruitment process is in place that attracts people with the appropriate type and level of experience to perform the work.

- There is appropriate cross-training of staff to increase motivation and productivity.

- There is a reward system in place to acknowledge the contributions of extraordinary employees.

- Supervisors understand their supervisory role and have the necessary skills to manage other employees.

- A conflict resolution policy and system for resolving conflicts among employees, volunteers, and board members is in place.

Monitoring and Evaluation of the Organization

Monitoring means keeping an on-going record of an activity as it happens. It can tell you if youth-led changemaking team activities have been implemented according to your plan. It is important to monitor your work, because regular checking gives you the information to manage things. For example, if there is a problem, you are more likely to be able to minimize any potential damage if you can find out about it as soon as possible. Monitoring also provides information for reporting and being accountable for other group members, partners, and anyone affected by the activity.

Evaluation is judging the values or effectiveness of your youth-led changemaking team. It is a way of assessing whether the activities have achieved their objectives and how. Evaluation is very important. If your project is successful, you will find it easier to do more. If it is less successful, you will need to make changes and measure whether new activities are achieving their aim. There are always lessons to be learned from any activity, whether it is successful or not. It is important to record and understand these to avoid making the same mistakes again.

Try to answer these evaluation questions.

- Have you helped change things?
- Is the situation better than before?
- If so, by how much?
- Have you accomplished your objectives?
- How have your efforts changed the big picture?
- If you have accomplished what you set out to do, did it go as you anticipated?
- If you did not accomplish what you had intended, why not?
- What would you do differently next time?
- Are the people and organizations involved in your group happy with the results of their actions?

Recordkeeping

The youth-led changemaking team should keep simple records about their activities through checklists. The youth-led changemaking team should regularly complete checklists. It will provide information about a wide range of things, for example:

- Who is attending activities?
- What accomplishments have been made?
- What targets have been missed?
- What lessons have been learned?
- How many meetings were held?
- Who attended the meetings?
- What were the decisions taken regarding the organization?

- Who was responsible for what activities?

Social and Financial Audits

As the organization grows, consider carrying out social and financial audits. This doesn't have to be too burdensome, but it is good practice to have an annual review at the end of the year which shows how the social side of operations went alongside the financial, giving it equal importance and demonstrating why the organization is a changemaking organization. The social and financial audits can help a changemaking organization identify strengths and risks, complaisance and non-compliance with laws, and areas that require improvement. Without reliable external social and financial audits, an organization has no concrete way of justifying their significance.

How to Establish a For-Profit Organization/Company

The following are the steps to establish a profitable organization:

Selecting an Inspiring Company Name

The name of the organization should be chosen carefully. The name of the organization should be unique, and easy to remember and communicate. It is better to avoid any name which is confusing and requires interpretation. The name of the organization should not be a hasty choice. The name of the organization plays an important role in the success of the company, as it often stays in the memories of your customers. It speaks volumes about the nature of your business.

Gathering Information About Types of Registration

The next step is to gather information about the options available for setting up a private organization. There are many types of registration available for the registration of private companies. A private company can be comprised of one or more members. It is obligatory for every company to declare itself as a sole proprietorship, corporation, or partnership. This information can be obtained directly from the government office or from the consulting companies. It is always good to have a meeting with someone who has actually gone through the process of registration recently. It can save time and resources.

Going Through the Requirements For Setting Up a Private Organization

There are some basic requirements to be met before setting up a private company. This includes defining purpose, paying fees, filling out forms, providing an office address, signing a commitment letter, and sharing information about shareholders (in case you are going to start in partnership with someone).

Developing Memorandum or Constitution

The memorandum or constitution provides basic information about how the company will be run by you or the directors. It will be the rulebook of the company.

Filing the Registration

The next step is to send the information about your company to the registration office. A fee will be charged to set up a private company. It may take a few weeks to get the certificate of your registration. The registration office may check or visit your office for verification.

Opening a Bank Account

After the registration of your company, the next step is to open a bank account to keep a complete record of your financial transactions. If you are running a single-member company, you can operate the bank account. If you are partnering with someone, then you have to open a joint account.

Getting Your Tax Numbers

The tax treatment for non-profits, for-profits, and social enterprises varies from country to country. It is important to acquire all required tax numbers, licenses, insurances, and permits at the beginning. The best way to get information is to have a meeting with an expert.

Appointing Director(s)

Depending on the size of your available funds, you can appoint a director of group of directors to run the company alongside you. Your company should have at least one director. The director will be legally responsible for running the company and making sure plans are executed and monitored effectively.

Setting Up An Accounting System

It is important to set up a process to review the financial performance of the company regularly. There are many accounting software packages available on the market to track the business transactions effectively and efficiently. It is better to hire a specialist to manage the account of the company.

Setting Up a Website

It is important to use social media to promote the work of your company. No one will know your products or services exist if you do not tell them about it. Use social media to take orders and receive direct feedback about the performance of your company. It is important to communicate the benefits of your product(s) or services clearly to the general public. For-profit companies often use customers and their stories to attract new customers.

Chapter 9

THE CHANGE MAKER WORKBOOK-START TODAY AND JUMP INTO ACTION!

The purpose of this workbook is to turn the theory of the first few chapters into a practical change-making experience for you.

Our curriculum is aimed at helping young people to go from students-in-waiting to students-in-action; from dependents to effective contributors, from victims to leaders, and from sheltered to shapers of society.

We can only do this with your help. So, take this material and run with it. Try it out. See what it can do for you. Be inspired, search for the answers within yourself, and you will come to know the truth that there is great potential lying dormant within you. It's time to awaken this potential. You are the one that you have been waiting for to manifest the world that you always dreamed of.

Changemaking Self-Assessment and Belief System Check: Are You a Changemaker?

I firmly believe that those who know themselves seldom fail. Knowing yourself is the beginning of changemaking. Changemaking is not possible without self-awareness. Unfortunately, our families and schools have not been very successful at helping children discover the changemaker within them. Helping children and young people understand that they are equally blessed and gifted provides a solid foundation for changemaking. It is a universal truth that, if young people don't use their inherent changemaking abilities, they will lose them.

Nothing is more disastrous in the lives of young people than thinking that they are born without gifts or changemaking abilities. This demeaning self-appraisal pushes young people to think that poverty and deprivation is in their DNA. They start playing the victim. It forces young people to reach depressive levels of despair. Many young people judge themselves by their wealth, power, luxuries in life, position, external appearance, and relationships. They try to develop their identities or find out their talents through thrill-seeking activities such as one-wheeling or over-speeding. They don't realize that they can also develop a new identity and find out their real abilities through changemaking. They don't need to expose themselves to serious physical and moral harm.

Many young people delay their changemaking journey because of limited education and skills, as well as financial resources. In my changemaking journey, I have found out that, in real life, you are not appraised by the level of your knowledge and skills, but by your determination, fearlessness, resolve, and patience. Those who prefer to operate from their memories seldom achieve something big. Those who use their powers of imagination seldom lose. When you plan to begin your changemaking journey, it is important to know your character strengths.

Strengths and Weaknesses Self-Assessment

1) *Review each quality and select a range. 1 indicates weakness while 10 indicates strength.*

Quality	Range
I like to challenge myself to do new things.	1 2 3 4 5 6 7 8 9 10
I am capable of imagining new ideas.	1 2 3 4 5 6 7 8 9 10
I am passionate about my goals.	1 2 3 4 5 6 7 8 9 10
I have a spirit of adventure.	1 2 3 4 5 6 7 8 9 10
I have a strong urge to achieve.	1 2 3 4 5 6 7 8 9 10
I am self-confident and self-reliant.	1 2 3 4 5 6 7 8 9 10
I am goal-oriented.	1 2 3 4 5 6 7 8 9 10

I am innovative, creative, and versatile.	1 2 3 4 5 6 7 8 9 10
I am persistent and I don't give up easily.	1 2 3 4 5 6 7 8 9 10
I am hardworking and energetic.	1 2 3 4 5 6 7 8 9 10
I am a positive thinker.	1 2 3 4 5 6 7 8 9 10
I am willing to take initiative.	1 2 3 4 5 6 7 8 9 10
I am able and willing to commit myself.	1 2 3 4 5 6 7 8 9 10
I am trustworthy.	1 2 3 4 5 6 7 8 9 10
I am open to opportunities.	1 2 3 4 5 6 7 8 9 10
I work well with other people.	1 2 3 4 5 6 7 8 9 10

Table 20: Self-Assessment

2) After you have rated yourself in the categories above, see in which categories you scored below 6. Use the following questions with each of the categories in which you scored below 6 to check your self-image and look for ways to improve and grow.

Q1: Is it really true that I am not _____ (enter the statement from above in which you scored below 6, e.g. *willing to take initiative*)?

_____
_____
_____
_____

Q2: Turn it around–Can I find three examples where I was _____ (e.g. *willing to take initiative*)?

_____
_____
_____
_____

(This is to show you that your personality is probably not 100% either/or. Rather, it is important to become aware that we acted in a way that supports our goals and our productive behaviors.)

Q3: In which ways could I demonstrate and strengthen this positive character trait/behavior more in the future (e.g. *think more positive*)? Think of at least three ways to do this.

_____
_____
_____
_____
_____
_____
_____
_____
_____
_____

Revealing the WHY

In this section, we will dig a little deeper into the type of problem you have identified and would like to work on changing.

Q1: What social problem would I like to address?

_____

_____

_____

_____

Q2: Why is this important to me?

_____

_____

_____

_____

Q3: What is the scale of this problem?

_____

_____

_____

_____

Q4: What damage is this problem doing?

_____

_____

_____

_____

Q5: What good is this problem preventing?

_____

_____

Creating an Empowering Outlook

This section is designed to help you reflect a bit more on your vision. An inspiring vision and heartfelt vision can be a very empowering force, because it helps you to recall again and again that you are working on something bigger than yourself and enhance your feeling of purposefulness. If you nurture your positive vision and connect to it on an emotional basis again and again, you will likely see yourself moving towards your goals over time.

Q1: Do I have a vision in life? What does it look like? What does it feel like? Remember that you can have a vision for different areas of your life, from family and relationships to health, social impact, spiritual abundance, financial abundance, and mastering what you enjoy doing.

Q2: What changes would I want to see in my country/community?

_____
_____
_____
_____
_____
_____
_____
_____
_____

Q3: What are my short-term and long-term goals to move towards achieving my vision?

Remember that it is mostly true that we *over*estimate what we can do in a week, but we highly *under*estimate what we can achieve in ten years.

So, when it comes to your long-term goals, allow yourself to think big and dream. Don't worry if you don't know HOW to achieve your long-term goals or your legacy goals.

All you have to worry about now is setting goals that truly excite you. This will likely be the case if you have an emotional connection to your goal and it inspires you. If the goal speaks to your heart, then it has real power. If it doesn't excite or inspire you, you might have to reconsider WHY you want it.

One last word of advice: The goals you set for yourself now can be changed. As human beings, we change. Some goals that might have been important to us five years ago might not be relevant to us anymore. This is okay. All it means is that we have evolved. This is why it makes sense to revisit your goals regularly and meditate over them to see if they still speak to your heart.

***Legacy goals (3 to 7 years)**–What would you like your life and your project to look like 7 years from now? What would be your ideal scenario? In this question, we don't ask what you think is realistic, but what you would ideally like to achieve.*

The Change Maker Workbook-Start Today and Jump Into Action!

Close your eyes and envision it. What does your vision look like? What does it feel like? If your mind jumps in, telling you that this is impossible, or that you can never achieve this vision, then quietly acknowledge that this is your old self and your memories of the past speaking. Thank your mind for its opinion, and then gently focus on the ideal future you want to experience. It is not necessary to know HOW this will come about.

Right now, it is about envisioning.

Then, when you have connected to your ideal vision for yourself in 7 years, you can start writing down your 7-year goals:

- _____
- _____
- _____
- _____
- _____
- _____
- _____
- _____
- _____
- _____
- _____
- _____
- _____
- _____

Long-term goals (1 year to 3 years)-*What are your 3-year goals? Are they aligned with your 7-year goals? Again, connect to what inspires you and then write it down:*

- _____
- _____

- _____
- _____
- _____
- _____
- _____
- _____
- _____
- _____
- _____
- _____
- _____
- _____

Mid-term goals (1 month to 3 months)-*Now, what would you like to achieve in the next 3 months? Are these goals in line with your 3-year goals? If so, good! If not, check whether they are conflicting with your long-term vision. Again, write your goals down and make an emotional connection with the goals and WHY you want to achieve them:*

- _____
- _____
- _____
- _____
- _____
- _____
- _____
- _____
- _____
- _____

- _____
- _____
- _____
- _____

Short-term goals (next 3 weeks)-*What do you want to achieve over the next 3 weeks? Write your goals for the next three weeks down. Then take an extra step and write the ONE* **NEXT CRITICAL STEP** *behind each of your goals that you can take right now to make a small step in the direction of your goals. Do this for your 3-week goals, your 3 month goals, your 1 to 3 year goals, and your 7-year goals.*

What is it that you could do to move yourself towards this goal? Is it to sign up for a class? Is it to research online on how to achieve your goal? Is it to start creating your product? Or is it to start practicing an instrument? Whatever your goal might be, if you know which next step you can take toward it, and you do this again and again, you cannot help but move towards your dreams.

- _____
- _____
- _____
- _____
- _____
- _____
- _____
- _____
- _____
- _____
- _____
- _____

We have found that an ideal time to review our long-term goals is at least once a month, and an ideal time to review our short-term goals is once a week.

You can also "connect" with your long-term goals in your daily visualization and meditation time. This can help you to stay in tune with your WHY.

Theory of Change Workspace

Q1: *What is my theory of change? How would you I to bring change to my society/country? What is my solution to the problem?*

_____
_____
_____
_____
_____

Q2: *What products or services will I provide, and to whom?*

_____
_____
_____
_____

Q3: *Are my products and services different from others in the market space, and if so, how? (e.g. Are they cheaper? More expensive? More accessible? More stylish? More appropriate for target group(s)? Of a better quality? Unique in packaging? Unique in customer service? Unique in the story that is told about the products or services? Do they come with a better guarantee? Are they easier to use? Do they work better/more easily? Is the education about the product/service better?)*

_____
_____
_____

Q4: What is the added value for my target group(s) if they buy my product or service?

Q5: How will I measure the social impact of my social enterprise?

You can use the attached form to measure the social impact of your social enterprise.

Q6: What are the activities that are necessary on a regular basis to provide value to my target group(s)?

Q7: Who will I need in my team, or as a partner, in order to provide these services? Who will they be? What should their background be? What should their role(s) be? What can I offer them in return for their time and/or resources?

Q8: *What are the resources I need in order to start my Social Enterprise? Do I know someone that has these resources available? Might I be able to make a deal with someone to gain access to the resources I need?*

Q9: *How will I sustain my activities? How will I make money to sustain my activities?*

Q10: *What will be the expenses that I might have to cover?*

Part 4

Chapter 10

SUPPORT THE CHANGE-WHAT IT MEANS FOR TEACHERS, FACILITATORS, AND PARENTS

Opening Hearts and Minds with Metaphors

Shepherd Work

Our work with young people is very similar to the work of a shepherd. The shepherd protects the sheep. He lays down his life for the sheep. He is responsible for the safety and growth of the sheep. Unlike others, he leads from behind and puts the sheep out front. When there is any danger, the shepherd rushes and takes the front line. He makes sure that the sheep are going in the right direction. He provides shelter to the sheep. He feeds the sheep. He brings the sheep to the best environment. He leads the sheep towards green pastures. He leads the sheep to still water so that they can drink without fear or drowning. He is accountable for every sheep.

He does not move forward unless all the sheep are satisfied. He shows extraordinary patience when the sheep want to play and hang out. He waits until the sheep finish. He protects them from danger and disease. He values every sheep. He does not leave any sheep behind. He knows if he leaves any sheep behind, it will be killed. On the other hand, sheep are always looking for guidance from the shepherd. Sheep cannot direct themselves without his support and guidance, as they can easily fall prey to predators. The good shepherd provides a sense of belonging to every sheep. The sheep hear and understand the voice of the shepherd and are willing to follow him.

Who is the shepherd among us? I believe that God has given parents, teachers, policy makers, politicians, and adults the role and position of the shepherd. They should encourage young people, rather than discourage them. They should trust young people rather, than distrust them. They should provide the best environment to young people to unlock their changemaking potential, rather than crushing them. They should lead them from behind, rather than leading them from out front. They should appreciate them, rather than curse them. They should give them a sense of belonging, rather than fostering a sense of isolation. They should gather them together, rather than exclude them. They should guide them to the right path, rather than force them to follow a wrong path.

They should help them explore career paths, rather than control them. They should take care of every young person, rather than focusing on a select few. They should provide young people with freedom from fear, rather than fostering fear in young people. They should stay with them at difficult times, rather than leaving them alone. They should be generous toward young people, rather than stingy. They should show mercy and care to young people, rather than punishing young people.

If you are a parent, teacher, social worker, policy maker, politician, religious leader, or adult, ask yourself: What kind of shepherd are you? What kind will you become?

Young People Are Like Seeds

I believe that young people are like seeds. Inside every young person is unlimited changemaking potential. This potential is unlocked in a carefully and intentionally created environment. The environment can be described as the soil. As there are different types of soils in which seeds grow, there are also different types of environments in which young people grow. We know what happens when a seed is sown into a hard and stony ground. The seeds that are planted in good soils produce great results. Similarly, when young people are provided with a rich environment, they grow in profound ways. As the seed will flourish when it is sown in the right soil, young people will unlock their changemaking potential when they are trusted and valued as equal partners. The environment plays a major role in the lives of young people.

There is a changemaker inside of every young person. The only way to bring out that changemaker is to make sure that young people grow up in a nourishing environment. When young people are not provided with the right environment, the changemaking potential inside of young people is trapped.

Similarly, when a tiny seed is not planted in the right environment, its potential to grow will be trapped. If planted in the right environment, however, this tiny seed will turn into a mighty tree and will bear fruit. But if you put a seed on your living room floor or dining table, the seed's potential to grow into a forest will be trapped. If you put the same seed in an open environment, the seed can turn into a forest.

If we want our children to become changemakers, then they should be placed in the right environment. The right environment is consciously created by everyone. Parents and teachers play a critical role in it. They must take care of their children like seeds. They must have positive expectations from young people. They must remember that, if they want their children to become changemakers, then the very first step is creating the structures that can support them to practice changemaking behavior *now*.

They should not just look at children and young people as someone lacking or limited. They must see and treat them as changemakers. When we envision every young person born with inherent changemaking potential, then this vision will become our daily motivation to create opportunities for young people to practice changemaking abilities and make it a reality. When I go to schools and communities, I see young people as changemakers, but others see them as problems to be managed or resources to be developed.

It hurts me to see that even our best parents and teachers are planting seeds in an environment that is not beneficial to unlocking the seed's potential, as they give very little space, opportunity, encouragement, or recognition to their children to practice their inherent changemaking abilities. They don't realize that there is no right age for changemaking. Their mental models affect children and young people in dramatic ways, whether we realize it immediately or not. When I look at the condition of young people today, I feel that they are reaping a large amount of limiting beliefs which they inherit from the society. Young people are not given a choice to become changemakers. They believe they are good-for-nothings and failures. They are out of touch with their changemaking abilities. We cannot harvest what we have not sown. We cannot do anything for our previous harvest, but we must commit ourselves to the present and future harvests.

The Canary Bird

Young people all over the world are facing staggering challenges. No single country has set up a large-scale mechanism to unlock the changemaking potential of young people intentionally. The recent unprecedented outbreak of youth-led terrorism incidents can be viewed as analogous to the canary bird, which is used to serve as an alarm system in underground coal mines.

The canary is used to assess the level of threat to life. The canary was always sent first to measure the airborne poisons. Canaries are best-suited for this because of their anatomy. When the canary is exposed to methane gas, it will die fast from poisoning.

The canary bird analogy elucidates the vulnerability of our young people. It acts like an early warning system. A large number of young people are desperately seeking attention and purpose. They are employing dangerous behaviors.

Disengagement, disconnection, and devaluation have created a fertile ground for dismal ideas. The number of young people involved in risky behaviors is mounting.

There is no billboard to show how quickly the number of disenfranchised young people is increasing. Young people, like canaries, are telling us through their behaviors what is missing in society.

The term "manufactured disaster" explains the reality of the current youth crisis. Our families, institutions, organizations, and communities have made the lives of young people miserable and impossible by excluding them from participation in meaningful and constructive activities.

I believe we are living on the edge of a volcano. It is time to dismiss the golden age-old maxim that "young people are just kids and are not capable of driving change". If we are not going to change our attitude towards young people, then we will continue to create environments conducive to the radicalization of young people by extremist groups. Young people are acting like a canary in a coal mine to tell us what is missing in society.

They are telling us through their behaviors that there is a huge youth engagement vacuum existing that is being exploited by the enemies of humanity by misusing the young people's changemaking potential to achieve their malign goals.

Terrorists and extremists are showing us, again and again, the potential and power that resides in every young person to affect the society. We must move away from our firefighting mode when it comes to dealing with youth-led terrorism incidents. We must understand that we need more than a military solution to combat youth-led terrorism. We should not forget that we have a record youth population today, greater than at any other time in the history of mankind.

We must move fast and collectively to transform the youth bulge into a youth boom by setting up mechanisms to harness and unleash the changemaking potential of our young people at all levels of society.

What is Required for This Model to Work and Build an Enabling Environment?

We need a broader youth-led changemaking movement in the world. We need a movement that engages a wide range of actors, and initiates departments, ministries, and organizations to build the field of youth-led changemaking. Educational institutions can play a major role in advancing the field of youth-led changemaking.

They can provide the leadership to create a sound eco-system for youth-led changemaking in their countries. It is in the educational institutions that we can find the largest number of children and young people. By integrating youth-led changemaking in schools, colleges, universities, and vocational institutions, we help incorporate youth-led changemaking in communities where these institutions are located. Youth-led changemaking can break the disconnect between schools and communities. Youth-led changemaking can be very instrumental in helping young people to apply what they have learned in classrooms. It would be a win-win situation for everyone. The best part of youth-led changemaking would be helping kids find new solutions to local problems, instead of only focusing on volunteering.

It is important to engage businesses and commercial companies to support youth-led changemaking. Youth-led changemaking can really help companies move up to a high moral plane. By bringing the private sector into the youth-led changemaking effort, we will further broaden the base of youth-led changemaking.

Philanthropists can make long-term investments in the field of youth-led changemaking. They can invest in innovative ideas. They can provide long-term capital, and managerial assistance and consulting.

Democracies can flourish tremendously when young people get the opportunity to contribute to shaping the civic life. Youth-led changemaking is a dynamic process by which young people can do just that.

Religious leaders can play a powerful role in promoting the concept of youth-led changemaking. They can inspire young people to serve as changemakers in their communities.

The support structures for youth-led changemaking are underdeveloped and fragmented. There is no country in the world that cannot benefit from youth-led changemaking. The thesis of this book is that countries where young people will be provided structured opportunities to practice changemaking abilities will accelerate their social and economic development process, while those countries where young people will not be provided structured opportunities to practice changemaking abilities will have to deal with the challenges of violence, stagnation, and poverty.

Youth-led changemaking has the potential to become a serious contender in development funding. Youth-led changemaking infrastructures are in place from the community to the federal level in all countries. There are many ways to establish and institutionalize the routes for youth-led changemaking.

Here are some specific ways to create an enabling environment for youth-led changemaking:

- Youth-led changemaking can be integrated into the curriculum of educational and technical institutions. Every child and young person should be given an opportunity to practice changemaking abilities. Youth-led changemaking should be made mandatory for every youth as part of their study requirements.

- Existing youth internship programs should be replaced with youth-led changemaking programs. Under internship programs, young people are provided with opportunities to get employment experience. It would be better if we encouraged and provided resources (similar to an internship stipend) to young people to start a youth-led changemaking project.

- Integration of youth-led changemaking into existing public entities at the national, provincial, and local levels can be undertaken. It will provide a ready-made framework to use youth-led changemaking as a strategy for nation-building.

- A national body on youth-led changemaking should be formulated with the objectives of promoting, documenting, and coordinating youth-led changemaking activities at all levels in the country.

- Enlisting support of media and celebrities for the promotion of the youth-led changemaking. Case studies demonstrating the impact of youth-led changemaking should be collected from the field for recognition and inspiration.

- Allocating one percent of the national and provincial budgets to youth-led changemaking.

- Establishing links with regional and international organizations working for the promotion of youth-led changemaking.

- Acknowledging the contributions of those who serve in youth-led changemaking programs.

- A national-level team of master trainers should be developed to train and engage civil society institutions in designing and implementing youth-led changemaking programs.

- Youth-led changemaking can be employed as a cost-effective strategy by the leading ministries and departments, such as women, education, health, environment, and skill development, to meet their developmental goals.

- Youth-led changemaking can be used as a tool for promoting national unity and fostering national development.

- Youth-led changemaking can be seen as a method of realizing local, national, and international commitments.

- Youth-led changemaking can be seen as an alternative strategy for engaging unemployed youth in community development, thus helping them to acquire the knowledge, skills, and attitudes that are required for any job.

- Youth-led changemaking programs can be developed and delivered through public and private partnerships.

- A youth-led changemaking foundation could be created and be linked with a venture capital fund gathered from major foundations, organizations, corporations, and philanthropists.

- A youth-led changemaking school can be set up to provide extensive and residential trainings to youth, civil society organizations, and youth-serving organizations.

- Support of well-established youth-serving institutions, such as Boy Scouts and Girls Scouts, could be enlisted for the expansion of youth-led changemaking programs.

Integrating Youth-Led Changemaking Model in Educational and Vocational Institutions

Educational and vocational institutions are uniquely placed to advance the concept of youth-led changemaking. It is therefore important to recognize educational and vocational institutions as major and powerful actors in the youth-led changemaking field-building process. It would be highly unrealistic to imagine that youth-led changemaking would thrive in educational and vocational institutions without concerted and intentional efforts. There are several vantage points from which to launch the youth-led changemaking movement in educational and vocational institutions:

- Educational and vocational institutions have so much to offer in the form of students, faculty members, parents, intellectual resources, and physical infrastructure to foster a culture of youth-led changemaking.

- There is a growing pressure on educational and vocational institutions to contribute directly to addressing social and economic challenges.

- Youth-led changemaking provides an exciting opportunity to educational and vocational institutions to stay relevant to present and future needs by helping students practice changemaking abilities.

- The importance of educational and vocational institutions in facilitating students to address local and global challenges is widely acknowledged.

- The youth-led changemaking provides an opportunity to create a community-based infrastructure of students, faculty members, and institutions that provide leadership and inspiration to broaden the impact of youth-led changemaking.

I would like to suggest a five-stage youth-led changemaking implementation framework for educational and vocational institutions.

This implementation framework is based on my experience of introducing the idea of youth-led changemaking to over 1,200 educational and vocational institutions and institutionalizing the idea of youth-led changemaking in over 225 institutions.

The implementation framework shows that for youth-led changemaking to take place, educational and vocational institutions must make a conscious effort to implement, encourage, and support the framework. I believe that youth-led changemaking is inevitable. Changemaking is a common desire that runs through all young people, regardless of their age, gender, education, or location. Youth-led changemaking is a multidimensional process. The following framework provides useful steps to educational and vocational institutions to initiate and embed youth-led changemaking in a systematic manner.

Here are the 5 stages:

1. **Defining** (creating urgency, mobilizing top-level commitment, and modeling)
2. **Empowering** (environment scanning and infrastructure building)
3. **Engaging** (showing quick wins and pathfinding the future course)
4. **Aligning** (leveraging and developing new systems)
5. **Institutionalizing** (embedding changemaking in process, culture, and curriculum)

Defining Stage

Youth-led changemaking is a compelling idea, but translating that idea into effective practice requires focused attention and commitment. One of the major challenges of building the field of youth-led changemaking is the inadequate knowledge base. There are no professors, institutions, or guidelines available in the field of youth-led changemaking. Although the concept of youth-led changemaking is gaining a lot of momentum and attention, the concept of youth-led changemaking is neither broadly nor well understood.

My implementation framework begins by finding an influential channel to introduce the concept of youth-led changemaking to the top leadership of an institution. It is important to make sure that the channel of introduction is trustworthy. This channel could be an organization, beneficiary, or partner. I also use print media to find interested partners to advance the concept of youth-led changemaking. During my first meeting with the leader of the institution, I have to do three things:

1. Firstly, I want to unearth the existing gaps and needs in the field of youth-led changemaking within the institution.

2. Secondly, I want to create a sense of urgency regarding the need to start youth-led changemaking policies and programs.
3. Thirdly, I want to communicate the benefits of starting a youth-led changemaking program to students, faculty members, and the institution.

I tend to highlight the following points:

- The real success of your university does not come from producing more graduates, but from producing changemakers.
- We need to find a way to unlock the changemaking potential of young people. Investing in youth-led changemaking provides endless opportunities to your students and the university.
- We are living in a highly entrepreneurial age where winners are not assessed by their abilities to memorize things, but by their ability to drive change.
- Our educational institutions are on auto-pilot, as they heavily rely on repeating knowledge and skills, instead of creating, inventing, and innovating something new.
- Educational and vocational institutions offer the greatest overlooked and sustainable resources to rebuild our communities.
- Youth-led changemaking offers the best way for educational and vocational institutions to enrich the learning process of students.
- Youth-led changemaking provides the most credible route to employment.
- Youth-led changemaking is a cross-cutting strategy that intersects youth development, community development, civic activism, social development, and institutional development.
- Youth-led changemaking helps educational and vocational institutions build bridges with communities.
- Youth-led changemaking often elevates the quality of teaching and learning. It provides students with hands-on competencies in their fields.

After sharing these thoughts, I try to uncover the issues faced by the institution to promote youth-led changemaking. I ask about their priorities, capacity, and issues that the institution might face while implementing the youth-led changemaking program.

I ask them about the potential people and departments who could be involved in taking a lead role in it. After listening to their views, I focus on sharing the work of my organization. I explain our vision, our track record, what kind of services we offer to young people and youth-serving institutions, what kind of results we have achieved so far, and I share many examples of youth-led changemaking projects.

This helps move the discussion forward and makes a connection with the institution. I always prefer to lead this stage. I held the first meeting with the representatives of over 1,200 educational and vocational institutions. It is not that I mistrust the abilities of my staff members to inspire people and organizations to join us, it is more about taking responsibility to open the door for youth-led changemaking. I believe that every great partnership begins with a single meeting. Your ability to build rapport, trust, and hope heavily influences the outcome.

If everything goes well in the first meeting with the leader of the institution, I begin the planning process with the leader to build a foundation for our relationship with the institution. I encourage them to nominate a faculty member(s) to coordinate things with us. I share ideas on how to select a focal person(s). I encourage them to seek expression of interest from within the institution to find an interested faculty member(s) for the job.

Empowering Stage

The empowering stage is focused on two things: The first thing is to identify strengths and weaknesses in the institution with regards to offering youth-led changemaking opportunities. The second thing is to build the infrastructure for youth-led changemaking. This stage aims to develop a changemaking ecosystem within the institution, and to create a team which works collectively to make youth-led changemaking the new norm and expectation within the institution.

This stage begins by carrying out a campus scan in collaboration with the nominated faculty member(s). We have developed a specialized questionnaire (attached) to gauge the level of understanding about the concept of youth-led changemaking. It explores the level of inclusion of youth-led changemaking activities in the culture and curriculum of the institution.

After the campus scanning, a changemaking team comprising of faculty members and students who can seed youth-led changemaking is created. The purpose of creating a changemaking team within each institution is to have a core team that has passion and relevant skills in planning, implementing, and evaluating changemaking activities within the institution. A key feature of the training is that it is experiential in nature. Young people participate in a two-day changemaking competition to create a social and economic value in society. Young people are provided Rs.100 (US$1) to initiate an idea of an activity that produces social and economic benefits. This activity helps show quick wins to the institutions. It also helps create social acceptability of the idea.

Engaging Stage

This is a vital stage in advancing the concept of youth-led changemaking. It is a stage where the institution takes the responsibility to create an environment for youth-led changemaking. In this stage, the institution engages faculty members and students in a wide range of youth-led changemaking activities. Faculty members and students understand the need, urgency, and benefits of youth-led changemaking. The top leadership, along with faculty members, decides what to focus on as an institution. The institution develops a clear vision and shared responsibilities to achieve it. The institution develops a road map to create, deliver, and capture value in the field of youth-led changemaking. The institution identifies potential funding opportunities for youth-led changemaking from within and outside the institution. The institution rolls out small-scale youth-led changemaking competitions. Everyone in the institution develops a strong sense of purpose and ownership. They develop standardizing performance measurement tools and build new pipelines for future engagement. It is a demanding stage, as the institution gets involved in pathfinding to embed youth-led changemaking within the institution.

Aligning Stage

This stage aims at designing and refining structures which ensure that everybody goes in the right direction. The current structures and systems are evaluated. The potential roadblocks are identified. In my experience, an overwhelming majority of institutions want to start youth-led changemaking programs, but very few institutions are actually capable of aligning structures to produce the desired results. Due to the inability of people to align structures, many institutions don't go beyond the engaging stage. The major problems get in the way of youth-led changemaking because of systems and structures. I had many long conversations with the faculty members of several institutions in which they tried to sell me the excuse that they are willing to support youth-led changemaking, but their systems and structures are their biggest stumbling blocks. My advice to faculty members is that systems and structures are designed to prevent bad things from happening; they are not designed to prevent *good* things from happening. I tried to convince them that systems and structures are things. They don't have the capacity to decide. They are created by people, and they can be replaced by people if they are not producing the right results. Aligning structures is the most difficult leadership challenge, because many of our institutions are on auto-pilot, as traditions have locked them in. Without aligning structures and systems of the institution, it is virtually impossible to make youth-led changemaking a top priority of the institution.

Institutionalizing Stage

Institutionalizing is the fruit of the first four stages. As we cannot have fruit without the roots, similarly, we cannot institutionalize the concept of youth-led changemaking in any institution without the defining, empowering, engaging, and aligning stages. Institutionalizing the concept of youth-led changemaking requires building the eco-system in which the practice of youth-led changemaking takes place. The eco-system includes human, financial, intellectual, physical, social, and political resources that can play an instrumental role in advancing the field of youth-led changemaking. The first four stages are aimed at addressing the inefficiencies within the eco-system. It is of no use to build the capacity of faculty members if the environment in which they function is not supportive. It is not possible for a single leader to do what it takes to advance the field of youth-led changemaking. It takes a family to build a family. There are many players in the field of youth-led changemaking at the moment. These players are not involved in designing and implementing strategic interventions to speed-up the development of the youth-led changemaking field. Institutionalizing the concept of youth-led changemaking requires a whole-campus approach. This means that all the major players within the institution must take deliberate steps to build the field. Institutionalization is achieved when the efforts of an institution go beyond the output to the process of engaging young people in changemaking. It is a formal process to inspire, reward, and manage young people involved in changemaking. This stage aims at integrating youth-led changemaking into the institutions' culture and structure.

Youth-led changemaking is the need of the hour, as the demand for learning problem-solving and social innovation is climbing everywhere in the world. Youth-led changemaking has the potential to transform an average campus into a changemaking campus. Educational and vocational institutions are uniquely placed to offer students much-required changemaking opportunities, infrastructure, financial assistance, and peer networks. Time is ripe to recognize educational and vocational institutions as major actors in problem-solving and social innovation through youth-led changemaking.

Bringing Youth-Led Changemaking to the Classroom

Youth-Led Changemaking is a form of experimental learning, where students learn by doing. Effective youth-led changemaking programs incorporate six critical stages:

1. Inspiration
2. Formation
3. Preparation
4. Action
5. Reflection
6. Celebration

Inspiration

The inspiration stage begins by holding an open session with the students to encourage and motivate them to practice their changemaking abilities. There are several ways that a teacher can inspire their students. A teacher can share stories of young changemakers, show short videos of young makers, and invite a young changemaker to share their story. The purpose of sharing the work of young changemakers is to communicate the benefits of changemaking to students and society, and to send a message that changemaking is possible at any age, and students should not wait to graduate before they become changemakers.

Formation

The second stage is to seek expression of interest from the interested students for participation in the changemaking competition. The students will be encouraged to submit their expression of interest in the form of teams. A student team should be comprised of no less than 3, and no more than 5 members.

Preparation

The Preparation stage involves seven steps:

1. **Terms of Engagement:** The teachers will explain the terms of engagement to all student teams. All student teams are required to read, sign, and submit the terms of engagement for the competition mentioned in the "Youth-Led Changemaking Competition Guidelines and Registration Form" (attached).

2. **Disbursement of Funds:** The teacher will disburse a small amount of funds to the student teams to begin their changemaking projects. The size of the funds should be very small. The idea is to stimulate the changemaking abilities of young people. In our work, we provide funds from Rs. 100 (US$1) to Rs. 5000 (US$50) to each student team at this stage. Funds can be arranged or provided by the schools to students on the condition that if there is any profit generated by the student teams, it will be distributed on the basis of the following formula: The student team will take 50% profit, the school will take 40% profit, and the teachers will be provided 10% profit for facilitating the students. If there is any loss faced by student teams, it will be borne by the donor (i.e. the school).

3. **Brainstorming (Identification of Problems):** The brainstorming session can be done by the students themselves or can be facilitated by the teachers. The purpose of the session is to identify problems, challenges, or opportunities.

4. **Prioritization of Problems:** After identification of problems or opportunities, students should be encouraged to prioritize the problems and determine which problem or issue needs urgent attention. The prioritization of the challenges, opportunities, or problems should be done by the students. The students should decide whether they would like to offer a product or service to meet the unmet service needs.

5. **Developing Goals or Objectives:** The next activity is for students to develop goals and objectives of the changemaking project.

Goals/Objectives	Learning Goals/Objectives
Benefits to school	Students will learn _____
Benefits to other students	Students will understand _____
Benefits to society	Students will be able to _____

Table 18: Developing Goals and Objectives of the Changemaking Project

6. **Develop:** The next step in the preparation stage is to develop or arrange a product or service that can produce social and economic benefits. This stage also focuses on developing a dissemination plan of the changemaking project by tapping local resources.

7. **Organize:** This is a very important activity of the preparation stage. It includes making small teams/groups, setting out roles and responsibilities, identifying a leader or leaders, and developing a timeline and work plan. Students are encouraged to brainstorm a list of tasks and determine their most logical sequence. Student teams divide responsibilities among themselves.

WHAT needs to get done?	WHO will be responsible?	WHEN does it need to get done? (Use dates)	WHO will need to be involved? (e.g. people on your team or outside support)

Table 19: Dividing Responsibilities Among Changemaking Team Members

Action Stage

The Action stage involves four steps. These include:

1. Executing the changemaking project as planned

2. Holding discussions with students and teachers to share progress and solve unanticipated problems

3. Acknowledging the efforts of students that are very active, and encouraging those that are shy or a little slow to perform

4. Monitoring the pace of the activities. Make adjustments to the initial plan as new information is gained and new circumstances are faced. It is important to keep the momentum of the changemaking project throughout the competition. A good youth-led changemaking project maintains good momentum throughout its lifespan.

Reflection Stage

The fifth stage of an effective youth-led changemaking project is reflection. It is a process by which students think critically about their experience.

It is carried out through a variety of ways, such as writing, talking, listening, and reading about their service experiences.

Much of what we learn in life comes from reflecting on our experiences. It requires that we provide structured time for students and teachers to **think, talk, and write** about what they did and observed during the changemaking project (forms attached). Without reflection, we lose a great opportunity to maximize student learning.

Celebration Stage

The sixth and final stage of the changemaking project is the celebration stage. This stage is carried out by conducting the following activities:

- Organizing a reception party
- Organizing an award ceremony
- Writing letters of appreciation for students involved in changemaking projects
- Providing certificates and cash awards to students
- Reporting to local newspaper publishers and news reporters to publicly recognize the accomplishments of students
- Organizing a changemaking exhibition to showcase the work of students

All Failures Are Not Equal

In my 20 years of working with young people, I have found out that the fear of failure presents a major stumbling block to unlock the changemaking potential of young people.

The fear of failure is putting off many young people from beginning their changemaking journey. Young people feel reluctant to try something in public. They are not sure how their efforts will turn out. The fear of failure causes many young people to do nothing. It stops them from unlocking, experimenting, and innovating. Many young people do not realize that it is impossible to live an impactful life without experiencing some kind of failure. Changemaking provides a great opportunity for young people to overcome their fear of failure and discover things about themselves that they would have never explored otherwise.

I believe there are two types of failure. One is *standstill failure,* and another is *failing forward.*

Standstill failure means a reluctance shown by people to get involved in new and challenging tasks. The fear of failure forces them to sabotage their prospects of success. Young people are mostly the victim of standstill failure. Standstill failure is an option, and not a requirement. It is the worst kind of failure. It is the result of poor self-judgment. No effort is required to encounter standstill failure. It tracks you down and hits you automatically. It keeps you in waiting mode. It keeps you guessing. It takes away your power to initiate and create. It fills your heart with fear, doubt, and mistrust. It instigates you to see every opportunity pessimistically. A large number of young people today do not want to fail "out loud". They want to play it safe. They prefer to wait. They are afraid to be rejected, and their need for outside approval and their fear of disapproval and "losing face" inhibit the expression of their natural changemaking spirit. Young people do not realize that their lack of initiative or desire to try something new will automatically qualify them for standstill failure. Standstill failure cannot be avoided even if you prefer to remain in your shell. It will come at you fast and furious.

Why do young people fall victim to standstill failure?

- Young people have inherited a very negative belief system from their environment.
- Young people have poor self-awareness. They focus on what they can't do, rather than what they can do.
- Young people think they will lose their respect and credibility. They will be seen as a loser.
- Young people prefer to operate from memory and not from imagination.
- Young people often find it difficult to see the positive outcomes that are possible.
- Young people are used to their daily routine and don't want to get distracted.
- Young people follow myths blindly.

In my work, I met so many young people living their lives in standstill mode. They blame society and the external environment for their failure. It is partially true. Society plays an important role in developing a weak belief system in young people. Our educational institutions made the false promise to many of them that a very good job would be waiting at the end of their educational career. Many bright, talented, and intelligent young people ended up living their lives in standstill mode. These young people were not born with the fear of starting something new. Their hearts and minds were conditioned in a manner to think and act pessimistically. It does not matter how educated, skilled, and talented you are if you continue to live your life in standstill mode.

It is also true that we are equipped with the tools to turn around our lives. We are in charge of our lives. We have a choice every day to decide what kind of life we want to live. Many young people are knocked down from inside so early in their lives, and therefore, it is very difficult for them to see themselves as valuable and capable of driving change in society. It is very difficult to find out that many young people are living their lives in standstill mode. In my opinion, the number of these young people is growing very fast. This number is not displayed in newspapers and electronic media or on billboards. These young people feel that they are not good enough. They are intimidated by the size of their problems. They are often involved in risky behaviors. They forget that God has placed the seeds of changemaking in everyone. This changemaking potential is not allowed to release. They have come to the conclusion that they are not good enough to start something of value. They do not realize that they are equally gifted and talented. God has declared them a masterpiece. They do not realize that they are truly blessed and can really bounce back from every situation in life. Their vision is restricted by their environment. Their negative thoughts are putting venom into their system. They forget to realize that they are blessed with everything they need to change their lives.

It is important that both adults and young people reprogram their mental infrastructure. We need a new mental infrastructure that can help us save the lives of many young people. We must get rid of obsolete and limiting beliefs. It is easy to build, improve, or strengthen physical infrastructure when needed. The physical infrastructure automatically seeks the immediate attention of people when broken, damaged, or weakened. On the contrary, the mental infrastructure is not visible, and does not seek immediate attention in case of malfunctioning. Our old mental infrastructure is no longer effective. When young people realize that this waiting game has not worked for them in the past and will not work for them in the future, they will see that it is time to say goodbye to caution and inaction. In the words of Norman Cousin, *"Death isn't the greatest loss in life. The greatest loss is what dies inside of us while we live."*

In my work, I have found that young people love to take initiative when trusted and admired. Their minds start transcending all limitations, their hearts start sending positive vibrations, their spirits become incredible, and their bodies perform exceptionally.

The other type of failure is *failing forward*. Failing forward helps young people discover their future. It is the best form of failure. It is a blessing in disguise. It is an educative failure. It brings us closer to our goal. It guides us in a new direction. It helps us improve. It takes us closer to success. It helps young people explore their changemaking potential in the real world. It helps young people reconnect with their inherent changemaking abilities. It paves the road to great achievement. Failing forward is our best teacher. If you fail while trying something bigger, then you are not a failure. Although the results show that you are a failure, in reality, you are not a failure. You learned what does not work. Remember the words of Thomas Edison: *"I have not failed. I have just found 10,000 ways that won't work."* Young people who prefer to fail forward are excited without fear of embarrassment. They refuse to accept second-best. They are always eager and enthusiastic. They want to go the extra mile. They accept failure, but they don't accept giving up. They see failure as a ladder. They don't wait, they prepare and perform. Failing forward helps us discover, showcase, and sharpen our talents. Socrates once said, *"To move the world, we must first move ourselves."* According to Charles Schulz, *"Life is a ten-speed bike. Most of us have gears we never use."*

Young people have to make a choice every day: whether they want to face standstill failure, or they want to fail forward. Young people must not forget that there is no success without a trial or failure. Failure should not be seen as your enemy; rather it should be seen as your best friend. Failure helps you to find the right direction. It prepares you for long-lasting success. It builds your character from the inside-out. It teaches you patience and resilience.

Strategies to Encourage Young People to Become Changemakers

Although already mentioned throughout this book, let us have a look at the specific strategies to encourage young people to become Changemakers.

Trust

Trust provides the shortest route to get positive results. Young people feel very happy when they are trusted. They actually thrive on trust. Our distrust in young people has already proved to be very costly. We have lost so many innocent lives due to our inability to build trust in young people. We can nurture trust in young people very quickly. It does not take any special qualification or course to feel whether you are trusted or not. I believe that the human heart is designed in a manner to pick up subtle clues from one another quickly. Young people are very quick to pick up on when they are not trusted. A large number of young people are growing up in a very low-trust environment. I have seen low trust in young people everywhere. It can be witnessed in their families, classrooms, and communities. Our survival is based on our ability to reach out and establish trust with young people. Without trusting young people and their potential, there will be no peace, prosperity, or stability. Over-trusting young people may result in some degree of disappointment at times, but a lack of trust in young people often results in high social and economic costs. Not trusting young people puts us at greater risk.

Every time I to talk to young people, my first priority is to establish trust with them. I designed a new youth-led changemaking model a few years ago to establish, extend, and restore trust with young people. I have engaged over 16,000 young people in that model to show people and organizations that young people want to be trusted. I did not put any conditions on the participation in the changemaking competition program. The only requirement to participate in the changemaking competition is desire. I did not look at their education level, skill level, or economic background. Instead, I looked at each young person as pure potential, capable of driving a change in their communities. I provided a small amount of money to all those young people who decided to begin their changemaking journey.

It worked very well in this case. Young people who are living in the most difficult conditions responded to my trust in them with great speed. They outshined young people from privileged backgrounds. In my conversations with young people, I tried to communicate to young people that I don't care what others think about them, all I know is that each one of them is equipped with changemaking abilities, and it requires just one person or experience to help them reclaim their power. My youth-led changemaking model has shown that the problem is not "out there", it is inside of us.

We must understand that young people cannot reach their potential without somebody believing in them. It is amazing to see what we can achieve when we believe in young people. Our major role in life is to install a positive belief system in young people. When the seed of positive belief takes firm root in young people, it cannot be blown away by the strongest storms. We need to ask ourselves a simple question: Are we helping our children and young people develop a positive belief system? Or are we just treating them as objects? Trust helps young people explore their true changemaking potential. We can't bring out the best in young people by mistrusting them.

I have demonstrated through my work the simple way to build trust with young people. A simple change in our attitude and expectations can be the beginning of building a long-term trust with young people. I encourage you to implement this model in your work; you will see an immediate impact on young people. You will achieve multiple outcomes.

Care

Caring is a desire and passion to help young people become changemakers. When I looked back at my professional life, I realized that the only thing which really helped me to begin my changemaking journey was my desire to bring change into the lives of young people.

I resigned from my first job because I did not want to continue with something that had no impact on young people. I heard so many young people say that there is no one who cares about them and there is no one who respects them. I did not sleep well for many nights. I felt very frustrated and stressed out. I started blaming myself. My mind was not helping me find a way to help those young people. Young people used to approach me with great expectations and hope, and I had nothing to offer to them. I used to pray to God to help me find someone who can help these young people. I never realized that one day, God would put me in a position to create an impact on the lives of many young people. I used to pray to God to help me find a new vision. I genuinely wanted to help young people. I can't leave young people, I can't ignore the cry of young people, and I can't use them to build my career.

I made a big decision in my life to resign from my job to find a better way to serve young people. I opened my first office in my car garage. I was super excited to the extent that I did not realize that the garage was not fit to establish an office. My garage was quite long and only seven feet high. There was no ventilation system.

Support The Change—What it Means for Teachers, Facilitators, and Parents

I realized very late why I used to have long discussions with people outside my office door, rather than inside my office. During the rainy season, water used to come inside and there was no place to sit. I used to invite people to my office so confidently. My journey started from a single community. Now, I have reached out and engaged over 1,200 educational institutions. I traveled extensively by road to meet young people and open the doors for youth-led changemaking. I have traveled to many countries to share my work.

I believe it is time for each youth development practitioner to candidly review their work and reject repetition and conventional approaches that make sense to them but do not lift up young people. Young people may forget what you teach them, but they will never forget how you treat them.

I know they might fear funding collapse and salary reduction. But they must not forget that it will never cost them as much as the number of young lives we are losing every day in our world. Genuine caring does not require any funding. Donors cannot reduce it. It requires commitment and honest reflection of our work with young people.

Appreciation

I believe that every one of us has the power to change the mood of another person simply by expressing positive emotions. During my first job, when I was interacting with so many unhappy young people lacking self-esteem, confidence, and self-belief, I found out that sincere appreciation is very powerful to lift the morale of these young people. When young people are appreciated, they are in a better position to harness their unrealized changemaking potential.

Young people should be encouraged and admired at every step. It affects their attitudes, performance, and spirit to work together. It will give them a very positive message that they are fully capable, that they are not judged, and that they can act without any external assistance. During my sessions with young people, I tried to communicate to young people again and again that they are very important, that they are wonderfully made, that they are strong and equipped, that they are fully capable of turning around their lives and the lives of many other people, and that they are blessed with changemaking abilities. It really makes young people feel very good and positive. Do you know a young person who committed suicide because they were appreciated a lot? Do you know someone who has started using drugs because they were appreciated a lot? Do you know someone on the street without shelter and food because they were cared for and appreciated a lot? Young people are telling us through their behavior what is missing in their lives. It is our moral obligation to respond to it. I know many young people who have saved the notes of appreciation from their teachers for decades. It is very sad that today, youth development practitioners do not use appreciation as a tool to invoke a positive mood and spirit among young people. When I started my organization, I did not have the funds to carry out my projects. I used to go to communities and use the power of appreciation unconsciously. It really helped me build a strong bond with young people. The gift of your attention and appreciation is the greatest gift you can give to young people. When a young person looks into our eyes and sees their worth, the foundation for changemaking is laid immediately. We must look at young people from the eyes of delight, and not from the eyes of suspicion.

Forgiveness

Forgiveness is better than charity followed by insults. It is a terse reality that a large number of children and young people are denied the basic rights of personhood because they fall short of an ideal. Forgiveness means that you accept young people as they are. You don't turn your back on them. Forgiveness means letting it go.

Forgiveness means you go back to young people again and again until the miracle happens.

Forgiveness means giving a second chance to young people. You might get disappointed at times when you trust young people, but you will live in constant distress if you don't forgive them.

Everybody makes mistakes. Our politicians make mistakes. Athletes make mistakes. Religious leaders make mistakes. Policy makers make mistakes. Why do we create a lot of fuss when young people make mistakes? Why do we adopt a very harsh attitude towards young people when they make a mistake? Why do we start painting all young people with the same brush?

Why do we try to get even with young people instantly? Forgiveness means giving another chance to young people. Many young people have committed suicide because they believed that they would not be forgiven by their parents, teachers, peers, and society. Every day, we see the consequences of not forgiving young people. When we choose not to forgive young people, we encourage hidden agendas and drastic outcomes. Forgiveness can be used as a powerful tool to heal, reconnect, and reintegrate young people as changemakers. When young people grow up in environments where they learn to forgive, it helps them develop a sound heart and mental health. On the flip side, if young people grow up in environments where they see forgiveness is not practiced, they tend to learn not to forgive others and themselves.

Forgiveness is the most vital tool to restore the relationship with young people and avoid terrible outcomes. I have found that forgiveness is the key to build sustainable relationships with young people. It repairs and strengthens our relationship with young people. Forgiveness helps young people develop positive behaviors.

Design of Youth-Led Changemaking Program

Youth-led changemaking is a unique public idea. It can attack many serious problems in society simultaneously. Youth-led changemaking provides a great mechanism to reintegrate out-of-school young people into society as useful citizens. The largest cohort of youth-led changemaking would come from educational and vocational institutions.

What should be the design of a youth-led changemaking program?

1. *Compulsory or Voluntary:* The decision whether to make a youth-led changemaking program compulsory or voluntary for young people depends on the size of the youth population, internal and external peace, and the security situation and challenges faced by your country. Countries that are facing serious internal threats, and that are lagging behind in meeting the basic needs of society and engaging young people in constructive tasks, would have no real problems in making youth-led changemaking a compulsory program.

2. *Income Generation or Income Consumption:* The striking feature of the youth-led changemaking program is its ability to engage young people in the creation of social and economic value at the base of the pyramid. The other youth volunteer programs consume a lot of wealth, as they have to arrange resources, wages, or stipends to engage young people in the creation of social value. Youth-led changemaking emphasizes the creation of double or triple bottom-line value to provide an incentive to both young people and their communities. Young people are

encouraged to put the mission first. For example, by coming up with need-based project ideas, or by providing products and services to people at a lower price. The performance of young people is assessed against the ideas they executed, the social impact they created, and the income they generated.

3. *Selective or Universal:* The beauty of the youth-led changemaking program is that it offers enormous returns to all young people. It sees every young person as a resource and capable of creating social and economic value in society. Unlike many other youth development programs, it does not focus on only engaging those young people who are educated and skilled, but all young people who were previously ignored and forgotten. It believes in the ideology that every young person is born with changemaking potential and requires an opportunity to unlock it. It is an inclusive program.

4. *Centralized or Decentralized:* The idea of youth-led changemaking can only be realized with intentional and rational planning. It requires decentralization. It may require a new bureaucracy at a federal level for supervision and regulation. Youth-led changemaking can be best implemented in collaboration with provincial and local ministries and departments.

5. *Open-ended or Closed-ended:* The youth-led changemaking program follows an open-ended civic process. It brings a massive shift in which youth engagement programs are designed and delivered. It does not ask young people to participate in pre-determined and pre-conceived programs. It gives the freedom to young people to lead the process from beginning to end.

6. *Limited or Long-Term:* A youth-led changemaking program provides an opportunity to young people to unlock their changemaking potential in a fixed period of time. This period can range from 1 month to 3 months. This period can be seen as a trial period for young people to learn more about themselves

and their strengths and weaknesses. During this period, young people need to solve a problem by using entrepreneurial principles. If young people feel that they have conceived and implemented an innovative idea, they can continue on with it.

Why Youth-Led Changemaking Should Be a Top Priority

A return on an investment measures the gain or loss on a policy. A youth-led changemaking policy or program offers multiple returns. Let's examine the effectiveness of a youth-led changemaking idea from different perspectives.

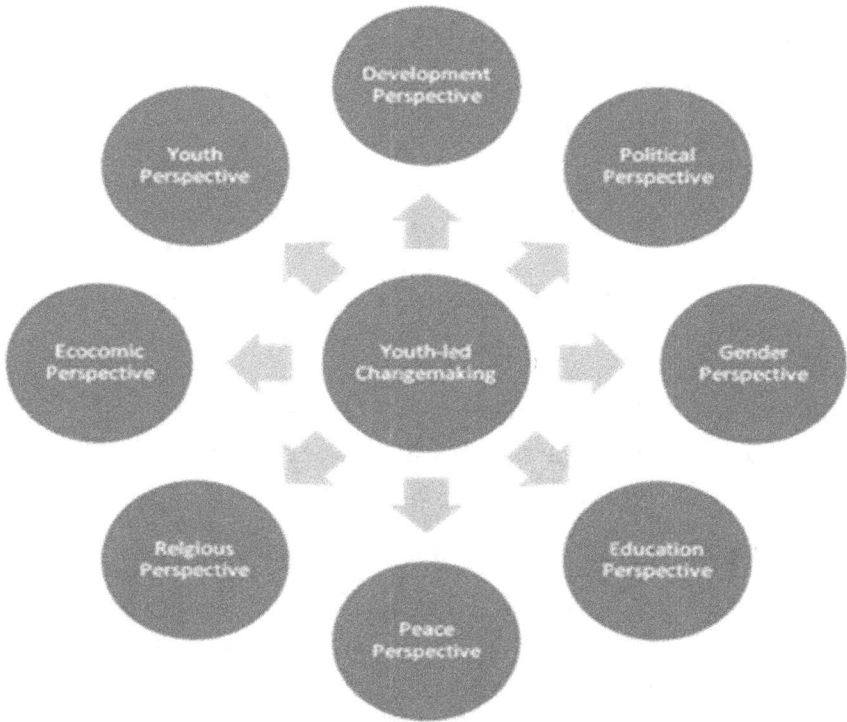

Figure 9: Multidimensionality of Youth-led Changemaking

Development Perspective

Take a look at some of the unmet service needs in the world:

- 758 million adults are illiterate – two-thirds of whom are women – and still lack basic reading and writing skills globally (UNESCO Institute of Statistics [UIS] data for 2014).
- 263 million children and youth are out of school globally (UNESCO Institute of Statistics [UIS] data for 2016).
- At least 2 billion people use a drinking water source that is contaminated with feces (WHO fact sheet, July 2017)
- Every day, 830 women die from preventable causes related to pregnancy and childbirth (WHO fact sheet 2016)
- 2.3 billion people still do not have basic sanitation facilities, such as toilets or latrines (WHO, fact sheet 2017)
- 36.7 million people are living with HIV at the end of 2016 (WHO, 2016)
- More than 1.3 billion people live in extreme poverty (less than $1.25 a day). 1 billion children are living in poverty. 22,000 children die each day due to poverty (UNICEF, 2014).

It is quite evident that we are seriously struggling to meet the service needs of our people.

We need to find a cost-effective way to meet the needs of society. Youth-led changemaking can play a significant role in addressing many of the above-mentioned service needs of society.

We have already seen that young people in various changemaking competitions conceived and carried out many innovative projects in diverse fields. Youth-led changemaking plays a major role in reducing the growing fragmentation in society. It brings young people from diverse backgrounds together. Youth-led changemaking should be seen as a major strategy for the social and economic development of the community.

Democratic Perspective

A genuine democracy requires *active citizens* and not *citizens in waiting*. Youth-led changemaking provides a great opportunity to restore youth action at a grassroots level.

It encourages young people to come together and solve real issues with entrepreneurial principles. The civic health index of many countries is showing a downward trend. Many countries are drifting away from democratic values. Youth-led changemaking provides a new mechanism to sustain the participation of young people. It ensures the participation of young people in the political process beyond election season, as it encourages young people to take collective action in the areas of the greatest need. A larger number of young people are feeling more isolated or socially excluded than before. The youth-led changemaking idea provides an opportunity to the disconnected youth population to reconnect with society and work collectively for the greater good. Instead of waiting for someone or asking someone to solve their local problems, youth-led changemaking encourages young people to create their own efforts that will address serious issues. Youth-led changemaking will help redefine the meaning of citizenship among young people. Youth-led changemaking provides the foundation for democratic institutions. Democracies will flourish only when young people will acquire the capacity to shape civic life.

Gender Perspective

Youth-led changemaking provides a great opportunity to unlock the changemaking potential of young girls. Young girls lack opportunities to lead and drive change in their communities.

Although the number of young girls enrolled in higher education institutions have increased recently, it has not put young girls in the driver's seat. There are very few opportunities available for young girls to design and deliver changemaking projects. There is no pipeline established to produce young female changemakers.

Youth-led changemaking presents an ideal opportunity to mainstream young girls into the local development process. We have seen in our work that when young girls were provided opportunities to drive change, they outperformed male youth. They showed extraordinary commitment, character, and intelligence to design and deliver changemaking projects.

Youth-led changemaking provides an excellent platform to increase the number of young female changemakers in the society. It will help young girls attract more funding and recognition for their efforts. Women represent more than half of the population in many countries of the world and they represent a large, untapped resource to bring change at a grassroots level. Youth-led changemaking offers a good alternative to female development organizations to shift their focus from education and training to the engagement of young girls in changemaking. We have seen that many organizations spend too much money on training and capacity-building of girls and women without providing them with opportunities to explore their entrepreneurial potential in the real world.

Education Perspective

We have already explained in detail about the value of youth-led changemaking for the existing education system. It will counterbalance the passive education that is being given to young people. It will transform an average educational campus into a changemaking campus. It will create and activate new spaces for youth-led changemaking. It will help millions of students every year experience the thrill of being a changemaker. It will help students discover their changemaking potential in the real world. It will break traditional institutional barriers to youth-led changemaking. It will break the disconnect between educational institutions and communities. It will provide students with an opportunity to discover their inherent changemaking abilities by confronting social problems.

Peace Perspective

It has been acknowledged globally that terrorist groups are increasingly recruiting young people into their ranks to disrupt society. Terrorist groups are an indication of our inability to inspire trust in young people. It is interesting to note that a large number of conflict-affected countries have a youth population of more than half. Terrorist groups are feeding the fires of terrorism with the blood of our young people. There is a pressing need to find a way to transform the youth bulge into a youth boom by unlocking the changemaking potential of young people. Our efforts have been restricted to listening to the concerns of young people, providing space to young people to voice their opinions, and developing a plan of action to prevent violent extremism. There is not a single coordinated effort to set up delivery systems that unleash the changemaking potential of young people. We have completely failed to create a permanent space for youth-led changemaking at any level of society. Terrorist groups are fully cognizant of our weakness and they are exploiting it by extending trust to young people. It is not enough to provide education and jobs to young people; we must also provide an opportunity for young people to develop a sense of usefulness and a sense of connection with society. Youth-led changemaking provides a remarkable opportunity to every young person to play an important role in making sustainable peace.

Religious Perspective

All religions believe in serving others, alleviating pain and poverty, and becoming more engaged. There is no religion in the world which discourages civic engagement. Youth-led changemaking can provide the first practical experience to many children and young people to serve others. It will provide the foundation to build a society on just principles. We have seen over the last few years that many countries are losing their capacity to engage children and young people in activities that can produce social, cultural, and economic change. Youth-led changemaking provides a great platform to reconnect children and young people to society. It will not only improve their spiritual condition, but also contribute to the well-being of society. Youth-led changemaking will help many individuals exert a positive influence on society. If a young person sees a problem in society, they will take an action to resolve that problem with an entrepreneurial approach. It will help many disconnected young people foster new relationships of trust and reciprocity with society. It will help young people break traditional boundaries and reduce hostility towards others.

Youth Perspective

We have a record youth population today. Our world is home to 1.8 billion young people. There are more young people between the ages of 10 and 24 today than at any other time in human history. 9 out of 10 young people are living in less-developed countries. Will these young people be able to unlock their changemaking potential? No single country has tried to set up a mechanism to unlock the changemaking potential of its youth. Young people present a huge underutilized resource. We need to take strategic steps to benefit from the abilities of these young people. It is not enough to invest in young people. The lives of young people will not change, no matter how many services we provide to young people, if young people are not seen as changemakers *now*. We have seen that education, skill development, protection against crime, and better health facilities have not brought significant changes in the lives of young people. Governments have failed to respond to this unprecedented challenge. They continue to see them as a liability instead of an opportunity. It is time to change our perspective about young people. Youth-led changemaking sees young people as a resource, an asset, and a force for social and economic progress and transformation. It helps young people drive change, and not simply follow change. It opens new opportunities and options for young people. It develops a sense of connection and purpose among young people. It enables young people to realize their leadership potential. It contributes to the development of social and emotional intelligence. It nurtures generosity and a sense of giving among young people. It offers a training ground for producing good citizens. It provides job experience to young people. It gives an opportunity for career exploration to young people.

Economic Perspective

Youth-led changemaking will boost the level of productivity of a country massively. It will offer a new source of innovation to society. Young people are the lead users of products and services. They often develop a strong desire to go one step ahead of others. Youth-led changemaking programs will provide them with an opportunity to identify the loopholes in existing products and services, and offer better products or services by using simple tools and materials. We have seen in our work that they focus on the fast delivery of ideas with less bureaucracy. It offers a service delivery mechanism to the poor and forgotten. It reduces youth crime and drug abuse. Youth-led changemaking will reduce youth unemployment. It will provide society with millions of workers and innovators at a very low expense. It will provide job experience to millions of young people. From a macroeconomic perspective, youth-led changemaking will contribute to improving the productivity level of young people, transferring knowledge, and dealing with a vast idle human resource in the best possible manner. Youth-led changemaking will offer products and services to people in need. The diffusion of knowledge from educated and skilled young people will promote economic recovery through the creation of innovative environments. This can lead to the creation of new job opportunities and economic development at a grassroots level. Youth-led changemaking will encourage young people to work in difficult conditions where many investors are reluctant to operate. It will enhance the quality of the labor force, but also inspires new business activities. Youth-led changemaking will be an infinite source of innovation at a grassroots level.

Financing Strategies for Youth-Led Changemaking

Youth-led changemaking can pursue multiple financing strategies:

1. Aligning Strategy
2. Allocating Strategy
3. Partnering Strategy
4. Crowdfunding Strategy
5. Earned income Strategy

Aligning strategy

This strategy aims at aligning existing structures of educational and vocational institutions and youth-serving institutions to support youth-led changemaking. This means that youth-led changemaking will be embedded in the culture and curriculum of educational and vocational institutions as a requirement. Educational and vocational institutions have a ready-made framework available to incorporate the concept of youth-led changemaking into their systems. This strategy will save a lot of financial resources, such as salaries of staff, space and utilities, administrative costs, infrastructure development, and other related costs. Staffing costs and infrastructure development costs represent the largest cost element. Educational institutions can use or allocate a small fee for youth-led changemaking. In our work, we use the physical and social infrastructure of educational and vocational institutions to engage young people in changemaking. We provide a small amount of funding of Rs. 5,000 (US$ 50) to each youth team (mostly comprising of 5 members) for changemaking. If we split this amount to a group of 5 members, it is only Rs. 1000(US$10) per person. It is not a very big amount to be invested by an educational institution. An average school, college, or university in Pakistan is taking more than Rs.1000 (US$10) per month from its students. Like YES Network Pakistan, the educational institutions can enter into a partnership with young people by investing Rs.1000 in each young person for starting their changemaking journey. The profit generated by the student teams should be equally distributed between student teams and educational institutions. In case of loss, the educational institution should bear it. The students of vocational institutions are often provided with stipends on a monthly basis. A small portion of that stipend can be allocated for changemaking projects by vocational institutions on the same conditions as given above.

Allocating Strategy

This strategy aims to allocate at least 1% of the national budget to youth-led changemaking. This can be done by attaching youth-led changemaking with public entities at the federal level, provincial level, or local level. Young people can be attached to different ministries and departments. The women ministry can encourage young people to carry out changemaking projects in the area of female empowerment. The health ministry can ask young people to carry out changemaking projects in the field of health in villages and hard-to-reach communities. The environment ministry can ask young people to design and deliver changemaking projects in the field of environment. Similarly, the education ministry can ask young people to design and deliver changemaking projects in the field of education for those children who are out of school. Public funding can also include funding from federal or local programs, such as poverty alleviation programs, internship programs, training programs, or capacity building programs.

Partnering Strategy

A key strategy for financing youth-led changemaking can be building partnerships with foundations, organizations, private businesses, corporations, and philanthropists. These organizations can provide access to very useful financial resources, including intellectual resources. These organizations can help advance the idea of youth-led changemaking at a national level by leveraging resources from different sources. Private companies believe that such contributions can improve their public image by putting them on a high moral plane. The other advantage of bringing a private sector on board will be opening new possibilities for young people to advance their ideas or seek employment opportunities from these companies in the future.

Crowdfunding Strategy

Funds for a youth-led changemaking program can be generated via crowdfunding. Crowdfunding has emerged as a great platform to build financial capital for a new venture. It pools together small amounts of money from a group of people that like your idea by using social media. Crowdfunding provides a quick way to attain funding for youth-led changemaking projects. It can help young people bring their products and services to the market quickly.

Earned Income Strategy

The striking feature of the youth-led changemaking idea is its ability to generate income through the sale of products or services rendered or work performed by the young people. You must have noticed in the results of the changemaking competitions given above that 88% youth teams were able to generate a profit on the amount invested in their project by providing need-based services to people of all ages. We have shown through our work that youth-led changemaking offers the most lucrative investment opportunity to people and institutions. Out of 16,000 young people engaged by YES recently, 88% were able to create social and economic value in a very short period of time. Young people were able to create a profit of 93.5% on the investment. It shows that youth-led changemaking is not only the best long-term investment, but it is a good short-term investment of money as well.

Chapter 11

RESOURCES AND TRAINING FOR FACILITATORS AND INSTITUTIONS

This chapter will explain the role of a teacher or a focal person in supporting young people to become changemakers. The benefits of youth-led changemaking are maximized when teachers facilitate students effectively. Teacher support is seen as the most vital component for unlocking the changemaking potential of students. The major responsibility of a teacher or focal person is to bring out the best in young people. Many young people don't know about their changemaking potential because nobody believed in them. It is amazing to see what we can accomplish when we believe in young people. It is painful to see that a large number of young people have a limited vision due to their environment. When we change their environment, we help young people change their vision. The Changemaking Competition provides a great opportunity for young people to expand their vision.

The Role and Responsibilities of the Teacher/Focal Person

The role and responsibilities of the teacher/focal person is divided into three parts:

Before the Competition

1. *Establish a Trust Account:* The most important responsibility of a teacher or focal person is to open a trust account in every

student. Without opening a trust account in every student, it would be extremely difficult for a teacher to inspire students to explore their changemaking abilities. The teacher should make every student feel special. A teacher can open a trust account in every student by simply looking at them with delight and hope. Every positive look, word, gesture, text message, or feeling is a huge deposit in the trust account of a young person. Every teacher involved in advancing youth-led changemaking should ask themselves: Am I making consistent deposits into the trust account of my students? Am I looking for ways to increase or strengthen the trust account of my students? Have I reached out to every student and made them feel that I really believe that they are born with changemaking potential and abilities? I personally believe that young people perform exceptionally well when their trust account is in surplus.

2. *Campus Scanning:* The focal person will carry out a campus scan to gauge the level of inclusion of youth-led changemaking in the culture and curriculum of the institute (campus scanning tool attached).

3. *Organize:* An introductory session on the concept of "Youth-Led Changemaking" with the faculty members and students. The purpose of the session is to create awareness about the concept of youth-led changemaking and inspire faculty members and students to participate in the competition. The focal person will share the benefits of the competition for everyone. The focal person will take feedback from the faculty members and students after the session (form attached).

4. *Identify:* The second task is to seek an expression of interest from the interested faculty members and students for participation in the competition. The expression of interest will be taken on the "Youth-Led Changemaking Competition Guidelines and Registration Form" (attached).

5. *Form Teams:* Students will be encouraged to participate in the competition in teams. A student team should be comprised of no less than 3, and no more than 5 members. Students are given the freedom to work alone as well.

6. *Terms of Engagement:* The focal person will explain the terms of engagement to all the student teams. Students are required to read, sign, and submit the terms of engagement for the competition mentioned in the "Youth-Led Changemaking Competition Guidelines and Registration Form" (attached).

7. *Conduct:* The focal person will conduct a baseline survey with the selected student teams (baseline form attached).

8. *Bank Account:* The focal person will provide their personal bank account details to YES for the transfer of funds. These funds will be provided to all the student teams.

During the Competition

1. *Conduct Meetings:* The focal person will conduct weekly meetings with the student teams to get an update on their progress and document their experiences. Student teams that are showing a lack of interest, or are slow in launching their changemaking projects, will be counseled.

2. *Submit:* The focal person will collect weekly reports along with 50% profit from the student teams for onwards transmission to the YES office. The focal person will have the power to disqualify any student team that is not following the terms of engagement for the competition.

3. *Take and Deposit Profit:* The focal person will be entitled to keep 10% of the profit collected from the student teams and deposit the remaining 40% into the YES account online as a donation from the student teams.

4. *Take Action Pictures:* The focal person will take action pictures of the student teams. The focal person should also encourage students to take action pictures of their activities at every stage of their project.

5. *Motivate and Encourage:* The focal person should encourage and motivate students to participate actively in the competition. One of the key responsibilities of a teacher or focal person is to motivate and encourage students. It will be very difficult to unlock the changemaking potential of young people without making them feel that you really believe that they are born with changemaking potential and abilities. Young people perform exceptionally well when they are genuinely trusted. It is important for a focal person or teacher to establish an emotional connection with each student and remain consistent in their interaction with all students. Encouraging words go a long way in helping students perform well and show resilience during tough times.

After the Competition

1. *Celebrate:* The focal person will organize a celebration event to appreciate the efforts of all the students. The focal person should invite parents and other notable dignitaries to attend the celebration event. The focal person will distribute certificates of participation to all the student teams.

2. *Document:* The focal person will document the whole changemaking competition in the form of a short video, documentary, or pictures. The focal person will collect the case studies of all the changemaking projects of the students on the prescribed format (attached). The focal person will also carry out an impact survey (questionnaire attached) of the competition.

3. *Feedback and Reflection:* The focal person will fill out the feedback and reflection forms to share their key insights, experiences, and ideas for further improvement.

Changemaking Competition Forms for Use in Your Institution

Before the Competition

You will find the following Changemaking Competition Forms:

- Campus Scanning Tool
- Baseline Survey Form
- Registration Form
- Student Feedback Form

For download at http://www.youthledchangemaking.com/before-competition-forms

During the Competition

You will find the following Changemaking Competition Forms:

- Weekly Reporting Form

For download at http://www.youthledchangemaking.com/during-competition-forms

After the Competition

You will find the following Changemaking Competition Forms:

- Reflection Report
- Individual Reflection
- Feedback Form
- Case Study Format

For download at http://www.youthledchangemaking.com/after-competition-forms

Part 5

Chapter 12

THE LONG-TERM VISION

Section 1: The Changemaking School

an essay by Ali Raza Khan on the vision for a Changemaking School

I have often been asked, "What's your endgame?" My answer is that I want to make Youth-Led Changemaking a top priority for all stakeholders. Guided by the belief that every young person is born with changemaking potential, I intend to open the doors for youth-led changemaking everywhere. I believe that the best way to achieve my vision is to work with educational and vocational institutions to create and multiply spaces for youth-led changemaking.

Our educational institutions reach out to the maximum number of children and young people. Unfortunately, our educational institutions have not been designed to produce Changemakers. They were designed to produce good servants.

There are so many defects in our educational system. I believe that without change in our educational system, there will be no change in the world.

I figured out two ways to address this challenge.

The first way is to transform the existing educational institutions, and the second way is to create an institution where I can demonstrate the effectiveness of my idea.

The Long-Term Vision

I have traveled over three-hundred-thousand kilometers by road over the last few years to inspire, sensitize, orient, and engage the representatives of over 1,200 educational and vocational institutions in Pakistan to create a new paradigm for young people where they are seen as a part of the solution, rather than as part of the problem. I have been trying my level best to transform existing educational and vocational institutions into changemaker campuses. A changemaker campus is one in which all the faculty members and students of all disciplines are required to think and act in an entrepreneurial way. I wanted to see every educational and vocational institution start to look towards the future in all activities, rather than be involved in the repetition of knowledge and skills. I believe that the high-level of expertise in diverse fields distinctively qualifies educational and vocational institutions to strive towards being one step ahead of times.

I have proven the effectiveness of my youth-led changemaking model. I have given enough evidence again and again of what happens when we treat youth as equal partners in development, and not as consumers.

I have learned from my work that when we demand obedience, compliance, and innocence from young people, we get obedience, compliance, and innocence, and when we seek solution and innovation from young people, we get solution and innovation in return.

Despite all that, I always feel that something is still missing in the way our educational institutions treat, educate, relate, prepare, and empower our children and young people.

Now, my deepest desire is to establish a **"Changemaking School"**. We need reformers and changemakers in all fields. We have so many problems, but we have so few changemakers.

I believe we can only achieve peace and prosperity by increasing the number of changemakers. Through my changemaking school, I want to provide a new paradigm to students to help them discover the champion within.

In my changemaking school, grades will not be rewarded on the basis of the ability of students to memorize things, but instead, students will be rewarded on their ability to think, create, invent, and innovate.

In my changemaking school, students will not be seen as future leaders, but instead, they will be seen as present leaders.

In my changemaking school, students will not be treated as empty vessels into which we pour our wisdom, but instead, they will be seen as the most promising resource to bring change in the lives of others.

In my changemaking school, students will not focus on personal achievement, but instead, they will focus on helping others achieve.

In my changemaking school, students will not just talk about the problems of society, but instead, they will interact with the problems of society.

In my changemaking school, you will not see pictures of students who have scored very high on examinations on the publications and front walls of the school, but instead, you will see pictures of students who are making a difference in the lives of others successfully.

In my changemaking school, teachers will not be rewarded on the academic performance of their students, but instead, by their ability to facilitate students in their changemaking journey.

In my changemaking school, every student will represent a solution, and no one will represent a problem.

In my changemaking school, students will not focus on knowledge and skill repetition, but instead, they will focus on turning their new ideas into reality.

In my changemaking school, students will not have self-serving goals, but they will have goals for the greater good.

Admission criteria: In my changemaking school, students will not be given admission on the basis of their academic record, performance, or economic status, but on the basis of their past contributions to society, as well as their passion and desire to bring change to society.

Curriculum: The curriculum of my changemaking school will not be static, but it will be very dynamic, as it will focus on the challenges being faced by my country and the world.

Teaching methodologies: In my changemaking school, traditional teaching methodologies will not be followed, but they will be based on reflection, imagination, creation, initiation, innovation, and collaboration.

Operating norms: In my changemaking school, operating norms will not be based on strict rules and regulations, but they will be based on appreciation, trust, care, and teamwork.

Assessment of students: In my changemaking school, students will not be assessed in the classroom, but they will be assessed in their communities by their changemaking projects. It will be a win-win situation for everyone.

Learning outcomes: The learning outcomes of my changemaking school will not focus on reading, writing, and memorizing facts, but it will focus on empathy, critical thinking, creativity, resolve, problem-solving, and team building.

Compassion, not competition: In my changemaking school, compassion, not competition, will be the driving force in students' success.

Faculty: The teachers of my changemaking school will be social entrepreneurs, business entrepreneurs, activists, doers, and people who are experts in *using* knowledge, not just teaching knowledge.

Fees: No fees will be charged to the students. Instead, students will be provided technical and financial assistance to bring change to their communities.

Revenue generation: The revenue generation model of the school will be based on working in partnership with students. Students will be engaged in creating social, economic, and environmental value through their social innovative projects.

Changemaker Title: Degrees will not be awarded to students after the completion of their 24 months of engagement in problem-solving, but instead, they will be given the title of "Changemaker".

Diversity: Students of my changemaking school will represent true diversity. There will be no discrimination on the basis of color, creed, sect, gender, or religion.

Ideas: In my changemaking school, ideas will be rewarded, and grades will not be given.

Graduation ceremony: The graduation ceremony of my changemaking school will be an occasion to celebrate the contributions of students to society. It will not be an occasion to celebrate what students have gained, but it will be an occasion to celebrate what students have given back to society. The graduation ceremony will not only be attended by the parents of the students, but also by the community members who have benefitted, or will benefit, from the changemaking projects of students.

I hope that one day, I will be able to establish my changemaking school. I have nurtured this dream inside of me for many years. Now, I am sharing it with others when I feel the greatest necessity to provide an alternative vision. My changemaking school intends to offer something which does not exist.

I am happy that I have created a changemaking school in my imagination. I know that it might be a challenge to establish it, but it's not impossible.

I know that one day, I will be able to create such a school in reality. It's the best way to live up to my passion and my dream. If you are tired of investing in outdated and ineffective youth development programs, I encourage you to help me realize my vision of setting a new trend in education. I promise that you will be proud of your investment.

Section 2: World Youth Engagement Campaign: Thinking Big, Thinking Global

an essay on the vision for Youth-Led Changemaking by Thomas Jakel

When Ali Raza Khan picked me up from my hotel in Lahore one morning in February 2017, it felt as if I had just met a long-lost friend. It was the first time I had met Ali in person, but the hospitality and the passion for youth-led changemaking that he shared with everyone around him made me instantly feel connected to him.

I had interviewed Ali via Skype. Now, I sat in a silver Corolla, which was not only Ali's car, but also his office, meeting room, and kitchen, driving toward Texila University.

Why was I there in Pakistan, only a few days after a blast in the center of Lahore, after many of my friends warned me of the security risk? Because I had finally come across someone who not only shared my vision, but was years down the path that I still wanted to travel.

From the moment that I first spoke to Ali on Skype, he has become an inspiration and a mentor to me, through his unshakable trust in the abilities and the potential of young people, and through the love he shares, and how he uplifts everyone around him.

Ali has, through years of experimenting and expressing an unrelenting drive and passion for uplifting people, innovated a trust-based engagement model for the youth that seems to be unique in its combination of simplicity, effectiveness, and scale.

So, my question is this: What would a world look like where not only tens of thousands of young people in Pakistan are given the opportunity to practice and discover their changemaking abilities, but hundreds of millions of young people globally?

This is not a rhetorical question. There could be a real possibility to find out.

Why would we want to find out?

Well, I guess it would be in all of our best interests to encourage the hundreds of millions of young people to use productive means to find purpose, joy, and the feeling of fulfilment that dedication to an inspiring WHY brings with it, through contribution to society, instead of looking for purpose and a sense of importance through potentially destructive means, such as drug abuse, crime, terrorism, overthrow, or uprising.

Is this just my personal opinion?

Possibly. But the Arab spring is an indicator of what can happen when the dreams and hopes of an entire generation of young people cannot be met by their governments.

We have many well-educated young people, but few changemakers and entrepreneurs that create jobs and opportunities through innovation and proactive action.

We have many people that look towards problems and feel defeated by them, denying their own power of being able to bring change and create different circumstances. What we need are more people who are independent and free, because they know that they can overcome challenges and create their own opportunities.

Someone who has practiced Changemaking abilities for a few years will not need a job. It might be unlikely that they will even be looking for a job. It is much more likely that they will look for a way to add value, and thus, create their own job, and possibly jobs for many others, while at the same time making a positive contribution.

Poverty and the problems we currently face in the world would be gone fast if we really helped young people unleash their inherent potential and discover their innate greatness.

Section 3: Gaining + Giving = Development

an essay on the balance of gaining and giving, and entrepreneurs with heart by Ali Raza Khan

Development is an ongoing process.

The process begins with our birth and ends with our death. The process of development, either positive or negative, cannot be stopped while you are alive.

Every person, family, community, or society has developed a kind of model of development. This model is based on their beliefs, values, training, education, and experiences.

Mostly, when we define development for ourselves or for others, we tend to take a very "objective" view.

This means we look at the financial position (such as bank balance, property, or material possessions,) and the intellectual position (such as degrees, diplomas, or skills).

We believe that the possession of wealth and education are the most important variables of development. Most of our development work, theories, and models evolve around these indicators.

We consider people or societies to be developed if they are scoring high in these two areas. The dark side of relying heavily on these two indicators is the creation of a society where division is made between and among people on the basis of their ability to gain from society.

Human beings are masterly designed by God. Human beings have infinite potential to gain and give. There is no data that exists in research which can tell us accurately what the maximum limit of gaining and giving of a person and society is.

The creation of man by universal intelligence is an act of giving. The foundation of every religion is laid on the principle of giving. God has created the entire universe on the principle of giving. If we are in doubt, then let us look at the sun, which gives light and energy to every living thing. Imagine a day without the sun. Look at the moon, which gives us fascinating and pleasant reflected light from the sun. The force of the moon moves the oceans. Look at the stars, which give us direction in the darkness of the land and sea.

Look at the oceans and the seas, which are committed to our service. We eat and get ornaments from them. Look at the mountains that give balance to our earth. Look at the sky, which gives us shelter and rain.

Look at the earth, which gives fruits and vegetables for our sustenance. Look at bees, which give us honey to heal our bodies. Look at the tree, which gives us oxygen and medicine. Look at the flowers, which give us fragrance, beauty, happiness, and emotional healing.

In short, God has instituted a natural law whereby a person who persistently adheres to the principle of gaining, and refuses to give gradually, loses the ability to perceive the truth and live a peaceful life.

In a nutshell, in all the religions and wise traditions of the world, human beings are advised to give in order to attain virtuous conduct. Those who refuse to give from what God has given to them get excluded from the grace of God. If we go against the law of giving, it will not only affect our development, but will also upset the balance of the world. If human beings are able to understand the wonders of God, then we will not attach any importance to worldly gains.

We have forgotten the basic principle of giving. We think that we are created only to gain as much as possible and as quickly as possible.

Had God designed humankind only for gaining from society, he would not have planted a heart in the human body. The human heart is the king of organs. The natural language of our human heart is compassion. The heart of the human body is not only a physical thing that pumps blood. It is a social thing. It connects to others. It is an emotional thing. It sends signals and vibrations, both positive and negative, to others. It is a spiritual thing. It connects you with God like a cell phone.

Our heart is strongly linked to all our body parts. Our ears, eyes, brain, and tongue work well when they receive positive signals from the heart. Our heart does not send positive vibrations automatically. If the principle of giving is not instituted in the upbringing of children, it will corrupt the heart. The heart will not be able to function positively. It will not understand and see things clearly.

Remember, it is not human eyes which lose sight, it is the human heart which loses sight. A heart which follows the principle of gaining obsessively loses inner stability and happiness.

Remember, we are on earth for a fixed term only. Death will take us over even if we live in fortified towers.

Remember, there will be no automatic teller machine (ATM) installed in our graveyards for us to keep track of our money when we are gone. So, why do we run so passionately after material possessions when we all know that one day we will die and leave behind all our possessions in the world?

We have chosen a wrong model of life and a wrong formula for development and happiness which begins and ends by following the principle of gaining blindly. With the burning desire to gain more and more, we are destroying our lives and our natural environment.

We use our minds for personal development and growth. We send our children to schools to gain more in life, and not to give more.

Today, we have more educated people in the world, but we are facing more troubles, more poverty, more hopelessness, and more helplessness than ever before.

Our education systems are filling our minds, but not our hearts. Regardless of where we live and what we possess, if you are not following the principle of giving in an organized and consistent manner, I can predict we will struggle to find happiness, meaningful relationships, and stillness of heart.

Giving is the best remedy for ailments and calamities. The value of a human being depends upon their power of giving. One who rushes madly after worldly gain runs the risk of encountering destruction in all spheres of life. Those who remain in gaining mode for a longer period of time impair their ability to give something back to others.

APPENDICES

i) COMMONLY ASKED QUESTIONS

Q1. What is a Youth-Led Changemaking Project?

A: It is a conscious effort of young people to discover their inherent changemaking potential by initiating an idea, activity, or process that produces social and economic benefits. In Youth-Led Changemaking Projects, social and economic benefits are intertwined. Young people are encouraged to use business principles to achieve social objectives.

Q2. How do you define an ideal Youth-Led Changemaking project?

An ideal Youth-Led Changemaking project has the following characteristics:

- It is youth-led.
- It signifies team work.
- It has an enterprise orientation (such as selling a product or service).
- It is comprehensive. Young people would have the opportunity to lead the process from start to finish.
- It takes an organic and bottom-up approach.
- It represents a solution.
- It aims at efficient problem-solving.
- It creates double (social and economic) or triple (social, economic, environmental, and spiritual) bottom-lines.

Q3. What are the major approaches adopted by young people for changemaking?

There are many approaches adopted by young people to drive change. Some of these approaches are given below:

- Social and economic benefits are unified. In other words, social and economic benefits are achieved simultaneously. Young people pursue an integrated approach.

- Social benefits overlap economic benefits. Young people put their social mission first.
- Economic benefits overlap social benefits. Young people put economic value creation first.
- Social and economic benefits are separated. The business activities are carried out to generate funds.

In short, social and economic values creation are the backbone of a Youth-Led Changemaking project. Young people are encouraged to adopt a balanced approach and make sure that the pendulum does not swing in one direction only.

Q4. What are the general domains of Youth-Led Changemaking?

There are many domains in which youth-led changemaking happens. These include: education, health, environment, agriculture, food, music, sports, information technology, fashion designing, visual arts, and entertainment. Young people are often the lead users of many products and services in many social settings. Since they are the lead user of many products and services, they already know a great deal about their strengths and weaknesses. It is interesting to observe that a large number of Youth-Led Changemaking projects follow an incremental approach towards changemaking. They prefer small advances, rather than major breakthroughs or disruptions to society. Youth-led changemaking is manifested in a new product, service, or process that they are unsatisfied with. Youth-Led Changemaking provides a remarkable opportunity for young people to refine an existing product or service by adding new components to it. Youth-Led Changemaking projects often come up with a new marketing strategy, training, and service delivery for a market segment that others have bypassed.

Q5. What is an ideal way to develop and execute Youth-Led Changemaking projects?

Young people often evolve their changemaking projects when learning-by-doing. They prefer to take a direct approach. They prefer customer feedback over detailed planning. They focus on speed and fast delivery. The idea of providing this opportunity to young people is to help them build their ideas with less bureaucracy. Young people are encouraged to use or reuse simple materials and tools. They develop and execute their changemaking projects in real conditions, encounter problems, make revisions in hours, and hit the market again.

Q6. How can I ensure the success of my project?

The best way to measure the effectiveness of your idea is to bring your potential customers on board from the beginning in the design of the product or service. It is easier to get people to support your idea if they are involved in it.

Q7. I am not a business student. Can I become a Changemaker?

Changemakers are required in all fields. We have a choice every day: whether we want to repeat the game all the time, or whether we want to change the game. There is a dire need to establish drivers of youth-led changemaking and innovation in all fields. We need change and improvement in every field. Young people provide an exciting source of innovation to society. We believe that young people have a natural tendency to open new doors of innovation at all levels. Youth-led changemaking provides an opportunity for young people to go first and experiment early and quickly in all fields.

Q8. What should be the size of the funding for a Youth-Led Changemaking Project?

The size of the funding should be small. The idea behind the Youth-Led Changemaking competition is to unlock the inherent changemaking potential of young people. Young people are encouraged to count on their inherent changemaking abilities (the ability to initiate, serve, imagine, choose, innovate, express, feel, collaborate, care, and appreciate). It does not require a degree or diploma, or a lot of funding

Appendices

to use our changemaking abilities. YES provides as low as US$1, and up to US$50, to help young people begin their changemaking journey.

The idea behind providing a small amount of funding is to activate or wake up the changemaker within each young person. Young people are encouraged to rely more on themselves and their natural changemaking abilities, rather than on funds. We have seen that many young people start and execute projects by not even spending a single penny, as they prefer to use their social capital or bring their idea, skill, and passion into the markets, instead of their problems and demands.

Q9. What should be the size of a youth-led changemaking project team?

It should be no less than 3, and no more than 5 members.

Q10. What should the duration of the Youth-Led Changemaking Competition be?

If you are running the competition for the first time in your school or community, the duration should not exceed more than 4 weeks. One key factor that can reduce the impact of your competition is its duration. Running the competition for too long may cause teachers and students to become distracted, whereas running the competition for a very short period of time can cause a high drop-out rate of student teams. The duration of the competition should be decided in consultation with teachers, as they will play a lynchpin role in the success of the competition. If teachers are over-occupied or distracted during the competition, it will impact the performance of students. It is recommended to hold the competition at a time when there is less academic pressure on students and teachers.

Q11. What should the role of a teacher in organizing the competition be?

The major responsibility of a teacher is to build trust with young people. Building trust with young people is the secret recipe to helping them discover the changemaker within. The Youth-Led Changemaking Competition requires a major shift in the role of a teacher from, "director or supervisor" to "facilitator and motivator". The roles and responsibilities of a teacher are divided into three phases: Before the competition, during the competition, and after the completion. Each phase has particular responsibilities. Please read chapter eight of this book for more information on these phases.

Q12. What should the judging criterion of the Youth-Led Changemaking Competition be?

The judging criterion of the Youth-Led Changemaking Competition is based on the following:

Indicators	Explanation	Marks
Social value creation	Number of people served, social impact or change brought	25
Economic value creation	Amount of income generated, how the income was generated	25
Type of Innovation	Incremental or radical	25
Personal Reflection	How well student teams reflect and document their experiences	25

Q13. Who can participate in the Youth-Led Changemaking Competition?

The Youth-Led Changemaking Competition follows a bottom-up and non-bureaucratic model. Anyone who is interested can participate in the competition. There is no criterion. The only criterion is to have a desire to participate. No presentation is required. No idea submission is required before participation. All those young people who are interested to participate in the competition need to form a team and fill out the registration form to receive funding and enter into the competition.

Q14. What are the benefits of the Youth-Led Changemaking Competition to students, teachers, schools, and communities?

The Youth-Led Changemaking Competition offers enormous returns to everyone. It helps students unlock their changemaking potential, develop a new belief system, increase confidence, establish a new identity, build new relationships, develop a sense of connection and usefulness, and become self-reliant and contributing members of society. It helps teachers to inspire trust in young people, apply new teaching methodologies (learning-by-doing), identify the hidden talents of young people, develop new insights, build new community partnerships with community members, get involved in other disciplines, and find new areas of research and publication. It helps schools reconnect with communities as places for public good, develop new partnerships, attract more students and funding, improve the quality of teaching and learning, improve visibility in communities, and offer hands-on competence to teachers and students in their fields. It helps communities accelerate social and economic development, develop a local service delivery mechanism, test new ideas, and reduce crime and drug abuse.

Q15. What kind of awards should be given to the top-performing student teams of the Youth-Led Competition?

It is important to offer something that will inspire students and teachers to participate in the competition with a full deck. This can include, but is not limited to, the following:

- Cash awards
- Certificates
- Medals
- Appreciation letters
- Features on social websites
- Opportunity to expand their ideas

Q16. Do you think that Changemaking is possible at a young age?

We are indoctrinated to believe in many untrue things. One of the myths we believe is that changemaking is not possible at a young age. In my work, I have thousands of examples of children and young people who embark upon a changemaking journey at a very young age. Many great changemakers in the world started their journey when they were in their teens. It is an open secret that changemaking is possible at any age. There is no pre-condition or specific age to become a changemaker.

Q17. Is it true that Changemaking is the domain of the privileged few?

Many of us believe that changemaking is the domain of the privileged few. I find this to be completely wrong. It is not the domain of the privileged few. It is the domain of everyone. Human beings are designed to create value and add value to society. It is amazing to see how many young people have given up so early in their lives, while they have forgotten that a goldmine lies within each of them. Everyone has the ability to deliver good and discard bad. I believe my work with young people, especially the disadvantaged youth, has busted the lone hero myth. Out of 16,000 young people, 88% of them were able to create a real social and economic impact.

Q18. What are the common challenges faced by schools while implementing the Youth-Led Changemaking Competition?

Challenges are present in everything we do. Youth-Led Changemaking is no exception. The most common challenges faced by schools are the following:

Challenge	Possible Response
Unsupportive institutional environment	Top leadership buy-in is the key to success.

Appendices

Lack of ownership from teachers	Develop an incentive system to motivate and reward teachers that facilitated students very well.
Inability of teachers to inspire students to become changemakers	Encourage teachers to see every young person with delight. Do not discriminate students on the basis of their academic record.
Negative perceptions about young people	Ample data is available on the internet that shows that when young people are seen as changemakers, they not only transform their lives, but the lives of others.
Lack of support from parents	Conduct a session with the parents to inform them about the purpose of the competition. Inform them that it is a very important activity to improve the self-belief of students. Ask them to encourage their children at every step.
Lack of self-belief among students	Share stories of young changemakers. You can access them at the following websites: www.yesnetworkpakistan.org www.seedthechangefoundation.org www.ashoka.org
Weak management of the competition	Share the role and responsibilities of teachers before, during, and after the competition. Encourage them to stay in close contact with all the student teams.

Too much help from teachers	It is observed that, often, teachers try to be too helpful, which prevents young people from experiencing the thrill of being a changemaker.
Absence of funding	There are many ways to secure funding for the Youth-Led Changemaking Competition: - Allocate a small percentage of fees for changemaking - Seek sponsorship from a private company - Organize a fundraising event - Attract a local donor or philanthropist to support the competition - Seek an interest-free loan from someone It is important to mention here that 88% of student teams that participated in the changemaking competitions of YES were able to make a profit. It shows that Youth-Led Changemaking is a most lucrative investment.

Appendices

How This Book Was Made

I wanted to write a book on youth-led changemaking for quite some time, but that *some time* turned out to be a *long time*. I was fully convinced that I had a great idea in the shape of youth-led changemaking. I witnessed the changemaking power of the most marginalized and socially-excluded young people very early on in my professional journey. I wanted to write a book on youth-led changemaking in order to stop the blind imitation of deficit-based youth development programs, to help young people realize that they are born with changemaking abilities inside them, to provide an alternative vision to parents, teachers, and policy makers, and to document my journey to the idea of youth-led changemaking. I also believe that God planted the desire of writing this book in my heart, and I was waiting for the right time to complete this assignment.

The reason that I delayed it was that I wanted to test my idea of youth-led changemaking in different educational and vocational institutions, as well as communities. I wanted to validate my idea in different social settings. My urge to write a book was increased after the successful testing of the youth-led changemaking idea with 6,000 young people studying in the state-owned vocational and technical institutions of Pakistan. I took my idea to leading educational and vocational institutions in Pakistan for further validation and consolidation. The results were amazing. The temptation of getting more specific data from the youth-led changemaking competitions carried out in a wide range of educational and vocational institutions could not be controlled. In a short span of time, I was able to engage over 16,000 young people from different social settings in changemaking competitions. Despite the fact that I was able to gather a lot of concrete data about the success of my model of youth-led changemaking, I was finding it difficult to take some time out from my work to develop a framework for the book. At that time, Thomas Jakel made a thrilling entry in my life and work. Thomas wanted to interview me to learn more about my youth-led changemaking work. I had never imagined that an interview on Skype would turn into such a meaningful and life-long relationship. After the interview, Thomas expressed his desire to join me for a couple of weeks to see my work in action. I was very happy to see his enthusiasm. I invited him to Pakistan. Thomas brought a sea of positive energy along with him, and his passion, desire, and commitment inspired me a lot. Here was someone willing to learn and contribute to the field of youth development, flying in all the way from Germany at his own expense, just to experience the power of youth-led changemaking in the educational and vocational institutions of Pakistan. Two days before his arrival in Lahore, there was a serious bomb blast which killed many innocent people. I thought that he might delay or postpone his visit to Pakistan. I sent him an email to learn about his travel plans and concerns. He immediately replied to me, writing:

"Yes, I heard about the explosion last night and I am deeply sorry for the victims and their families. I hope that you, your family, team members, and friends are safe. I am sad for the people directly affected, and my thoughts are with them. I am not concerned for my own safety, and the preparations are going well. I am looking forward to the stay. My thoughts on the event: If it was an attack, it just goes to show that we as a human race still have a long way to go to learn to live in peace with each other, and to learn to create for the benefit of all instead of destroying. I think the work you are doing, speaking to people's potential and sharing hope, can help with this learning process."

I was very delighted and relieved to read his email. When Thomas joined me in Lahore, I had an opportunity to take him to several educational and vocational institutions where youth-led changemaking competitions were going on. Thomas had the opportunity to meet and interact with several-thousand young people. He got first-hand knowledge, experience, and impact of my youth-led changemaking model. I also shared with him my desire to write a book on youth-led changemaking. Thomas liked my idea and offered his complete support in carrying out this project. So, we decided to write the book together. We immediately put a lot of energy into the development of the book. Thomas inspired me with his speed, the sense of urgency he brought to this work, and his commitment to it. For the first time, I concentrated on the book very deeply. Thomas developed an initial framework of the book based on my talks on changemaking in different universities of Pakistan and the results of the changemaking competitions. Then I started to work on the book, day and night. Thomas organized the work so well that it really helped me to pick up the pace, and to reflect on my 20 years of experience of working with young people. I thought many times that God was using Thomas to document my journey for something greater and impactful. So, over the next months, Thomas and I communicated our progress via email. Thomas was very quick to review my material, asked many questions, added his personal and professional experiences, and publicized my work in his social circles.

After only a few months of intense work, I am very glad to hold this manuscript in my hand. We both hope that you enjoy the read and apply its essence.

We hope you enjoyed the read. If you want to get in touch with the authors, you find their contact details below.

Ali Raza Khan
Founder and CEO
YES Network Pakistan
W: www.yesnetworkpakistan.org
E: alikhanmeets@gmail.com

Thomas Jakel
Co-Founder and CEO
YES Founders Foundation
W: www.yesfoundersfoundation.org
E: team@yesfoundersfoundation.org

www.ingramcontent.com/pod-product-compliance
Lightning Source LLC
Chambersburg PA
CBHW070932230426

43666CB00011B/2410